S0-BRH-501

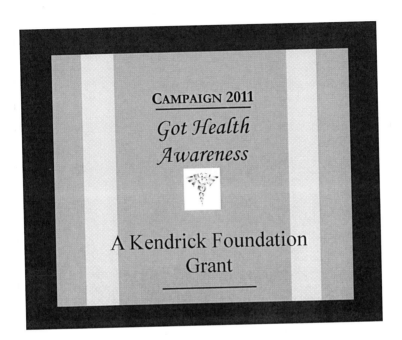

CAMPAIGN 2011

Got Health
Awareness

A Kendrick Foundation
Grant

DISCARD

MOORESVILLE PUBLIC LIBRARY
220 W. HARRISON ST.
MOORESVILLE, IN 46158
317-831-7323

Childhood
Psychological Disorders

Childhood Psychological Disorders

Current Controversies

Alberto M. Bursztyn, Editor

MOORESVILLE PUBLIC LIBRARY
220 WEST HARRISON STREET
MOORESVILLE, INDIANA 46158

Making Sense of Psychology
Carol Korn-Bursztyn, Series Editor

 PRAEGER

AN IMPRINT OF ABC-CLIO, LLC
Santa Barbara, California • Denver, Colorado • Oxford, England

Copyright 2011 by Alberto M. Bursztyn

All rights reserved. No part of this publication may be reproduced, stored in a retrieval system, or transmitted, in any form or by any means, electronic, mechanical, photocopying, recording, or otherwise, except for the inclusion of brief quotations in a review, without prior permission in writing from the publisher.

Library of Congress Cataloging-in-Publication Data

Childhood psychological disorders : current controversies /
Alberto M. Bursztyn, editor.
    p. cm. — (Making sense of psychology)
  Includes bibliographical references and index.
  ISBN 978-0-313-33696-6 (alk. paper) — ISBN 978-0-313-06406-7 (ebook)
1. Developmentally disabled children.   2. Children with disabilities—
Mental health.   3. Child mental health.   4. Child psychology.   I. Bursztyn,
Alberto, 1952–
  RJ506.D47C45   2011
  618.92'89—dc22   2010052070

ISBN: 978-0-313-33696-6
EISBN: 978-0-313-06406-7

15   14   13   12   11   1   2   3   4   5

This book is also available on the World Wide Web as an eBook.
Visit www.abc-clio.com for details.

Praeger
An Imprint of ABC-CLIO, LLC

ABC-CLIO, LLC
130 Cremona Drive, P.O. Box 1911
Santa Barbara, California 93116-1911

This book is printed on acid-free paper ∞

Manufactured in the United States of America

I dedicate this book to Daniel,
For the memories and strength of our old friendship,
For your tenacious spirit today

Contents

Series Foreword

The "Making Sense of Psychology" series is designed to provide readers with broad perspectives on some of the greatest challenges affecting the psychological growth and development of children, adolescents, and emerging adults today. The idea for the series grows out of the need for bringing the knowledge and current findings of researchers and practitioners to a wide audience of readers who interact with young people daily, readers who are concerned about and able to impact on their growth and development. The series provides a reliable reference source for concerned parents, teachers, mental health providers, youth counselors, and others looking for basic, practical information grounded within current research and professional practice. It provides a wealth of information together with informed, professional perspectives in a readable style.

The "Making Sense of Psychology" series supports, for example, the student writing a term paper on contemporary issues in childcare, the parent seeking an understanding of a child's disability or of risky behavior in adolescence, or the teacher seeking up-to-date, reliable, and expert information on the effects of family stress on school performance. The series explores the everyday, commonplace difficulties of growing up, as well as the more complex issues that young people face at home with parents, siblings, and other family members—at school, with friends in the community, and at work.

Each volume in the series provides readers with an overview of the topic that is the subject of the book, including a concise history and overview of contemporary perspectives of the topic. Readers learn about major theories and concepts and read how these theories and approaches are applied in real-life situations. The series volumes present the most important disputes and controversies in the field and explain, in jargon-free language, the issues involved. The "Making Sense of Psychology" series provides an entry point for readers to continue their research and learning. Resources for professionals and parents, including articles, books, organizations, and appropriate and dependable web sites, are listed.

Divided into three major groups of titles, the series "Making Sense of Psychology" presents today's concerns for today's researchers, including parents, teachers, mental health practitioners, and youth counselors. Series volumes are grouped under the following: *Making Sense of Child Psychology*; *Making Sense of Adolescent Development and Psychology*; and *Making Sense of Emerging Adulthood*.

Researchers and practitioners in the field of psychology, social work, psychiatry, and mental health who are studying major issues and concerns regarding the healthy development of children, adolescents, and emerging adults are invited to submit manuscripts. Also invited are parents, teachers, and others who wish to submit essays that describe their experiences with children, teens, and young adults for inclusion in the series.

Carol Korn-Bursztyn, PsyD Series Editor

Acknowledgments

The idea for this book emerged in the context of conducting a study of families whose children had transitioned from a *restrictive* setting—that is, a school for children with severe disabilities—to neighborhood schools. I placed the word restrictive in italics because these families, for the most part, did not object to the isolation by disability that the initial school represented; they viewed the specialized school as a necessary first step in their child's journey to social and academic integration. Although these parents were savvy about the special education system—some had moved to specific school districts because of the special education department's reputation—they still struggled with ambivalence about finding the right balance between home, school, and the demand of therapies. They obsessed daily about when to step in and when to let go as their children confronted new challenges and experiences. More that anything else, they worried about their children's emotional well-being in the more open and challenging context of a regular school; they wondered if the teachers, the school, the therapists, were doing enough, were doing the right thing, and questioned if they themselves were good parents. I'm thankful that they welcomed me into their homes and spoke openly about some of the most difficult issues in their lives. This book owes much to the knowledge, insights, and wishes they shared with me.

The book is also the product of collaboration and friendship. I approached the contributors hoping they would write specific chapters given their areas of interest and expertise; all of them happily agreed to participate. The ensuing process has been an enjoyable exchange as the evolving drafts provided a fruitful source of conversation and mutual education. In a number of cases the collaboration led to the question: What's our next project together? I thank them all and indeed I look forward to working on shared projects in the near future.

I am grateful to my colleagues and friends at Brooklyn College, and particularly to faculty in the school psychology and special education programs for the many conversations and discussions that inform my work and my teaching. I wish to recognize, beyond those who contributed to this volume, Pauline Bynoe, Florence Rubinson, Paul McCabe, Graciela Elizalde-Utnick, Laura Barbanel, Harriet Bredhoff, and Arline Levine.

Other colleagues who have influenced this project in significant ways include Christine Pawelski, at Teachers College; Carol Goossens, Amanda Caccavo, Janette Glover, Fran Prezant, Susan Friede, Rosemarie Zaso and Marcello Carnevale, at Abilities!; Emilia Lopez and Helen Johnson, at Queens College; and the CUNY Graduate Center.

I also wish to recognize Debbie Carvalko and the editorial staff at ABC-CLIO for their unwavering encouragement and conscientious dedication to the production of this volume.

This book owes the most to Carol Korn-Bursztyn, my wife, partner, editor and best friend.

Introduction:
What Is Disability?

Alberto M. Bursztyn

Disability occupies the shadows of our collective psyche. In a society that glamorizes vacuous celebrity, physical prowess, and perfect bodies, disability is the unwanted other, the aspect of humanity that evokes vulnerability and anguish—the opposite of our collective fantasized lives. Disability usually enters as unwelcome news and in its wake it tends to redefine individuals' and families' trajectories. Those affected generally face their challenges privately. A child with disabilities forces a detour; well-planned lives need to be rethought, carefree lives assume a new gravity, and families struggling with challenges may be brought to a breaking point. Parents of children with disabilities often find themselves in a new, lonely, and bewildering territory without a guide, map, or GPS.

This book is rooted in a desire to help parents, teachers, young people with disabilities, and others interested in disability disentangle some of the most controversial and unsettled contemporary issues regarding children with impairments. The book does not aim to be a comprehensive guide to disabilities or to provide definitive answers about specific diagnoses or treatments. Instead it is envisioned as a trail map through difficult terrain, encouraging the reader to understand the lay of the land and some of the landmarks one might see and experience along the way. For those who are interested, there are suggestions for further readings and resources at the end of each chapter.

How and why are childhood disabilities controversial? Controversy emerges in the context of change: when the old answers no longer suit the questions, when new knowledge is contested, or when new concepts challenge established categories. While disabilities have always been a part of the human experience, their nature and social meaning have not been constant; in fact, they are ever changing. Our understanding of disability is formed by prevalent cultural, religious, and scientific contexts. These broad spheres of meaning-making are far from static, and development in one is bound the affect the others. New treatments can offer hope for children and families, but these may not be universally welcomed within certain faith traditions, or they might raise concern about personal freedoms and privacy. Vaccinations are a good prism to interpret the confluence of social forces. For example, Jonas Salk's breakthrough in developing the polio vaccine was hailed as a triumph by the scientific community in 1955 and embraced by most families fearing the disabling and possibly fatal consequences of the disease. Today, though, some argue against polio vaccine as medical mandate due to conflicts with religious belief.

Many new parents, concerned that vaccination may precipitate the onset of autism in their young children, opt to avoid the diphtheria, pertussis, tetanus (DPT) or measles, mumps, rubella (MMR) inoculations despite the medical profession's strong endorsement of immunization. Poor understanding of the causes of autism and growing mistrust of institutionalized medicine heightens anxiety and opens the door to questioning medical knowledge and advice. As in this case, and many others, controversies emerge when different sources of knowledge assign conflicting meanings to specific conditions, procedures, and interventions. In fact, greater access to means of communication and resource-sharing has resulted in a worldwide proliferation of nontraditional treatments and methods.

Parents are now presented with conflicting advice and treatment options for their children. Some of those treatments may in fact be sound, but to the extent that they exist outside the mainstream they typically have not been adequately tested for safety and/or effectiveness. Parents of young children with disabilities must now consider a wide array of treatment choices, including some that have a cultish following and promise more than they can deliver.

Conflict is not limited to treatment; conditions associated with disability are themselves in flux. For instance, the current definitions of intellectual disabilities are markedly different from those accepted a generation or two ago. While for most of the 20th century psychologists could diagnose a child a mentally retarded on the basis of an IQ test score alone, current requirements demand a multidisciplinary and multitest approach that includes measures of adaptive behavior. The IQ score, while still required in most cases, must document a significantly more pronounced deficit than the earlier specified criterion for diagnosis. This shift in definition has had enormous implications because a broad segment of individuals previously identified as educable mentally retarded are now considered low average if they meet social functioning norms for their chronological age.

As this example suggests, a disability may be contingent on definitions subject to change and modification. In the case of a mental retardation diagnosis, the work of Jane Mercer in California was a catalyst for change. Dr. Mercer, an anthropologist, observed that individuals classified as mildly mentally retarded in school in later years were able to hold jobs, raise families, and were not noticeably different from their non-classified age peers. Her research questioned if disability could legitimately justified on the basis of a test score alone. Later, a court decision in California ruled that the IQ tests disproportionably assigned African American children to program for the mild mentally retarded and banned its use altogether. The guideposts for intellectual disability were shifted and therefore expanded the parameters of average range intellectual functioning.

The documented permutations of definitions of disability suggest mutability in the very essence of what we may consider to be the impairment in question. In the United States, legal mandates and court decisions have contributed to reassessments of disabilities and treatments. We often find, years later, that what may have been a controversial law or ruling in its day has set a new standard for what is popularly accepted as normal and routine.

In establishing parameters for identifying psychopathology, the mental health professions also reflect cultural shifts. Psychiatric disorders have been reclassified or omitted altogether as clinicians and researchers begin to differentiate disability from difference. Homosexuality is a case in point. Newer editions of the *DSM* (*Diagnostic and Statistical Manual of Mental Disorders*), published by the American Psychiatric Association, have ceased to classify homosexuality as a pathological condition. Empirical evidence based on a study by the National Institute of Mental Health influenced the psychiatric community to question the nature of sexual orientation. The *DSM* in 1973 stated that homosexuality in itself implied no impairment in judgment, stability, reliability, or general social or vocational capabilities. Other mental health professional organizations soon followed and discarded notions of homosexuality as inherently deviant. Interestingly, atypical sexual orientation in children continues to generate arguments within the mental health professions, and the matter is far from settled. Chapter 10 in this book addresses that controversy and explores the broader issues of atypical/nonconforming gender identity in children.

Although one social trend has been to expand the parameters of normalcy to accommodate greater human diversity, another trend has been to medicalize human experience. New disorders, some newly named, continue to add complexity to the compendium of humanity's emotional ills described in the *DSM*—which now has close to 900 pages. For example, nonverbal learning disabilities, shopping addiction, and binge eating disorder are relatively new additions. In the near future, social networking and/or gaming addiction may be recognized as diagnosable disorders as the APA readies the fifth edition of the *DSM*.

Among the changes proposed, Asperger syndrome may be edited out and subsumed under autism spectrum disorder. One could argue that as a consequence of the ongoing appraisal of what is psychopathological, we are also engaged in reassessing and setting the boundaries on what is normal. What emerges in our contemporary perspective on disability is a sense that drawing lines between ability and disability, or between normal and abnormal, is a somewhat arbitrary process. Social theorists refer to this process as *social construction*; in other words, something has a particular meaning because members of the culture agree on the significance of a term.

Thus the particular meaning of a disabling condition is tied to how a society names it and treats it. Members of other cultures may not share those meanings; they may not even have a word to describe it. This cultural discrepancy in categorizing is often observed when school officials try to explain to a recent immigrant family that their child has a learning disability. In many cultures learning disabilities are not a construct; therefore, parents may fail to understand the impairment. What may be a disability in one social context, dyslexia for example, might not register as a disability in nonliterate or agrarian societies where fluid reading is not essential to meet adult social expectations.

Disability—A Matter of Degree

Most conditions that we associate with disability occur in a continuum of severity. Not all children with autism are incapable of social interaction, not all children with cerebral palsy have difficulty speaking. Rather, we observe broad variability in abilities within conditions, and we find that diagnosticians may disagree in their efforts to classify specific children within categories of disability and degree of severity.

Considering the degree of severity of disability in childhood is particularly challenging, because young children's neurological systems are not fully developed, and the potential for further growth may be difficult to estimate. While exercising caution to restrict unrealistic expectations, we often encounter children who have defied professional pronouncements, such as "She'll never talk," or "He'll never walk unassisted." In these situations one could ask, to what extent have the love, care and treatment the child received account for beating the odds? Or one could question if the professional's judgment reflected dated knowledge of the condition affecting the child. In either case, with the evolution of understating about specific disabilities, and newer therapies and adaptive technologies, there is greater likelihood that children with disabilities will achieve their cognitive, social, and emotional potential.

Disabilities are not fixed qualities; some individuals with clearly identified, visible, and severe disabilities function well in the world of the nondisabled; they approach their conditions as simply another challenge. Stephen Hawking in science, and Chuck Close in art, for example, are not known for their limitations but for their enormous talents. Most nondisabled people in their respective fields have not achieved what these and other disabled individuals have accomplished. But without pointing to exceptional cases, more and more children with disabilities are able to live full lives as adults because education and networks of support continue to expand to accommodate their needs, and society as a whole recognizes their rights to full participation and engagement. Disability is not simply a challenge to be overcome by individuals but a task and requirement for change for society at large.

Dimensions of Disability

In an ontological sense, disabilities are recognized as having a physical dimension in the body of the child, but their presence is felt in the context of interaction between the child and the social world. The World Health Organization (WHO) describes disability in the following way:

> *Disabilities* is an umbrella term, covering impairments, activity limitations, and participation restrictions. An impairment is a problem in body function or structure; an activity limitation is a difficulty encountered by an individual in executing a task or action; while a participation restriction is a problem experienced by an individual in involvement in life situations. Thus disability is a complex phenomenon, reflecting an interaction between features of a person's body and features of the society in which he or she lives.

The World Health Organization's approach considers the limitations of the body but pays close attention to how these impact activity and participation in a social realm:

> These domains are classified from body, individual and societal perspectives by means of two lists: a list of body functions and structure, and a list of domains of activity and participation. Since an individual's functioning and disability occurs in a context, the ICF (International Classification of Function, Disability, and Health) and also includes a list of environmental factors.

Contextualizing disability serves to reframe disabling conditions, discarding older perspectives that understood disability strictly as biological or medical concerns affecting a finite minority of a population in need of special care. The contextualized definition implies that disability is a condition that can affect anyone in the course of a lifetime. In this way, the WHO places disabilities on par with diseases by shifting the focus from cause to impact. Using this framework, disabilities in childhood must be considered not only as specific impairments but, more globally, as conditions that affect a child's capacity to engage and participate in the social realm. What makes a child disabled is not the impairment per se, but its impact on her capacity to be a full participant in her familial and social world.

The U.S. government's policies regarding Supplementary Security Income (SSI) for families raising children with disabilities also clearly focus on the functional impact of disability. Eligibility criteria disqualify earners and specify severe limitations on other functional activities for at least 12 months duration. The following are SSI guidelines for parents:

Your child must meet all of the following requirements to be considered disabled and therefore eligible for SSI:

- The child must not be working and earning more than $1,000 a month in 2010. (This earnings amount changes every year.) If he or she is working and earning that much money, we will find that your child is not disabled.
- The child must have a physical or mental condition, or a combination of conditions, that results in "marked and severe functional limitations." This means that the condition(s) must very seriously limit your child's activities.
- The child's condition(s) must have lasted, or be expected to last, at least 12 months; or must be expected to result in death.

If your child's condition(s) results in "marked and severe functional limitations" for at least 12 continuous months, we will find that your child is disabled. But if it does not result in those limitations, or does not last for at least 12 months, we will find that your child is not disabled.

Despite increasing attention to the functional aspects of disability, the psychiatric and educational establishments in the United States continue to be driven by definitional categories that construe disability as a defining characteristic of the child. For example, classifying a child as ADHD does not require clinicians to evaluate the familial and/or educational environments where the disability is noted. The disability, in that framework, resides within the child and disregards the context where the presumed disability interferes with function. The medical approach, equating mental disorders with other physical illnesses, is resistant to change in a society where health benefits and reimbursements for treatment are tied to specific diagnoses. Finding that a child acts ADHD in one context but seems well adjusted in another would potentially challenge the diagnostic entity and disqualify eligibility for treatment. The same could be said for a child who shows autistic features that qualify him for services, but if treatment helps diminishes the outward manifestations of the disorder his eligibility for services may be discontinued.

The medical model defines normalcy as the lack of pathology. While on first appraisal this statement suggests a cautious approach to diagnosis, in practice it creates a false binary; children are either ADHD or not, they are emotionally disturbed or not. In effect the medical model lacks nuance and fails to adequately consider the degree of impairment—it reifies the pathological label. This is unfortunate because we know from clinical practice and life experiences that emotional states are not immutable or uniform; rather, we know that under changing contexts a child may be more or less well adjusted. In fact, psychological conditions in children are usually not like diseases caused by identifiable pathogens but instead may be reactions to environmental stressors. Thus the medical approach to mental health lacks sensitivity to contextual conditions and functional adjustment in various settings.

The U.S. Department of Education, following a medical paradigm, lists 13 categories of disability that qualify a child for access to special education services. These categories are specified in the Individuals with Disabilities Education Act (IDEA), the Federal law that mandates school districts to guarantee free and appropriate access to public education for all children with disabilities. The IDEA disability categories, under which 3- through 21-year-olds may be eligible for services, are:

- autism;
- deaf-blindness;
- deafness;
- emotional disturbance;
- hearing impairment;
- mental retardation (intellectual disability);
- multiple disabilities;
- orthopedic impairment;
- other health impairment;
- specific learning disability;
- speech or language impairment;
- traumatic brain injury; or
- visual impairment (including blindness).

While there may not be much disagreement regarding identification of children with physical disabilities and health or sensory impairments, the identification of children with emotional and behavioral challenges is inherently more complicated. Moreover, since these conditions, as described by the Federal laws, do not match psychopathological diagnoses encoded in the *DSM* or International Classification of Diseases (ICD), there is ample room for disagreement.

In this volume, we are particularly drawn to the controversies in childhood disability that focus on emotional, social, and behavioral concerns, that is, the psychological dimensions in childhood disability. We identify topics where the field of childhood disability remains unsettled or where new questions and research compel us to reconsider established paradigms and to think or act differently. In addressing specific topics, the contributors to this volume seek to explain critical and controversial issues highlighting the state of knowledge and the nature of opposing arguments among specialists in various disciplines. Each chapter is enriched with case studies and examples from practice.

In the first chapter I describe sociological and psychological perspectives on the field of child disability. The chapter addresses the evolution of disability concepts and highlights the dynamic nature of disability as a human condition and as a social phenomenon. The nature of disability and its impact on the family system and schools is explored through the vantage point of children, their parents and siblings, and educators. In the second chapter, Dr. Yoon-Joo Lee and I explore the role of culture and traditional beliefs in defining and understanding disability. The chapter includes brief accounts of our own experiences with disabilities as lenses into other cultures and frames of reference. Dr. Lee narrates her experience of growing up with a disability in South Korea, and I recount my difficulties in the early grades while growing up in Argentina. We also explore a number of cultural and religious beliefs associated with traditional ways of understanding disability and its causes and how social forces contribute to the development of identity.

The third chapter, by Elizabeth Scanlon, delves into one of the most salient and conflicted diagnosis in our time, pediatric bipolar disorder. This chapter describes the features of bipolar disorder in children and provides a window into the latest discussions regarding mediation and treatment options. Dana Freed revisits ADHD in the book's fourth chapter. ADHD is the most frequently diagnosed pediatric mental disorder in the United States and the one most tied to drug therapy, yet questions regarding the likelihood of over diagnoses and the potential harmful effects of medication continue to cause disquiet among parents of children carrying this diagnosis.

Autism is addressed in two chapters. Dr. Jeanne Angus describes the shifting nature of diagnosis and assessment. She reviews the latest developments in assessment and clinical examinations and describes the current hypotheses regarding the origins of the disorder. Dr. Carol Korn-Bursztyn provides a narrative of treatment modalities and their implied theoretical assumptions, drawing from her work with children and families challenged by autism spectrum disorder (ASD).

Dr. Harold Golubtchik addresses the confounding educational label emotionally handicapped/disturbed (EH/D) and describes the experience of a particular school established to meet the needs of students labeled EH/D. The eighth chapter, by Dr. Jennifer Foster, explores treatment options for students identified as EH/D, including the spectrum of residential and home-based programs.

The chapter written by Suzanne Huber deals with food allergies and related disorders and explores the psychological effects of these disabilities. Concerns about the potential deadly effects of exposure to widely available foodstuffs, such as peanuts, create unique parenting challenges. These disabilities, which seem to be ever-more common, affect children development by heightening the sense of danger and vulnerability.

The chapter authored by Drs. Eliza Dragowski, María Scharrón-del Río, and Ms. Amy Sandigorsky investigates the rationale for gender identity disorder (GID) diagnosis and explores gender-atypical conditions in childhood. While homosexuality is no longer associated with psychopathology, GID continues to be listed in the *DSM* as a diagnosable condition. Arguments for maintaining the diagnosis include the notion that the label offers parents access to third-party payment for therapy—the purpose of therapy is assumed to focus on the parents need to accept the child's gender identity. Clearly this is still a controversial diagnosis that can be tangentially related to atypical sexual development. The authors describe the current thinking regarding disorders of sex differentiation in children and their psychological implications.

The conclusion focuses on disability and parenting, with emphasis on how family relationships both affect and are shaped by disability. In that chapter I also address how families raising children with disabilities interact with schools, and particularly with the special education teachers, clinicians, and administrators.

Childhood disability presents challenges not only to the child and her family but also to the broader social network where they live. The extended family, neighbors, nondisabled peers, shopkeepers and hairdressers, everyone who interacts with the family could play a constructive and supportive role. Unfortunately, despite substantial gains, children with disabilities are still often excluded from being full participants in their communities. Exclusion is sometimes by design—such as when making requirements for participation in an activity contingent on demonstrated ability in specific tasks. At other times it may be lack of attention or consideration—like an outing on a boat that precludes wheelchair access. In writing this book we hope to contribute to a fuller understanding of the issues and needs of children with disabilities and families raising them.

References

American Psychiatric Association. (2000). *Diagnostic and statistical manual of mental disorders* (4th ed., text rev.). Washington, DC: Author.

Mercer, J. R. (1973). *Labeling the mentally retarded: Clinical and social system perspectives on mental retardation.* Berkeley: University of California Press.

Supplemental Security Income. http://www.ssa.gov/pubs/10026.html.

U.S. Department of Education. http://idea.ed.gov/explore/view/p/,root,regs, 300,A,300%252E8,c,.

World Health Organization. http://www.who.int/topics/disabilities/en/.

CHAPTER 1

Parents, Children with Disabilities, and Social Integration

Alberto M. Bursztyn

The way we talk about disability—the words we use, the tone of voice we effect, the reactions we anticipate in the listener—reveals the common discomfort and anxiety that surrounds human frailty and difference. The uneasiness is magnified when we speak of children with disabilities. Our culture is prone to assign individuals to categories, and the disabled have the unfortunate status of being defined culturally by their limitations. Race, religion, gender, and other social categories focus on specific personal attributes and/or beliefs, but none is as disempowering as disability—which places individuals into a group by virtue of their presumed lack of ability or their need for care. Disability is a social category of exclusion.

It is instructive in this regard to trace the evolving vocabulary of disability in the English language. Cripples, gave way to the handicapped, who later became disabled, or exceptional, and lately to individuals with disabilities. Some insist on the term *individuals with differences.* Contemporary disability rights activists would prefer to talk about challenges rather than disabilities, and others object to the mere effort of differentiating people with disabilities from those who ostensibly don't have them—or don't have them yet. After all, they point out—we are all likely to become disabled sooner or later.

The trouble with making disability disappear by simply seeing it as another form or degree of difference in human experience is that we may overlook the particular and central challenges that shape the identity of young people growing up with specific sensory, cognitive, emotional and/or physical challenges. Could we make things better by describing a child who is blind as being in a continuum with another who needs corrective lenses to see the board? They are both visually challenged, but the child who needs glasses may experience the world similarly to the child with 20/20 eyesight, whereas the child who is blind—even more so if the child was born blind—will live in a space where sounds, touch, and smell will play a greater role in defining experience. For the child who is blind, inability to see will inevitably become a core element of identity, whereas the child who wears glasses, or perhaps contact lenses, may not internalize limited vision in the same way.

Here lies a paradox: The more we seek to eliminate disability by seeing it as simply a manifestation of individual differences in a human continuum, the more we may delegitimize the centrality of individual limitations in identity formation. This tension was not lost on Miguel and Laura Perez, Carolina's parents. Carolina, a 10-year-old child with cerebral palsy that affected her movement and speech, had been educated for most of her life in a school serving exclusively children with physical and heath disorders. In the third grade, her parents brought her to the neighborhood school to continue her education among nondisabled peers. However, Carolina continued to use the pool and other services available through the specialized school. Mr. Perez explained that Carolina is learning at the local school like any other child on their block, but, he added, "her body belongs in the specialized school." The family anticipated and understood that although Carolina was making strides in developing a social network in her new school, she would always be seen as different, and she needed to accept her condition as an integral part of her identity. Maintaining connection with children experiencing similar challenges gave her perspective on her limitations and helped her cope with her feelings of being sidelined in sports and other physically competitive activities in the regular school.

Raising a Child with Disabilities

The awareness of individual differences emerges early in human consciousness. We learn whose voice is soothing when we are in distress, and whose voice is a prelude for active play. We soon learn that a sibling may be an exciting presence but cannot feed us. As children identify the members of their immediate family and other caregivers, they also form strong emotional bonds that not only guide development but form the basis of future dispositions, character, and identity.

As children grow, they are celebrated for their accomplishments. "He walked at nine months!" Or, "She spoke in full sentences at age two!" "She could throw a ball like a boy!" "And he would read stories to his sister when he was still in kindergarten." The stories are different for those children who cannot perform as well as their siblings and peers. Children growing up with a disability are more likely to experience anxious parental expectations and veiled sadness. Of course, when the child with cerebral palsy takes a first step unsupported, or the child who has severe autism takes a change in daily routine in stride, there is likely to be an outpouring of affectionate jubilation, but also one that betrays the long wait, the worries, the doubts about whether this was just a fluke rather than sustainable change. Thus parental worries permeate childhood—often resulting in children's feelings of self doubt or, less frequently, in reactive independence. Even when the family does its best to protect the child from feelings of inferiority due to limitations, the encounter with typically developing peers and siblings is likely to accentuate the sense of difference and unfairness.

Family therapists speak of homeostasis, the tendency of all systems, including families, to maintain or restore equilibrium. A family affected by a disability seeks to restore the lost balance, but the child's needs change the parents and the nature of their families in profound ways. Parents might be drawn together and support one another and the child; many times the added stress contributes to the relationship falling apart. Laura Marshak and Fran Prezant have written eloquently about the stresses of raising a child with disabilities and focus on how couples need to renegotiate and adjust their relationship to meet the new and evolving family needs. Their perspective suggests that couples must be prepared to reassess and revisit the needs of all family members because the challenges of disability are not restricted to childhood but are lifelong.

Rather than denying or minimizing difference, parents and siblings can be more helpful by fostering the child's acceptance of difference while highlighting the child's strengths. Children respond to the parental view and acceptance of the disability and internalize the often unspoken message. Oscar's mother said about him, "He has the sweetest smile in the family. Having Down's syndrome does not restrict your emotional life and capacity to feel. He is more sensitive than any of my other children." In a similar vein, Rachel's mother said, "She always knows when I need a kiss," about her daughter with Rhett's syndrome.

Adjustment requires parents to abandon their original dreams and hopes and instead reframe, reassess, and embrace a more realistic set of hopes and expectations. An allegory written by Emily Perl Kingsley, and widely quoted by parents of children with disabilities, addresses the initial confusion and subsequent acceptance of having a child with a diagnosable disability. She describes pregnancy as the euphoric feeling of planning a vacation to Italy— a destination full of exciting possibilities. But several months later, as the plane lands, the flight attendant says, "Welcome to Holland." The feeling of disbelief and disappointment, the shattered dreams and fantasies associated with Italy must be abandoned. One must deal with a new, inescapable reality that, after all is not a ". . . horrible, disgusting, filthy place, full of pestilence, famine and disease. It's just a different place." Learning a new language, getting a new guidebook, and learning to appreciate the tulips and windmills are part of coming to terms with the unintended change of course. Ms. Kingsley writes that the lost dream of Italy is a source of pain that will never go away, but she poignantly concludes her short essay this way: "But . . . if you spend your life mourning the fact that you didn't get to Italy, you may never be free to enjoy the very special, the very lovely things . . . about Holland."

Much has been written about the sequential stages of mourning, which are implied in the loss of the dreamed child. Drawn from studies on grief and bereavement, these stages suggest a progression from disbelief to acceptance; the grieving process is described frequently in self-help books and special education textbooks. The five stages may be summarized as follows: shock and denial are the first reactions—a parent may say "This can't be happening to me," or "The doctors don't know what they are talking about, my child will be fine!" A subsequent stage may be colored by anger as the parent lashes out—"Whose fault is it? I'll bring those responsible to account!" The stage that follows, usually described as bargaining, may consist of conversations and promises to God or another higher power that could heal the child. At these stages parents may engage in a frantic search for a miracle cure; but depression might follow as the parent feels increasingly helpless, exhausted, and abandoned in the subsequent stage. The final stage is acceptance or resignation, when the parent gains perspective and balance and learns to cope with the situation.

I interviewed a number of parents of children with severe disabilities for a study focusing on transitions from one educational context to another. They echoed many of the features of the stages described above, but most notably there was no clear sense of sequence or a notion of final acceptance or resolution. More typically, parents described a fluid emotional journey, with inescapable return to anxiety every time the child's school or child-care arrangement needed to change or when new challenges emerged as the child developed.

The parents I interviewed were a resilient and resourceful group; some of them had carefully chosen the school district they lived in with their children's education and care in mind. Yet the strain and pain of raising a child with severe disabilities was often heard in their responses and remarks. One mother said eloquently:

> There is frustration for the parents. It is more than physical. Okay, when you have a disabled child, you feel frustrated and then you learn to adapt to the situation, but you never accept it. When I see my daughter with other kids I say, Oh my God . . . I cry without the tears.

Another mother expressed a similar sentiment about her child with a degenerative genetic condition. She said "the life of a child with special needs is not normal." And then she added:

> The difficulty is always there, but one has to hope for the best, but if there is something that presents itself like another setback. I have to deal with this on a daily basis. Sometimes one feels depressed or tension—in fact, there is always this tension of what will happen tomorrow or what could be happening even now. Anxiety, that is always present, but we have learned to overcome.

Another parent described her emotional state as colored by pervasive sadness and exhaustion. She expressed how at each stage of her boy's development she and her husband have had to make difficult decisions about how to address not only their child's changing needs, but the whole family's way of life.

Parents understood that their own despair might affect their children negatively; they sought to maintain their calm and protect their children from negative feelings. As a parent of a child with traumatic brain injury (TBI) said,

> the first and number one thing is to have patience. That is one thing you have to have is a lot, a lot of patience. I'm learning that sometimes you can lose it, but yet right away you pick it up again. If you don't have patience, you cannot deal with it. Then you need psychological help yourself. You need a lot of patience and try to make him feel normal.

Parents raising children with physical disabilities and health impairments become aware that the child's disability will affect not only the child's physical being, but also her psychological health, including self-concept and interpersonal relations. While the initial emphasis is justifiably focused on treatment and therapies to ameliorate or cure the condition, parents must weigh how these interventions become formative experiences and building blocks of the maturing self. The time and effort dedicated to therapies and treatments inevitably interfere with other tasks of childhood, such as play, developing peer relations, and simply unhurriedly enjoying a recreational activity. When the primary preoccupation of parents is to rid the child of her disability, the consequence may be that the child sees herself as damaged and that parental love is conditional on her commitment to therapy. Under those conditions the child may rebel against treatment when she concludes that treatment is not a cure, or begin to sabotage it in a passive-aggressive way. In more extreme cases it can be the root of depression and helplessness. For the child to develop an emotionally healthy self, she must feel that parental love is not tied to therapy and be given sufficient time and opportunities to be regular kid in the family. But even when parents are conscious of their child's needs and do their best to cushion the difficulties they are likely to encounter, they can not anticipate or prevent emotional setbacks. Sharon, the mother of a teenage girl with motoric difficulties and cognitive delays, described her child's meltdown:

> Stacy was always an anxious kid, but in many ways she has always been very high in the school setting . . . she could go with the flow even if she was more an observer than a participant academically. She would find someway and the teachers would make her feel included. . . . As time went on, that started falling away when she realized that, you know, she started having greater realizations about who she was in relationships with other people with more ability, and part of what happened here was that she gave up. She was one of those kids that people would say don't stop trying and work themselves

to the bone. I also think that she was working to please people as opposed to doing it for something more . . . somewhere along the line
she quit, she just stopped being herself and was out of it. It was very
scary. . . . She regressed to a place I had not seen in a long time.

Sharon and Pete, Stacy's parents, reassessed her school placement and
therapy schedule and soon after made significant changes to accommodate Stacy's changing physical and emotional needs.

For parents, the educational and therapeutic options entail not only a
division of labor but also agreement on a specific course of action. It is
not uncommon that one parent will be more involved than another or become more hard driving than the spouse, thus leading to conflict within
the couple. To the extent that parents are aware of and comfortable playing different roles, the child will recognize the role each parent plays and
will respond accordingly. The following example is based on a conversation with a young family whose only daughter is affected by a muscular
syndrome.

Dad:	I want to push her, and you don't.
Mom:	No, and I want to protect her. So there you have it. The first half of the sentence belongs to him, and the second half of the sentence belongs to me.
Dad:	She'll fall, and I'll say, just get off your butt and let's move on, and she'll say, "Oh, Jodi . . . if she's hurting herself, she'll stop falling." I take her outside, we're playing baseball, riding a bike, you fell, you're okay, let's keep going, move on.
Interviewer:	What continues to be a challenge for your family?
Dad:	How much to protect.
Mom:	Yes, because we both realize that, you know, sometimes I give in to the fact that he's pushing and sometimes he gives into the fact that I'm mothering.
Dad:	It depends on the situation.
Mom:	It depends on the situation.
Interviewer:	Does it in anyway impact the family unit?
Dad:	No. Do we sit there and scream at each other about it? No, nothing like that. . . .
Mom:	No, no. (Interrupting) We laugh at each other. We do the good cop, bad cop routine. That's what we call it. We do it a lot. We do it a lot you know just to try to achieve the results or sooth the . . . like if she's mad at him be-cause he's pushed her too hard, then I'll come in and go, "Ah, you know, I understand." And if I'm being too mothering, he's like, "Uh, you know your mother, she's all over you" (laughing). So you know what I mean. He says "Just ignore her."

The previous scenario suggests a rather harmonious balance but one that can be easily disrupted as the child grows older and the perceptions and expectations change. Another couple we interviewed was extremely dedicated to finding the best therapies for their child, but as the preferred treatment required periodic long stays in Europe, the husband, who stayed behind caring for the other two younger children, spoke with resignation about the loss of balance in the family. A mother told me that her family's greatest success in still being together. She added:

> A lot of parents get separated, divorced, because it is very hard on the marriage. It's very hard on the kids. We still have it together. Our kids come first, and hopefully there will be a time for us, but right now, you know, I have had to give up my job and my husband works a lot of hours.

Attending to their children's special needs requires substantial planning and structure. Beyond considerations about access and mobility, parents needed to manage complex therapy and services schedules. A major transition, such as changing schools, presents serious challenges to the routines that families had adopted; therefore, change was approached with hesitation and caution. A mother in our study said:

> Well, we have a very structured life. That's what happened. We know that are the things that we have to do with her. For example, if we are going shopping, if we're going to do things for fun, we have to structure them. We have to plan. We manage improvisation, but it can't be that much. Then during the week, she goes for swimming classes, she goes for therapy, so all that is integrated. We have a very tight schedule. I'm always worried that something can go wrong, like the bus not coming or our van breaking down.

Change of school, for most of these families, was a difficult and carefully weighed decision. Attending to their children's special needs require substantial planning and structure. Parenting a child with health and physical needs presents a broader set of challenges than parenting a typically developing child. The necessary and ever-present concern for the child's physical well-being often evolves into a protective stance that limits the nature and quality of interaction between these children and their typically developing peers. This parental stance often extends to protecting the child, not only from physical injury or disease but also from emotional injury. It is not unusual for parents of children with disabilities to seek a school that offers a safe, protective, and sheltering environment, fearing that their children will be taunted or humiliated by their typically developing peers.

Yet parents often value their child's wish to be part of a larger social framework and begin to search for a balance between protectiveness and exposure, between isolation and integration. The parents interviewed in this study generally leaned toward maximizing the child's engagement with same-age peers and, in general, sought to promote the child's sense of self-worth and efficacy by normalizing their lives. For instance, a mother of a boy with cerebral palsy stated: "I try not to make my kid feel that the disease is more serious than what it is. Let them feel that they are normal kids, just like other kids." Parents raising children with disabilities face the challenge of mediating the world for the child, searching for the right balance between engagement in the world and protection from the world, between trusting the child's capacities and doubt.

An aspect of disability that requires attention is that the impairment is generally not shared with family members—it tends to be unique to the child and distinguishes her from siblings. This embodied difference does not preclude full membership in the family, but the nature of the impairment can become the family's center of gravity and parental concern. The consequences for siblings are far reaching; the child with disabilities will drawing disproportional attention, and this asymmetrical focus may be read as disproportional love. Typically developing siblings will generally understand the vulnerability of the affected brother or sister and will quickly learn to be a parent-helper, a much appreciated role. But the forbidden and suppressed thoughts and jealousies may linger and eventually undermine the sibling relationship. Guilt also tends to grow in families when parents and typically developing siblings blame themselves, justifiably or not, for the affected child's condition. Guilt and dread could spring from entirely irrational and unconscious sources yet may have a real impact on the quality of interactions.

Although a significant proportion of siblings of children with disabilities choose to enter helping professions in adulthood, some speak with ambivalence about their having grown up in a home where they felt less important or less loved that their impaired sibling. Even when the impairment is psychiatric or behavioral in nature, the siblings could be similarly affected. Jacqueline, the younger sister of a youth with early onset bipolar disorder, complained in therapy that her brother was given preferential treatment at home and that she was always at the receiving end of her parents' frustrations and despair. Even when he was abusive toward her, she felt abandoned by her parents who struggled to make sense of his outbursts.

Children with emotional and other less-visible disabilities encounter thorny social challenges, not the least within the home, as in Jacqueline's case. Because they may not at first stand out within a peer group and the nature of their disability might be masked, when the manifestation of the disorder becomes evident, it is often misunderstood. Thus children with behavioral disorders pose a different kind of parental challenge in promoting social integration. For these parents there are greater concerns that the child's behavior may be interpreted as a manifestation of poor parenting, with the attending sense of shame. A child that hits, tantrums, makes odd sounds, or runs around aimlessly stands out in a playground, restaurant, or movie theater. These families must contend with critical stares, unsolicited advice, and other potential humiliations; under those circumstances, parents of children who exhibit unusual behaviors commonly seek the refuge of seclusion, with potential exacerbation of atypical behaviors.

For these children, navigating the social world could be as daunting as it is for children with physical disabilities to get around in the physical world. The experience of peer rejection, an ever-present concern for parents and children alike, could also trigger more pronounced symptoms of the disorder. Social situations that trigger anxiety and stress in children with Tourette's syndrome and children with autism spectrum disorders (ASD) lead to more overt tic behavior and more self-stimulation (*stimming*), respectively. Also, children with poor impulse control might act out when they feel slighted or snubbed. Parents of children with these types of challenges soon learn to plan recreation and socialization activities with care and be attuned to the child's capacity to sustain social engagement. A mother of a third-grade girl with Asperger syndrome explained how her daughter's emerging social life is orchestrated and supervised:

> When you have a disabled child, you are always running late. There is no room for socialization except in school. They do a lot in school (the child is in an integrated classroom part of the day), but after school there is nothing. For her birthday I sent invitations for the kids to come over to watch TV. Boys and girls, a nice group of kids came over. I prepared popcorn and the house nice for the kids. They loved it. I took a picture of Katy with her friends and all of them were very, very nice. . . . But it's something she was complaining about the other day; they don't invite her.

Disability is an isolating condition; breaking out of isolation is contingent on many individual and family factors, but in order for children with disabilities to become full members of their communities, society also needs to change.

Disability and Society

Contemporary and emergent views on childhood disability are clearly leaning in the direction of maximum integration and participation, with the eventual goal of independence and self-reliance. It has not always been this way. Older generations drew sharp lines between those who were considered normal and those with handicaps. The child with severe disability was more likely then to reside in an institution than be raised at home. Until the 1960s it was common practice for pediatricians and other professionals to recommend residential placement for children with severe sensory, physical, or cognitive deficits. Children born with Down's syndrome or other severe cognitive or physical disabilities were commonly separated from their families, often at the hospital's nursery. The standard medical advice was to tell the sad parents that the child would ruin their family's life and that they should go home and try again.

To understand contemporary approaches and attitudes toward child-hood disability in the United States, one must revisit the Willowbrook ex-posé. Willowbrook was a New York State funded major residential facility for the disabled in Staten Island, a cluster of large buildings in a pastoral setting within the New York City limits. The serene exterior belied the hor-rific conditions to which the residents were subjected. Geraldo Rivera, then a young intrepid reporter for a local TV station, broke in with cameraman who later released the footage, documenting appalling, inhumane and de-grading treatment of children and adults with disabilities. Residents were seen naked and idle, others were screaming, rocking and bound, most were filthy, and some were naked and covered in excrement. The smell was nau-seating. Children were ostensibly in school, but no learning was taking place; instead they were being warehoused, neglected, and poorly nour-ished. The staff-patient ratio was inadequate to feed the residents, and the dining hall scenes were barbaric. Practically forgotten by society, overextended caretakers supervised an institution more reminiscent of a medieval asylum than of a late 20th-century residential facility. Willow-brook and multiple other institutions like it were a low priority to the po-litical establishment and were chronologically and severely underfunded.

Willowbrook was for the disabled community what the Stonewall riot was for the gay and lesbian rights movement and the Selma-to-Montgomery marches were to the civil rights struggle. It was a critical historical moment that changed the social discourse; the plight of the disabled brought forth a sense shame and, later, sympathy. There was no going back; Willowbrook was to be closed forever, and most of those neglected people with disabilities came to live in neighborhoods, in family homes, in supported residences in practically every neighborhood. Not everything went smoothly; some tragi-cally ended up homeless in the streets of New York, and many neighbor-hoods fought fiercely against organizations setting up residences in their back yards.

Still, Willowbrook cast a long shadow. Advocates and parents gained a foothold on policy forums, and their efforts facilitated the passage of sweeping educational reform. The Education for all Handicapped Chil-dren Act of 1975, also known as Public Law 94-142, gave birth to the spe-cial education system we now take for granted. It guaranteed a free and appropriate public education for all. It also championed the least restric-tive environment principle; it was now the responsibility of local school districts to create the programs and provide the supports that children might need. School administrators could no longer deny access to children with disabilities. Parents now had more options for their children's school-ing; children with disabilities returned to families and communities.

Each society's policy on childhood disability is a reflection of its values and priorities. Consequently, as societies change, so do their approaches to addressing children with special needs. In fact, as women, minorities, and children's rights come into focus in the context of addressing historical in-justices, concurrent concerns for the rights of individuals with disabilities inexorably lead to greater access and accommodations. There are clear parallels between the enhanced status of the disabled in a given society and the quality of civil rights for all. Historically, the opposite is also true, and there is no clearer example than the Nazi regime's early extermination of individuals with severe disabilities—a program that was not only endorsed but also carried out by the German medical establishment while Hitler consolidated power. The widespread euthanizing of severely disabled persons was the first step in human history's most brutal campaign of persecution and genocide. At that time, many states in this country had an active sterilization program targeting minority persons with below-average intelligence.

In the United States today, and in most of the industrialized world, there is a growing consensus that children with special needs should be integrated into society to the maximum extent possible. Warehousing children with disabilities in institutions and orphanages is still practiced widely in poorer countries, but the emerging trends point to greater community access and acceptance as parents and educators advocate for justice and change.

There are cultural and historical similarities between the struggle for civil rights and the emergence of an assertive disability rights community. Both, at their inception, sought to redefine and expand individual freedom and facilitate access where it had been denied. But the work has not simply been limited to changing society; just as critical has been the self-empowerment of those who have suffered debilitating discrimination and prejudice. In this sense, the cultural forces shaping change in the context of disability may be more layered than those typical of the civil rights; women's liberation; and gay, lesbian, bisexual, and transgender (GLBT) movements. Special education has been shaped primarily by advocates—especially parents, educators, and policy makers who for the most part are not persons with disabilities. Within universities, disability studies have gained a foothold as an academic discourse, focusing on disability as a interpretative framework and as a dimension of identity. Concurrently, and gaining strength, groups of people with disabilities are coming together to advocate for themselves. Their views of special education and traditional treatment approaches are not necessarily positive, because they represent attempts to expunge aspects of their identity. An interesting example of such a group is the loosely organized Aspies for Freedom. This group of people, who have been diagnosed with ASD or Asperger syndrome, rebel against therapies focusing on reshaping behavior. They make the case that society must become more open to different ways of being. Their Web site states the following:

> We have the view that Asperger and autism are not negative, and are not always a disability. . . . We know that autism is not a disease, and we oppose any attempts to "cure" someone of an autism spectrum condition, or any attempts to make them "normal" against their will.

We are part of building the autism culture. We aim to strengthen autism rights, oppose all forms of discrimination against aspies and
auties, and work to bring the community together both online and
offline. (Aspies for Freedom, n.d.)

The challenge to place the onus of acceptance on society in lieu of changing the individual with disabilities is most clearly evident in Deaf culture.
Deafness is seen by the largely hearing world as a disability, yet individuals who communicate effectively through sign language and participate
actively in a similarly capable community make a persuasive case that deafness is not impairing to their capacity to live fulfilling and healthy lives. The
Deaf community challenges the rest of us to recognize the implications of
applying the label *disabled* to a child by virtue of not conforming to a cultural norm. To the extent that those norms could be redefined, the meaning
of disability will change.

It is undeniable that free public education, support for community-based
services, and, more recently, legislation to facilitate access for individuals
with disabilities (American's with Disabilities Act of 1990) in employment
and other settings, have improved the lives and prospects of persons with
disabilities. Technology, in particular, has open new possibilities for social
and employment integration as personal mobility and work-site location
become increasingly disconnected from requirements of work. Assistive
technologies also contribute to expanding capabilities and communication; yet, these sociological currents and technological innovations say little
about how they affect individual identity and personal narratives.

In a social world organized by categories, there is the added danger of
essentializing common denominators; that is, limiting individual options
to assert a personal narrative because of the pressure to conform to membership in designated categories. In the case of the disabled, educators,
medical personnel, and mental health workers have defined those categories of disability for the purpose of treatment. Michel Foucault, the French
philosopher, would add that those categories also serve the purposes of
monitoring and control. Internalizing an identity as special education student, therapy client, or medical patient implies that the child is adopting
a view of self that is partly defined by a need to be remediated, treated,
or medicated. This deficit-driven view of the self can be diminish self-
efficacy and lead to self-perception as damaged or abnormal if the child
has not developed other sources of identity and strength.

Tom Shakespeare, an English disabilities studies scholar, notes that the
discourse on people with disabilities can take two meanings. When "identifying" is used as an active verb it implies uncovering or discovering disabled people. In that sense the identifier is external to the identified; such
would be the case when professionals assess and diagnose a disability. The
second meaning is found in the reflexive form of the verb, as is when one
identifies oneself as disabled. In such a case one stakes a claim as part of a
group or community of persons with disabilities. These semantic differences

draw the dividing lines between the assignment to a social category and the assumption of a personal and group identity.

Shakespeare has written about disability and identity, focusing both on categorization from above, societal, and identification from below, in the personal realm.

The social model focuses on dismantling barriers that may prevent the disabled from full inclusion in society. In this regard, the removal of physical barriers as well as prejudices aims to integrate those who suffer from the stigma of disability. In the social model encompasses all those affected by social prejudice, the individual with disability as well as his family.

A more political stance defines those with disabilities as members of a minority group. As such, persons with disabilities can argue for access and accommodations based on their status as an oppressed minority. Although this posture is consonant with the social model, it emphasizes identity politics in the course of gathering power.

A third approach to disability is as a category of social policy. In this regard, disability is a statutory construct, such as those for access to benefits or accommodations. It is tied to the legal processes and definitions that construct disability rather than to the person with impairments. Similarly disconnected from personal experience is the fourth approach, which constructs disability as the outcome of definitions inherent in social research surveys. The number of people who can be classified as suffering from a specific disorder in a particular region does not provide a useful context for understanding the experience of the disorder by the individuals included in the study.

The fifth category identified by Shakespeare relates to disability as a cultural construct; in his view this offers the best options for individuals' narratives and experiences to be integrated in self-identity. The tension between being defined and categorized by others and the need to form a personally meaningful narrative is a salient feature of the experience of disability. He concludes that disability identity is about telling stories, having the space to tell them, and having an audience that will listen. These views can help children with disabilities and their parents understand that the challenges of disability are not exclusively linked to therapies, access, or advocacy but more profoundly on how to develop a meaningful identity, drawing from the unique biographical narrative within the shared family and cultural contexts.

References

Appiah, K.A. (1994). Identity, authenticity, survival: Multicultural societies and social reproduction. In A. Gutman (Ed.), *Multiculturalism: Examining the politics of recognition.* (pp. 149–163).

Aspies for Freedom. (n.d.). "About AFF." Retrieved July 7, 2010, from the Aspies for Freedom Web site: http://www.aspiesforfreedom.com

Harry, B., Klingner, J., Carmer, E., Sturges, K., &. Moore, R. (2007). *Case studies of minority student placement in special education.* New York: Teachers College Press.

Ong-Dean, C. (2009). *Distinguishing disability: Parents, privilege, and special education.* Chicago: University of Chicago Press.

Shakespeare, T. (1996). Disability, identity and difference. In C. Barnes & G. Mercer (Eds.), *Exploring the divide* (pp. 94–113). Leeds, UK: The Disability Press.

Skrtic, T. M. (1995). *Disability and democracy: Reconstructing (special) education for postmodernity.* New York: Teachers College Press.

Webb, N. B. (2001). *Culturally diverse parent-child and family relationships: A guide for social workers and other practitioners.* New York: Columbia University Press.

CHAPTER 2

Understanding Childhood Disabilities through Culturally Diverse Families' Perspectives

Yoon-Joo Lee and Alberto M. Bursztyn

Introduction

Our work with families of children with special needs in diverse contexts and our own personal experiences with culture change, school, and disability inform this chapter. We also focus attention on how the culture shapes beliefs, attitudes and programs for children with disabilities. Dr. Yoon-Joo Lee, the first author, was born in South Korea and came to the United States as a teenager with her family. She completed high school in Texas. She currently serves in a board of directors for a nonprofit parent advocacy agency for Korean American families of children with special needs. Dr. Alberto Bursztyn also arrived at the United States as a teenage immigrant; he came with his parents from Argentina and completed high school and higher education in New York City. Both Drs. Lee and Bursztyn are members of the graduate special education faculty at Brooklyn College and often teach a course on families and disabilities to students in teacher education.

Through our shared experiences as teacher educators—specifically, preparing special education teachers—we often consider the challenges of working effectively with children and families from linguistically and culturally diverse backgrounds. Different cultural communities embrace narratives on disabilities that have been shaped by history, tradition, folk beliefs, and faith practices. In a global sense, diverse families with special needs may have different understandings, explanations, and remedies for various conditions; therefore, we need to recognize that disability is not simply an objective condition but also a social characteristic of a person, influenced by culture, religion, gender, class, and other factors.

MOORESVILLE PUBLIC LIBRARY
220 WEST HARRISON STREET
MOORESVILLE, INDIANA 46158

These culturally informed perspectives mediate how people make sense of disability and respond to people with disabilities. Values and stigma are often associated with people with disabilities, but these are far from uniform across impairments, cultures, and traditions. The cultural context that communicates explicit as well as subtle cultural and religious messages contributes to shaping life experiences for people with disabilities and their families. Although perceptions of disability change across and within cultures, these changes appear glacial to those most directly affected. Within our professional roles we often encounter divergent understanding of needs and priorities. We are also aware that the perspective of the child's parents, particularly when they agree with school recommendations, often generates tensions with extended family and community members who hold views on the child's disability grounded in the group's traditional beliefs.

Values, attitudes, and beliefs regarding disabilities vary across cultures and within cultures. Moreover, these views are not static but are constantly changing and evolving, and they are increasingly molded by secular, technological, and Western influences. Consequently, one may encounter multiple simultaneous interpretations of a specific disability or condition. For example, while there may be little argument regarding a child's inability to hear as measured by a competent audiologist, the meaning of deafness for the child and the family could vary radically if the child is born to deaf parents or to a hearing couple. Within a proud Deaf community there may be some members who feel relief that the child resembles the parents in every respect; while for hearing parents the child's condition is likely to be seen first as a disability and second as medical and educational challenge.

Based on current research and clinical experiences working with families of children with disabilities from diverse cultural backgrounds, we identified several themes illustrating the intersection between culture and disability in childhood. Specific case studies and anecdotes illustrate our narrative. We begin with autobiographical narratives of disability.

Yoon-Joo's Story

As a person with a physical disability—cerebral palsy—growing up in two different countries—Korea and the United States—I have felt and embodied how cultures play a significant role in shaping the experience and identity of people with disabilities. One thing that Koreans consider extremely important is *saving face,* and each family member is responsible to uphold the family's good name. If an individual does not achieve success and attain a desirable social standing, this is considered to bring shame to the whole family. In that hypercritical and evaluative context, a person with disabilities is often perceived as an embarrassment within the family; it is not unusual for family members to hide the person with disabilities from the public. I painfully recall when I was young, one of my aunts was getting married to a man from a high-status family; my grandparents didn't want me to attend the wedding ceremony. My parents were really disappointed and hurt by other family members' responses. But from the perspectives of other family members, my visible physical disability was not something they wanted to show in a public event such as a large family wedding. As I reflect on past events, I realize how family reputation in Korean culture is largely based on others' perception of the family; disability is interpreted negatively and casts embarrassment within the family.

Koreans strongly emphasize obligations and care for other family members. The oldest son is expected to take responsibility for his aged parents. In this cultural context, a person with disabilities is more likely to be perceived as a burden and a responsibility to other family members. Because my parents have always encouraged me to be independent, I had never thought about being dependent on my brother when my parents would be unable to look after me anymore, but I noticed my brother had a different perspective. When my brother was in a serious relationship with his girlfriend and wanted to talk about the marriage, one of the first things he discussed with her was whether she was okay with a fact that he had a sister with a disability whom he might need to look after. When I heard that my brother had this conversation, I found it very interesting because this showed how he perceived his role as a guardian, even though it was never explicitly discussed. Although at the time I was already an advanced graduate student in the United States, he was still following a deep-rooted cultural expectation that defined his role as the caretaker of weaker family members.

When reflecting on my experience as a person with disabilities, I often think about how I have encountered stigmatization, and how my cognitive and intellectual abilities have often been underestimated. I was perceived in a negative way, at least initially in school settings; how others responded to me directly related to how well I performed academically. This might be due to the fact that educational achievement is highly regarded in Korea. My junior high school experience was mostly about explaining to others that I could do well on the tests, despite my physical disability. I still remember how difficult it was to be the only student with disabilities in a huge public school. Back then, most students with disabilities attended segregated special education schools, and only few students were mainstreamed into regular schools without any formal support. I had attended a specialized elementary school for children with cerebral palsy (CP), but my mother had other plans. I believe my mother recognized my potential to follow along the general education curriculum. My parents' goal for me was to be admitted to a four-year college. Even though she didn't tell me explicitly, I could sense that she just wanted to try out a regular school for me. She believed that if I kept attending special education schools, the teachers in these schools would have lower expectations. When she shared her decision to send me to a regular junior high school,

I was very anxious and did not want to face the world where I would be visibly different from others.

My mother was very supportive and determined to advocate on my behalf. In the beginning of every school year, she arranged for a conference with teachers to explain to them the nature of my disability, which did not mean I was cognitively or mentally challenged. The first year in the junior high school was painfully challenging, because it was the first time in my life that I was the only student with disability in the midst of 2,500 teenage girls.

I believe that the social network of children with CP was a foundational experience for me. Since all my elementary school friends had CP, during that time I felt accepted as who I was. Someone from the outside might object to this kind of environment as inappropriate segregated, but, reflecting back, this experience helped me become more capable when I was finally mainstreamed. In the beginning, mainstreaming was challenging, but whenever I faced difficulties I remembered how well-regarded I was in the academic and social network of children with CP. This helped me discern when my typically developing peers began to see me beyond my disability. Perhaps paradoxically the segregated environment was a foundation for social inclusion for me.

In the regular school, my seventh-grade homeroom teacher was not happy about the fact that I was placed in her class, and let me know about it in an indirect way. It was not because she was worried that I might be disruptive and present challenging behaviors; she was concerned that my grades might lower the average of her class and that her reputation as a teacher might be undermined as a result. It took two months for her to realize that I was not the one who brought down the average grade. If I did well on the test, this teacher would show my report card to rebuke and pressure others to do better. I did not like that type of attention, because I didn't want to stand out. Still, my academic performance became the standard that others used to judge me. Through my grades, I felt a consistent need to prove to others that my physical disability did not mean I was slow. When comparing my experiences in Korea and the United States, I realize that in the United States I was not as concerned about the need to prove my worth to others through my grades. GPA is not the standard by which students evaluate each other in U.S. schools, but in Korea it was the key to being accepted.

When my grades showed that I was capable of following the general education curriculum, teachers' and peers' perceptions began to change. In the beginning, it was difficult for my peers to see me as who I was beyond the disability. My most vivid and painful memory of the first year in junior high school was watching my peers looking at me as if they had never seen a person with disabilities. When the homeroom teacher assigned one girl to sit next to me, she put her head down and began to cry. She didn't tell me directly why she was crying, but later that afternoon I found that she cried because she thought my disability was contagious and that she would catch disability from me. The homeroom teacher had to ask another student to sit next to me. As I recall events during the first year of junior high, I realize how my homeroom teacher often intervened to make sure that I would not be isolated or bullied. She made sure someone from the class was watching me, especially during field trips. Even though I understood her good intention, I resented it because I felt like she was assuming that I would not have any friends.

From my personal experience, I recognize the significant role of culture in my life story. Because Koreans value education highly, my parents pushed me to pursue a doctoral degree. Educational achievement is a key to inclusive education, social integration, and employment. But in Korea, the stigma associated with my physical disability did not end because I was employed and was able to live an independent life. Just a month ago while I was visiting my parents in Seoul, I decided to join a local fitness club so that I could continue to exercise during my vacation. Back in the United States I had never had a problem joining a gym; a sales representative typically explains the policy regarding safety and liability, and I sign the contract and pay the membership fee. I had a totally different experience in Korea. At first, the owner of the gym was reluctant to accept my membership. After my father explained to him that I had a regular gym membership in the United States and was used to working out in the gym, the owner accepted my membership under the condition that my father would accompany me while I worked out. Recently, the Korean government has passed legislations to ensure equity and inclusion for people with disabilities. The society is becoming more accepting, the education services for children with disabilities resemble the contemporary American model, and in some areas are even better than in the United States. Yet my own recent experience made me realize once again how people's perception of disability, rooted in cultural beliefs, cannot be easily changed through progressive legislation or policies. My frequent visits to Korea convince me that, although the laws protect individuals with disabilities in Korea, my disability would have raised greater concerns to employers than it would in the United States.

Living in the United States may also attest to my acculturation to this society. My parents have been supportive, loving, and strong advocates; their commitment to my growth and education has been unwavering. Yet, living away from them blunts their tendency to be overprotective—the Korean approach to family—and affirms my very American sense of independence and individualism. After 20 years of living in the United States, I realized how Americanized I have become. My experience as a person with a disability has changed over time as I became more acculturated to the U.S. culture, values, and beliefs. To a certain extent, culture has a stronger hold in forming my identity than disability. For example, regardless of my disability, I would still be reluctant to move permanently back to Korea. As we will further elaborate in this chapter, the identities of persons with disabilities are shaped by multiple and complexly intertwined influences.

Alberto's Story

I describe my early school experiences in late 1950's Argentina in order
to highlight how notions of disability are grounded in historical and cultural expectations. Our family resided in working class neighborhood in
Mendoza, the neat and unhurried capital of a province bordering the ma-
jestic Andes Mountains. Children attended relatively small neighborhood
schools staffed by teachers who had graduated from the *escuela normal*—the
local, specialized secondary school for academically competent girls. My
first elementary school was Mariano Moreno, a short walk from home.

When I began first grade, most of my classmates were encountering organized instruction for the first time as six-year-olds. I, however, had attended a private kindergarten the previous year and looked forward to
a continuation of that experience. Encouraged by my parents and a kind
teacher, I happily engaged in identifying letters and numbers, shapes and
colors. Although still unable to read, I was competent with number concepts, showed excellent conduct, and got along well with peers; my report
card suggested solid progress by the end of the year.

Second grade was an entirely different challenge. My most vivid memories of that year include seeing my mother through the classroom's open
door speaking with my teacher in the hallway, while I jumped from desk
to desk in a mix of defiance and glee. My classmates celebrated my performance with a raucous chorus of laughter and screams. That year I had be-
friended the older boys in our elementary school; they had been left back
several times and some were sporting the beginning of a mustache. Possibly because I showed such daring contempt towards authority, these older
boys saw me as a kindred soul and took me in as a mascot. During recess
we engaged in forbidden activities, such as chicken fights, that routinely
would lead to my sitting outside the principal's office while my despair-
ing parents were notified.

Both my parents were professionals with high academic expectations
for my older sister and me. My sister was a precocious child who learned
to read without formal instruction at four; she was academically gifted
and enjoyed school. Her teachers and my parents expected me to follow in
her footsteps. But I struggled with reading and felt inadequate at school
and later at home as well. My parents worried about my school behavior and learning difficulties; they suspected that something might be wrong
and took me to various specialists. My father was particularly concerned
about my hearing, because both of my mothers' sisters were profoundly
deaf. The family doctor saw nothing wrong with me. A psychologist who
administered the House-Tree-Person Test (the test requires the child to
draw same) concluded that I had above average intelligence but could not
explain my learning difficulties. She recommended calm, patience, and
practice, and suggested that as I matured I would learn to read.

My sister took the recommendations to heart and sought to preserve
the family's reputation by helping me to become a fluent reader—and to

prevent my being left back. We spent long hours together filling notebooks with letters and numbers, which I tended to reverse. Despite our joint efforts, I could not crack the code. Without signs of academic progress and still unruly in class, my mother pleaded with me to pay attention and to be respectful of the teacher.

Since my second grade teacher was a novice who struggled with classroom organization, my parents hoped that in third grade I would settle down in a new classroom and learn what I had not mastered the previous year. The third grade teacher was indeed a more experienced educator; her classroom was quiet, busy, and orderly—except for me. I continued to show promise as a rebel. My behavior stood out in this classroom in even greater relief as my classmates busily completed assignments while I showed little inclination to follow instructions. Out of the classroom, I still associated with the school's incorrigibles and kept my mother busy making frequent school visits to speak with the teacher and administrators.

Pained and embarrassed, my parents arranged for a transfer to another neighboring public school within the first two months of the school year. At Federico Moreno, the third grade teacher monitored my behavior closely as I sat near her desk. Without my old classmates as an appreciative audience, my provocations and defiance quickly subsided. I behaved more appropriately, but my work in reading and writing was still deficient. I remember that period as permeated by a sense of injustice. Why was reading so easy for my friends and so difficult for me? I thought I was simply not smart enough, and I hated school. Although I ceased to be a behavior problem and thus relieved some of my parents' embarrassment, they continued to worry about my lack of progress.

During that year we moved to a neighborhood in a developing area of the city. Since my academic difficulties persisted, my parents enrolled me in Avelino Maure, the recently built school near our new home. At eight years of age I was short, a little pudgy, and well mannered. I also and had a rich vocabulary that belied my reading difficulties. I could do the math with ease, but I read well below grade level and did my best to avoid reading. Mrs. Jofre, my new teacher, took an immediate liking to me and was encouraging in a way I had not experienced in school before. Under her guidance I learned to read. Possibly her way of instilling confidence, her ability to understand what type of help I needed, my desire to please her, and maturation were all implicated in my rapid progress toward the end of third grade.

She continued to be my teacher the following year, as she looped with the class to fourth grade. During the second year in her class I excelled, and my self-concept improved together with clear evidence of my improved academic performance. Although my underlying learning disabilities did not disappear, I was able to compensate increasingly well. By the end of sixth grade, at graduation from elementary school, I had the grade's highest GPA. The troubled and troubling student I had been would live on only as a family legend. In retrospect, a most salient aspect of my story is the critical role a competent and dedicated teacher played in developing my reading skills and in transforming my self-concept. Another child, from a family with fewer economic resources, less cultural capital, and without access to a talented teacher, would have followed the well-worn pattern of being left back multiple times—like my older friends in my first elementary school—and eventually dropping out.

Telling this story to my graduate education and school psychology students often challenges their perceptions of difficult or bad children in their schools. I remind them that one cannot predict the trajectory of children with difficulties; provided with the right help, they may become professors (professors who need more time to read students' papers.) Considering how my learning and behavior problems would be understood and treated in contemporary American schools leads to interesting insights. A culture six-thousand miles away and half a century ago provides sharp contrast to current practices. Perhaps it was my good fortune that certain labels had not yet entered the medical and educational lexicons at that time. I would have certainly qualified for a diagnosis of attention deficit hyperactivity disorder (ADHD) and most likely for oppositional defiant disorder (ODD) as well.

Now I understand that dyslexia was my primary disability, and that my disruptive behaviors were secondary effects. I could not succeed as a student, but I found other ways to assert my presence in school while checking out of competing with sister. The lack of options within local schools compelled my parents to transfer me three times in one school year. Now we would discourage frequent school changes, but in my case it was a fortuitously effective approach. A child with my profile today, in all likelihood, would be identified as in need of special education and possibly psychostimulant medication as well. Given the severity of my maladjustment to the classroom environment, it is possible that I would also have been identified as emotionally disturbed in addition to learning disabled. Alternatively, in a more optimistic and proactive scenario, a child with my academic and behavioral profile would be identified early and provided with an intensive program centering on early literacy skills and phonemic awareness. That type of early and effective intervention could have averted most the difficulties I experienced in the early grades.

Our current understanding of disabilities incorporates perspectives from medicine, psychiatry, and psychology. Although regrettably our special education models veer too often in the direction of medicalized and pharmacological interventions, still, school failure and behavioral difficulties are understood as a call for help. In my childhood, medicine and psychology were not seen as relevant to the work of schools, and there was no safety net. Stated simply, all children who were physically able to, attended school to the point where they could no longer succeed. As they encountered increasing difficulties and failures they were likely to be held back. After several instances of being left back, children stopped attending school; it was not unusual that they would begin work in childhood or adolescence, some as newsboys or shoe shiners, others helping in stores or on farms. Although education was compulsory until the sixth grade, authorities did not enforce the law. Moreover, the system was built on the assumption that secondary education was not for everyone, and only those with academic potential were expected to attend.

Currently, Argentina's education laws and practices provide for greater support for students with learning difficulties. Yet, special education is mostly reserved for children with severe disabilities who are educated in specialized schools. The notion of a continuum of services with regular education is gaining favor, but does not reach the comprehensiveness of American practices. Until relatively recently, the concept of learning disabilities was not fully accepted by educators, and psychotropic medications are still rarely administered to children in Latin America. However, psychotherapy is widely accepted in Argentina, and learning problems tend to be explored first as manifestation of psychological needs or family dysfunction; learning problems are likely to be framed in psychological terms first, before other causes are considered—family dynamics become a locus of exploration and intervention. In contrast, our orientation toward learning difficulties in the United States is more typically focused on neurological processes; therefore, the child's brain is the locus of study, and therapies rarely involve the family. Despite these differences, taking a long view, one may conclude that Argentina's education of children with disabilities resembles the contemporary American model more that its own past.

Dimensions of Cultures and Disabilities

Tom Friedman, the author and *New York Times* columnist notes that we live in an increasingly flat world as mass media, travel, and the Internet promote an homogenizing effect across cultures and contribute to narrowing traditional divides. Anthony Kwame Appiah, the Ghanian philosopher and cultural theorist, has written insightfully about how Western influences are assimilated in Africa and other parts of the developing world. The adoption of technology, particularly the means of communicating and computing among peoples who lived in relative isolation just a generation ago, has narrowed the divide between wealthy and poor nations. Moreover, the movement of people migrating across national boundaries is unprecedented in our history, and in its wake there is an intensifying rate of intercultural exchange.

In order to explore how disability is interpreted across cultures, we use the framework proposed by Geert Hofstede, the noted Dutch organizational sociologist, in 1980. His typology consists of four dimensions of culture that describe the widely observed diversity of communication patterns, beliefs, and behaviors across the globe and has been widely applied in international business and other fields. Hofstede was interested in identifying critical differences in the ways that people in various societies understood their worlds and what essential patterns of thinking and feeling guided their choices and actions. He noted that cultural patterns are well established by late childhood and determined the choice of symbols, values, and rituals. The noted sociologist Pierre Bourdieu described *habitus* in a similar way; as a set of dispositions inculcated by the society on the subjective structures of the individual. Both scholars conceive of this process as largely unconscious and as a requirement for effective participation in a given society.

Power Distance: How Do We Respond to Organizational Power

Hofstede named the first dimension Power Distance; it refers the degree to which organizational and institutional power is accepted or challenged. Individuals in high power distance societies are comfortable with large status differentials and implicitly accept that not all are created equal. Social relations in high power distance societies also reflect this stratification of power in family customs, teacher-student interactions, language use—which requires greater use of formality—and organizational practices that emphasize title and position over teamwork. In low power distance societies, there is greater expectation of accountability and egalitarianism, interactions within organizations are more informal and familiar, and language may be stripped of formalisms.

In the United States, a society with low power distance, equal treatment and access for people with disabilities are seen as basic rights. Even if the culture does not always live up to its ideal, accommodations for people with disabilities are part of the legal code, and parents are empowered to take legal action on behalf of their children. In cultures with great power distance, like most Arab countries, individual rights of children with disabilities lack the legal mandates and cultural imperative of egalitarianism. It should be noted that high power distance societies are also more likely to be tradition-bound and have weaker legal protections for women, homosexuals, and foreigners.

Individualism-Collectivism: Do We Function in a Group or as Individuals?

The second dimension described by Hofstede is the Individualism-Collectivism continuum. A key feature of this dimension is the degree to which a culture functions of the basis of the self, or the group. Hofstede found that high power distance societies were much more likely to collectivistic and vice-versa. A collectivist society places great value on group membership and establishes significant psychological distance between in-group and out-group individuals. Absolute loyalty to the group is a central organizing value of those societies. Conflicts are resolved through intermediaries and other face-saving maneuvers. In contrast, individualistic societies place greater value on individual choice and free-dom over loyalty. Individuals are expected to resolve problems on their own and are personally accountable for their actions. Also there is greater fluidity between in-group and out-group membership, and confrontation is commonplace.

The implications of this dimension to people with disabilities are profound. One can easily recognize the survival advantage of collectivist societies for a person who might not be able to support himself or herself. The group tends to take care of its members. Collectivistic cultures place strong emphasis on the importance of family values and the critical role of family members in dealing with people with disabilities. In most Spanish speaking countries and Asian societies, the extended family takes part in providing support for the individual with disabilities. Mexican American parents, for example, might prefer that their adult child with cognitive disabilities should live at home rather than in a supported living arrangement. Strong family unity is prized over independence.

Yet because collectivist societies are more rule-bound than individualist ones, the social status and options available for a person with disabilities are restricted by tradition and concern about the individual reflecting poorly on the group. The first author's experience of exclusion at a wedding in Korea, a family event where the two extended families would come to meet and be formally joined, reflects the concern about controlling the family's image and reputation. Disability was traditionally understood in Korea as the ancestors' punishment for a transgression.

Individualistic societies, such as the United States, rely more on institution than on in-group affiliation for support of individuals with disabilities; however, they allow and prize individual initiative and self-advocacy. Therefore, a child challenged by a disability is still expected to achieve her potential. The educational system values movement toward becoming self-supporting and independent; the hallmark of success is living independently of one's parents.

Achievement-Nurturance: Is Social Status Earned or Received?

The third cultural dimension is Achievement-Nurturance, originally labeled Masculinity-Femininity; it concerns gender roles and the degree to which gender-specific behaviors are rigidly defined or flexible and negotiable. Members of masculine (MAS) societies believe that men must be assertive and women nurturing. There is a high social prohibition against acting in nongender assigned roles. Male behavior is associated with achievement and ambition, and public symbols of male power, such as wealth, are celebrated. In these societies there is great concern with controlling women's behavior and enforcing their subjugated status.

Societies that score low in the MAS cluster show greater ambiguity regarding gender roles and demonstrate flexibility in the negotiation of social tasks. These societies also show greater interest in quality of life—rather than symbols of achievement—and more concern for the unfortunate and destitute. Sexual inequality is seen as detrimental to the social good.

Issues of gender and disability are particularly salient in traditional agricultural societies. In an agrarian setting, physical ability is an important attribute for both sexes, when contrasted with technologically advanced societies, where cognitive abilities prized. For example, Pakistani mothers we interviewed consider their daughters to be more disabled if they have mild physical impairments compared to impairments that do not interfere with an ability to take care of a household, such as deafness. Moreover, in societies where gender is a category of exclusion—that is, it limits an individual's access to privileges such as voting, driving, or owning property—having a disability further restricts access and lowers social status; in effect, a woman with a disability is doubly handicapped.

Achievement-Nurturance differentiation in societies suggests that the intersection between gender and disability may result in differential expectations and prospects for boys and girls similarly challenged by disability. One of our graduate students explored bias during the assessment process of young children with developmental delays whose families immigrated from Yemen, Jordan, and other Arab countries. Her study illustrated how many of the children's behaviors that may be considered as atypical in American culture may be typical in Arab cultures. After reviewing the evaluation reports with the mothers in her native Arabic, she concluded that certain behaviors that might appear to indicate disability or delay can be interpreted differently based on cultural expectations. The girls in this study were "very quiet and preferred solitary play to the company of peers" according to the evaluation reports. One girl was noted as "tending to communicate via nonverbal means such as eye gaze, facial expressions and body movements." However, the mothers attributed their daughters' shy and quiet behaviors as typical, since girls are expected to respect and listen to others. It is the norm within the Arab community for girls to be quiet and shy. On the other hand, the evaluators noted that boys were often "aggressive," "impulsive," and "tending to hit when upset." Their mothers, in turn, were not worried about these behaviors and attributed them to male cultural values of independence, self-reliance, and an ability to defend oneself. Again, in Arab cultures, a boy's aggressive behavior is not necessarily viewed as a delay. A mother from Yemen stated that it was "favorable," as she wanted her son to be able to "protect himself." These responses suggest that some cultures may be more accepting of boys' externalizing disorders, including ADHD and ODD, and less concerned with girls' internalizing disorders, such as anxiety and depression.

When addressing gender roles, the mothers' responsibilities in child-rearing are often discussed. In traditional Korean culture, where gender roles were rigidly defined, mothers' nurturing responsibilities extended to the child's health at birth. The term *Tae Gyo* refers to prenatal care and encompasses the self-discipline required by a pregnant woman to ensure the delivery of a healthy baby. During the pregnancy, mothers are told to look at pleasant things, eat good food, and think good thoughts. While this cultural tradition offers clear advantages to newborns, the practice has a dark side. Mothers of children with disabilities often feel guilt and blame themselves for their children's difficulties; they believed that poor Tae Gyo caused the child's impairment or illness. The following story, for which we are indebted to Dr. Hye Jun Park, illustrates this point.

Mrs. Kim had four boys who received special education services. Her boys had developmental delays and received services from early intervention services. Mrs. Kim faced a great deal of resistance from her husband and other family members because she took an active role of advocating for her sons and insisted on getting services as early as possible. She was not a fluent speaker of English, but she understood her legal rights in the United States and wanted to access the best services for her children. Her three older children were only a year apart.

She related that while she was pregnant with her second and third children, she went through financial and emotional hardships. She stated that she didn't receive help or sympathy, even from her husband. When she was pregnant with Ben, her second boy, her husband's business went bankrupt, and the family experienced great deal of stress. She felt sorry for Ben and believed she made him that way. She told to one of the teachers during an assessment meeting

> I didn't provide a good Tae Gyo for Ben. My husband was really angry and frustrated and I had to endure all of his anger as well. But with no reason, my husband began to blame my unborn child who was growing in my belly. He always told me he was unlucky and he brought us all bad luck that we had to go through this hardship. It was so hurtful for me and I cried a lot after my husband told me this over and over. I begged my husband not to say that because our baby was listening, but he didn't listen. So when he was born, I immediately sensed that his first cry was different. I felt like his crying sounded different from my first son. For me it sounded like really angry. His crying was always distinct from other children and he was not a happy child at all. His crankiness and crying seemed to confirm my husband's beliefs later. He has not been loved as much as David (first child). I tried to make up for it by paying more attention to him, but his younger brothers were only a year apart after him. So basically, I haven't paid much attention to any of my boys.

Even three years after her child was born, Mrs. Kim's interpretations of her children's special needs were traced to her stressful pregnancy with her second child. Such cultural folk beliefs implicitly blame mothers when children are born with disabilities, the subsequent stigmatization and isolation may lead to greater tensions with family members. In many Latin American countries, the father may bear the responsibility for birth defects or birth marks if he had not satisfied his wife's cravings (*antojos*) during pregnancy.

Recently in Korea there have been an increasing number of movies and TV documentaries that portray successful lives of people with disabilities. These stories often highlight strong dedication of parents, specifically mothers. These media portrayals affirming the idealized maternal role, in turn, influence how mothers perceive themselves. In 2005, a movie about a marathon runner who had autism was a big hit in Korean box-office sales, and the actor who played the main character won the best actor award in Korean film. People were impressed by a poignant human story and valorized the mother's determination to help her son with autism. But an interesting observation about this movie is that his father and other family members were rarely portrayed or mentioned in the film. This screenplay focuses only on the mother's dedication and devotion raising her child with disabilities. One of the mothers participating in the Korean parents group articulated this social expectation:

> 결국은 다른 사람의 도움을 받기는 하지만, 특수교육을 시키는 것
> 도 애를 키우는 것도 전부 엄마의 몫이거든요. 다른 사람의 도움 없
> 이는 안 되는 건 사실 이에요. 하지만 엄마가 애를 짊어져야 하는
> 건 몫이기 때문에 아이의 미래도 엄마가 만들어 주워야 한다고 생
> 각하거든요.
>
> *Even though there are a lot of professional supports available for families, the mothers have the ultimate responsibility of raising children with special needs. It is true that the mothers can't do anything without support from others. But they are ultimately responsible, and their job is to create best opportunities for their children's future.*

This sense of exclusive responsibility is also connected to a deep sense of guilt for the mothers when their children with disabilities are not improving.

Implied mother's guilt upon the birth of a child with disabilities is by no means exclusively observed in Korea or in traditional societies. In the United States, from the 1950s through the 1970s, the cause of autism was traced to *refrigerator mothers,* a term coined by the prominent psychiatrist Bruno Betleheim. He theorized that autism was the result of a failure of attachment cause by a cold and rejecting mother. Although that theory has now been largely rejected by mainstream mental health professionals, a whole generation of mothers was unfairly and cruelly stigmatized. To a lesser extent, attachment theory today may figure in the understanding of certain psychological disorders. The quality of mother-child attachment is a pivotal building block in human development and has been shown to have long-lasting effects. However, one needs to be concerned that attachment theory can be misapplied in relation to specific emotional disorders.

Not all psychopathology is rooted in attachment difficulties. Broader questions might be to what extent any society is prone to blame mothers for children's disabilities, and to what extent mothers themselves assume that burden. It seems that where children are the exclusive responsibility of mothers, children's disabilities, particularly those of an emotional nature, are more likely to be traced to poor mothering.

Uncertainty Avoidance: How Do We Respond to the Unknown?

The fourth dimension identified by Hofstede is Uncertainty Avoidance. High scores in the Uncertainty Avoidance Index (UAI) indicate that the culture has a propensity to avoid ambiguity and feels threatened by uncertainty. These cultures look askance at dissent and typically impose more structure when they feel threatened. Members of high uncertainty avoidant cultures hold consensus as an ideal and focus on adherence to rules rather than in novel thinking; there only one accepted Truth or path that all members must follow. Contrastingly, cultures with low scores on the UAI have high tolerance for dissenting views and may even encourage divergent thinking. Ambiguity in structures and procedures does not generate a sense of crisis; the unknown is understood more as a challenge than a source of anxiety. Emotions are typically suppressed in the course of disagreements.

Since cultures that score high on UAI experience anxiety about the unknown, they generate and enforce rules to control social behavior in the face of uncertainty. This characteristic tends to have negative effects on people with disabilities. The development and progression of children with disabilities are, by nature, uncertain processes. The urge to define and classify children on the basis of early identification of disability may result in long-term restrictive placements. Moreover, cultures that focus on controlling the behavior of individuals hold narrower expectations of normal functioning and may act punitively against individuals who do not conform to social norms. Children and youths with emotional challenges are particularly vulnerable in those contexts when they display nonsanctioned behaviors.

South Korea, a country with a high UAI score, and places great emphasis on individual conformity to social norms—the conditions in North Korea are substantially more restrictive. The first author's experience of not living within the defined expectations of a person with disabilities was atypical and provoked discomfort and anxiety for many around her, from the classmate who feared contagion to the more recent incident at the fitness club in Korea.

Uncertainty Avoidance is not necessarily tied to a society's wealth or level of development. Germany, which has a high level of literacy and enjoys one to the highest standards of living in the world, scores high in the UAI. Its neighbor, Denmark, which has similar levels of education and wealth, showed one of the lowest scores in Hofstede's study. The score differential suggests that Danes are more open to differences of opinion and are more tolerant of ambiguity. Not unsurprisingly, on a European poll that included the question, How much at ease do you feel when you are close to someone with a disability? Danes indicated high level of *comfort*, while Germans frequently indicated *ill at ease* when close to persons with disabilities.

Other researchers have suggested that some societies will show a higher score in the UAI when they are in the midst of rapid change. Conditions that create uncertainty foment fear of the future and are associated with greater social control and restricted individual freedoms. These conditions are particularly problematic for families of children with disabilities and for individuals with disabilities, because social integration hinges largely on increased tolerance and acceptance. In such a dynamic change situation we may expect to observe tensions between those who embrace change within the culture and those who feel threatened. Since the struggle for recognition of rights for the disabled is part of a larger social change agenda, these initiatives are less likely to succeed in societies fearing the unknown.

Thinking beyond Hofstede's Framework: Internal Versus External Control

Other anthropologists, cultural psychologists, and social scientists have expanded and/or critiqued Hofstede's model and proposed others of their own. We find the framework proposed by Trompenaars and Charles Hampden-Turner useful when focusing on disabilities. Their model offers seven dimensions—the one most pertinent to our topic focuses on how societies assign cause to life events. They distinguish between attribution emphases on internal control versus external control. Internal control, also known in social psychology and *field independence* suggests that individuals see themselves as independent agents, capable of affecting the course of their lives and bearing most of the responsibility for the choices they have made. Societies where the prevalent outlook is external control (field dependence) have a less autonomous view of events and believe that God, fate, or powers beyond their control have the most influence on the course of their lives.

Cultures and religions adhering to an external control worldview affect families and individual with disabilities in two major ways. First, it helps parents, and later the children themselves, view the disability as a matter beyond their control, and they therefore may be less conflicted about accepting the limitations or challenges. An external control perspective also ameliorates self-blame and may frame the disability as serving a noble purpose. Second, and in a more negative way, this outlook also suppresses the impulse to bring about change—both in the individual and in society— because effort is not seen as likely to change the situation. In extreme cases it may be seen as interfering with divine plans.

External control worldviews are evident in religious and folk beliefs that trace the disability to previous generations. Within some Asian cultures, such as Indian, Korean, and Chinese, a child's disability is believed to be a punishment for sins committed by the parents or ancestors. This folk belief is related to people's general outlook toward the life. In Chinese culture, each life is often viewed as a link in a chain from the past to the present. Similarly, the Hindu belief in Karma, or payment for past deeds, implies that the family accepts the child's disability as penance to redress the wrongdoings of the past. Also in some Indian cultures, the evil spirit or bad energy can cause a child to be born with a disability.

The notion that disabilities connect a family and community to ancestors was at the core of a case that reached the U.S. Supreme Court. A judge had ordered a Hmong family to arrange for corrective surgery for their child's clubfeet and hip displacement. The child, Kou Xiong, was born with congenital deformities that affected his movements, and the Fresno Social Services Department, following a doctor's recommendation, pressed for surgery against the parents' wishes. The Hmong Council, representing the family, believed that corrective surgery would interfere with the natural order and terrible thing would befall the community. They cited how in prior occasions, where surgery was preformed against the shaman's recommendations, tragedies unfolded. The family's lawyer lost every appeal, all the way to Sandra Day O'Connor's ruling. However, despite the legal defeat, no surgeon was willing to perform the operation without the family's consent because, as time passed, the risks for Kou increased and the outcome of surgeries was uncertain. Kou himself did not want to be separated from his family. Reviewing the psychiatric evaluations that indicated how the family may be ostracized as a consequence of the medical procedure, and that Kou would feel responsible if anything were to happen to his siblings, the original judge cited "grave psychological risks" and vacated the case against the family.

Religion and Folk Beliefs: Recurrent Topics in the Discussion of Cultures and Disabilities

Religious beliefs often provide explanatory frameworks for children's disabilities. In many Latin American countries, where Catholicism is practiced by the great majority of the population, such as in Argentina, Santo Domingo, and Mexico, many parents of children with disabilities explain, "*Es la voluntad de Dios*" (It's God will), "*Es el destino*" (It is fate). Another common expression, "*Es lo que Dios me dio*" (It's what God Gave me) implies that the parent was selected for this particular task and must accept God's plan. Families with these religious values may forgo treatments and therapies for their children with disabilities since they are rather fatalistic about outcomes. The focus on the afterlife justifies, and to an extent exalts, suffering in this life.

A clear expression of this religious outlook was demonstrated by Mr. Malek, a devout Muslim from Bangladesh and father of Masoud, a child with disfiguring birth defects. Upon enrolling Masoud at school for kindergarten, Mr. Malek indicated concern that the other children may stare and taunt Masoud. School support staff sought to reassure the father that the child would be well cared for in the school and described to him services available for the child, including speech and occupational therapies. Knowing that the family had limited resources, many children, and that Mrs. Malek spoke no English, one of the social workers identified a path to access specialized treatment, but her efforts were dismissed by the father. Mr. Malek explained that it was God's will that Masoud should have his impairments. He said, "Allah made Masoud like that, that's His will. Who are we to change Allah's plan? It's wrong to do such a thing!" The social worker reluctantly accepted the father's perspective but wondered if the mother and Masoud himself would have considered the corrective treatment options.

A Closer Look at a Religious Community and Disability

Among Orthodox Jews, views on disability have multiple origins; some are associated with rabbinic writings, others are more clearly rooted in folk belief. An example of understanding derived from rabbinic writing is the notion that all human beings are endowed with a God-given soul (*neshamah*), and since no soul is superior to another, all persons, regardless of ability, should be equally respected for their connection to God. (A similar belief is prevalent among many Native American cultures). Since Orthodox Judaism is practiced through the fulfillment of mitzvoth (good deeds) and prescribed rituals; it is not uncommon that individuals fear the consequences of not adhering properly to all the traditions and requirements. Consequently, concern about bringing to light a healthy child is underlined by concerns with rituals and proscriptions. When we asked a number of orthodox women what they do to ensure the birth of a healthy baby, most mentioned following the required rituals. Rebecca, for example said: "To produce a healthy baby it is important to take your vitamins and follow the rules of *niddah*." She explained: "When a woman is menstruating, she is separated from her husband. If there is contact when the woman is menstruating, an unhealthy child can be produced." The belief that an unhealthy baby is born as the result of not following the rituals surrounding menstruation (*niddah*) implies that the disability may be a punishment for the parents' transgression.

More clearly rooted in folk belief is the fear that coming in contact with a misshapen person or an unclean animal during pregnancy can damage the developing fetus. This belief is also loosely rooted in the notion of separating the ritually clean (*kosher*) from the unclean (*treif*). Pregnant women are expected to adhere closely to all the ritual requirements of cleanliness (*kashrut*) to ensure the health of the fetus. Another concern during pregnancy and early life is the potential damaging effect of the evil eye; a superstition shared by Jews, Arabs, and most Mediterranean cultures. This superstition is based on the fear that certain individuals, driven by envy, can inflict injury or bad luck. Newborns are thought to be particularly susceptible and need to be protected—generally with a talisman. A kinder view on disability, also emerging from folk belief, considers that the person with a disability is the embodied soul of a Jewish sage (*tzadik*) who has returned to this world to complete an unfinished task. This myth is particularly interesting because there is no clear basis for the belief in reincarnation in the Jewish faith. In pragmatic terms, however, children with disabilities are often hidden from sight because they may negatively affect the marrying prospects of their siblings. In a society that prizes intelligence and learning, cognitive and emotional impairments are particularly troublesome for families; although presently greater acceptance and accommodations are being promoted by influential figures and institutions. These brief observations hint at the complex interactions between various sources of belief about disability within a single community. As is true in most societies, disabilities, and their prevention, are understood in multiple, mutable, and sometimes conflicting ways.

Conclusion

The framework proposed by Hofstede and other related ideas we addressed in this chapter explored how disability is interpreted across cultures. As shown in many examples, the experience of disability is influenced by a complex interaction of culture, economic status, gender, religion, exposure to media, and myriad other factors, including the subjective understanding of one's condition. We sought to highlight that there is much variability, not only across cultures, but also within cultures. Cultures are fluid systems and are constantly changing, even within societies that seek to resist change. Attitudes toward people with disabilities are changing globally due to internal social movements, generational changes, access to technology and media, and Western influences. The Internet is both an agent of change and an instrument for greater access for individuals with disabilities and their families. As parents gain new information about different kinds of disabilities and treatment options, they often question traditional and folk beliefs regarding their of children's functioning and development. Moreover, new information about therapies catapults many parents to an activist role, thus accelerating change within their own communities.

Globalization is changing the status of people with disabilities within societies. Through the ongoing process by which economies and cultures are becoming more integrated, the Western conceptions of mental health, illness, and disability are more likely to shape experiences of people with disabilities in non-Western countries. Western medicine, in particular, influences not only how certain conditions are treated, but, as some have argued, they also influence the very expression of medical conditions. The growing incidence of children identified and treated for ADHD in Central America is an example of both growing awareness of the condition in countries where it was relatively rarely identified before and a new market for multinational pharmaceutical companies.

Treatments for disabilities and the transfer of knowledge about different options reflect a two-way movement between East and West, traditional and modern understandings. For example, acupuncture and herbal medicines, originating in China, have traveled west and are often considered as treatment approaches for individuals with disabilities. Also Conductive Education (CE), a low-tech method originating in post–World War II Hungary, is gaining influence as a promising treatment approach for children with physical disabilities in the United States and much of the industrialized world. Similarly, meditation, yoga, and relaxation techniques rooted in Indian traditions are increasingly adopted in the treatment of individuals with emotional disabilities and addictions.

Families' perspectives in understanding their children's disabilities are diverse and multifaceted, influenced by traditional beliefs, historical circumstances, social trends, and present level of knowledge. Disability is not a fixed or immutable entity, it does not belong to medicine, psychology, or rehabilitation therapies; rather, it is best understood as an evolving aspect of the human experience that is subject to reinterpretation by the individuals affected and their own communities.

References

Appiah, K.A. (2006). *Cosmopolitanism: Ethics in a world of strangers.* New York: Norton.

Artiles, A.J., & Trent, S.C. (2000). Representation of culturally/linguistically diverse students. In C.R. Reynolds & E. Fletcher-Jantzen (Eds.), *Encyclopedia of special education, Vol. 1* (2nd ed. pp. 513–517). New York: Wiley.

Bourdieu, P., & Wacquant, L.J.D. (1992). *An invitation to reflexive sociology.* Chicago: The University of Chicago Press.

Bursztyn, A.M. (2007). Multicultural school psychology: Directions for future research. In E. Lopez, G. Esquivel, and S. Nahari (Eds.), *Handbook of multicultural school psychology: An interdisciplinary perspective* (pp. 639–658). New York: Erlbaum.

Freeway, A. (2002). *Results of European poll of attitudes toward disability.* Retrieved from http://www.disabilityworld.org/11-12_02/il/poll.shtml.

Friedman, T.L. (2005). *The world is flat: A brief history of the twenty-first century.* New York: Farrar, Straus & Giroux.

Hampden-Turner, C., & Trompenaars, F. (1997). *Riding the waves of culture: Understanding diversity in global business.* New York: McGraw-Hill.

Harry, B. (1992). *Cultural diversity, families, and the special education system.* New York: Teachers College Press.

Hofstede, G. (1980). *Culture's consequences: International differences in work-related values.* Newbury Park, CA: Sage.

Jones, B. (2003). *Childhood disability in a multicultural society.* Oxon, UK: Radcliffe Medical Press.

Leyser, Y. (1998). (1994). Stress and adaptation in Orthodox Jewish families with a disabled child. *American Journal of Orthopsychiatry, 64*(3), 376–385.

Multicultural Disability Advocacy Association. (2004). *Opening doors booklets.* Retrieved from http://www.mdaa.org.au/publications/openingdoors.html.

Park, H. (2003). *Transitions from home to preschool special education programs: Experiences of four immigrant Korean families of children with special needs.* Doctoral dissertation, Department of Curriculum and Teaching, Teachers College, Columbia University, New York.

Renteln, A. D. (2004). *The cultural defense.* New York: Oxford University Press.

Wormnæs, S., & Olsen, M. (2009). Mothers' hearts speaking: Education enlightens, empowers and protects girls with disabilities. *International Journal of Special Education, 24*(1), 64–74.

CHAPTER 3

Conflicts and Confusion: Current Understandings of Early Onset Bipolar Disorder

Elizabeth M. Scanlon

Alex, age 16, was diagnosed with obsessive compulsive disorder (OCD), Tourette's syndrome, and attention-deficit/hyperactivity disorder (ADHD) by age five. His atypical behaviors began as early as one year of age, when he started throwing temper tantrums that lasted for hours during which he screamed, cried, hit, and was inconsolable. At three years of age he placed a box of pasta on the stove and turned it on so that he could cook it for dinner, nearly setting the house on fire. His parents report that throughout childhood he only slept for three-hour intervals and that they would wake up to find him running back and forth through the house, undeterred by their commands and pleas to stop. At school, Alex's teachers reported that he would not follow directions, experienced periods of extreme hyperactivity in which he could not sit still or concentrate on work, and was unconcerned with other children. He was determined eligible for special education services in kindergarten. At home and in school Alex was frequently in trouble for using foul language, refusing to do something unless it was his idea, and having explosive tantrums in response to the word *no* or denial of a desired object. He obsesses about toys and is so compelled to obtain them that he was once caught shoplifting at the mall after his mother told him she would not purchase the toy for him.

Currently, Alex is in his junior year at the local public high school and continues to receive special education support for academics; he attends lunch, gym, chorus, and vocational classes in the mainstream. He has few friends and complains sometimes about feeling lonely and sad. Alex has been asking his parents repeatedly if he can take a drivers education course, not accepting no for an answer. He spends much of his free time playing video games in his room, and his parents report that he will occasionally laugh hysterically without any apparent stimuli. He can be heard talking to himself, and he often mutters about the good and bad guys. He has stated some suicidal and homicidal ideation, but he reportedly does not have a plan. He currently takes medication to treat OCD and Tourette's. Two months ago he was hospitalized after a hallucinatory episode at school in which he became violent. Alex was placed in an in-patient adolescent psychiatric unit at the hospital for one week; during that time the doctors diagnosed him with Psychotic Disorder Not Otherwise Specified and began treating him with an antipsychotic medication that caused the hallucinatory symptoms to subside. His parents have done some research online and are questioning if their son has bipolar disorder. They have mentioned to the psychiatrist that there is familial history of bipolar disorder. The psychiatrist is hesitant to diagnose Alex and has given only vague responses to the parents' inquiry.

Diagnosis and Psychiatric Treatment

Childhood's most misunderstood disorder—that's how early onset bipolar disorder is commonly described, and for good reason. There is a great deal of confusion about bipolar disorder (BPD) in children, but none greater than the experience the child with BPD has just trying to navigate daily life. Children with bipolar disorder, like Alex, live in a world that frequently fails to understand them. The experience can be isolating, terrifying, maddening, and confusing—feelings that may only prove to exacerbate their already labile mood states. They feel intensely, and in the process of expressing feelings the only way they know how, they may break things, hurt people, or endanger themselves. Their perceptions of situations and intense goal-directed activity can skew the facts of the situation, leaving them genuinely confused and consequently enraged by the world's failure to respond to their needs. In this state, they may revert to an earlier, more primitive fight or flight response in which every *no*, every denial of goals feels threatening and they must either fight for what they want at any cost or unleash their frustration at others or themselves.

When their tantrum ends and they survey the damage done to the people they love as well as to personal possessions, many of which may belong to them, they feel remorse. Children with bipolar disorder do not understand their own actions, behaviors, or feelings much better than the family and friends who witness them. These children will feel that their reactions were justified, even if the consequences indicate otherwise. Because children only know the world through their discovery and experience of it, what they feel and how intensely they feel it is what they know as normal. Therefore, the world's response to them is what is jarring. There is uncertainty about their family's inability to understand and meet their needs and a genuine, intolerable pain associated with that experience. Combined with the side effects of medications that make them feel unwell or unlike themselves, these children may never feel at rest or at home in their own bodies. They might feel self-conscious about taking medicine or exploding in public. The *experience* of the child with bipolar should not be neglected in the midst of the many other aspects of the disorder. The child is, after all, still a child, and for the most part, a misunderstood child.

For many years it was believed that BPD exclusively affected adults, a belief propagated by the psychological theories that were dominant at that time. Its emergence as a disorder of childhood has been complex for a number of reasons, the most prominent of which is its unique symptomology in children and how that differs from the symptoms exhibited by adults. Furthermore, it is unclear whether childhood symptomology is a precursor to the adult disorder or a cluster of comorbid disorders appearing in concert and overlapping with early onset bipolar disorder. This chapter will endeavor to briefly explore the issues and controversies as well as the implications for children and families.

Bipolar disorder is a mood disorder that causes alternating periods of depression and mania. Researchers have not yet determined the cause, but most believe it might be a combination of genetics, minor brain abnormalities, and environmental factors such as extremely stressful life events. It is therefore considered a biopsychosocial disorder. Although much is known about the adult form of the disorder, its childhood presentation is still shrouded in mystery and uncertainty. First acknowledged in the mid-19th century as a disorder that affects children, it made its mainstream debut about 150 years later. The intervening century traces a muddled trail of discovery and conflicting views on diagnosis, symptoms, and treatment.

Childhood is a time of rapid growth and development during which the biological and psychosocial processes actively mesh within and around the child. As a result, mental health disorder symptoms emerge in the context of that growth and development and can appear differently than they do in the fully developed adult. One of the hallmarks of bipolar disorder in adulthood is a major depressive episode. This is also frequently the first sign of the disorder in children. While both children and adults experience depression, the symptoms typically associated with depression—prolonged sadness, low energy levels, loss of interest in pleasurable activities—are not always present in children. Depression in children can emulate adult symptoms, but it may also be expressed differently. Child psychiatrists identify severe irritability, anger, or frustration as pediatric depression. The other hallmark of bipolar disorder, mania, can similarly appear one way in adults and another in children. For example, both adults and children will exhibit high energy, excitement, and grandiosity, which means individuals may feel that they can perform superhuman feats or that they are, in fact, superhuman. In children, grandiosity is more typically exhibited in a know-it-all attitude toward parents and teachers or a belief that they are above the rules. The child with BPD may react with an explosive and even violent response when told "no" by an authority figure. Adult and early onset bipolar disorder may share some overlapping traits, but can appear very differently at varying stages of development.

In fact, differences in symptoms even occur *within* childhood. Children under age nine tend to be primarily irritable and emotionally labile. After age nine, children exhibit euphoria, excitement, paranoia, and grandiosity. Children of all ages may also experience a decreased need for sleep; impulsivity; inattention; reduced frustration tolerance; a propensity for risky activities; decreased inhibition; hypersexuality; and explosive, angry outbursts. In their most severe form, mania and depression can lead to psychosis, which may include delusions and auditory or visual hallucinations. The inability to regulate emotions and the dizzying pace of racing thoughts may incapacitate a child's rational decision-making, planning, organizing, or judgment abilities—thought processes that are linked to executive functions.

School can be particularly challenging because it places demands on the child's executive functions, problem-solving ability, and appropriate peer interactions. As a result, children with bipolar disorder frequently have difficulty achieving academically and are often referred for special education self-contained classes or services. They may struggle particularly with mathematics; speech fluency; reading comprehension; processing issues involving working memory; sequencing; planning; estimating time; written expression; cognitive, emotional, and motor abilities; deciphering nonverbal social cues; and visual–spatial tasks, which all rely on those executive functions mentioned previously. Lack of success in academics combined with the sheer demands of an environment that is not well suited to the child's needs, and compounded by difficulties interacting with peers, can make school life a very difficult and confidence-reducing experience.

When psychologists, psychiatrists, physicians and other qualified practitioners diagnose individuals with mental health disorders, they refer to the *Diagnostic and Statistical Manual of Mental Disorders, Fourth Edition (DSM-IV)*. The *DSM-IV* is a manual that outlines in clinical terms the type of symptoms, severity, and duration that individuals must exhibit to meet the criteria for a psychopathological disorder. Currently, the *DSM-IV* makes mention of bipolar disorder in children; however, the criteria used to diagnose a child are largely based on adult symptoms. Children often fail to meet the stated criteria because the symptoms may present differently.

One significant difference in symptom presentation between adults and children is the frequency of cycling between moods. Adults who experience bipolar disorder have distinct periods of suffering from depression and separate distinct periods of experiencing mania, with well-defined recovery periods between them. The mood disorder itself is named after these two opposite poles of emotion. Whereas depression makes a person feel hopeless, sluggish, and sad, mania introduces a high level of energy, elation, and grandiosity. Empirical research studies suggest that adults cycle through these two poles of feeling and energy levels at a much slower rate than children do. The *DSM-IV* diagnostic criteria specify that the child must experience these distinct mood states for a duration of time that closely resembles the adult symptomology, making the diagnosis in children more difficult.

For example, the *DSM-IV* states that a manic episode must last for one week. Many children experience the ups and downs of depressed and elevated moods several times within 24 hours, and with little to no periods of recovery. This is called *rapid cycling*. Not every child cycles through emotions rapidly, but a large number, as many as 70 percent, do—which makes the symptoms appear very different than the typical adult presentation.

Rapid cycling can occur at such a high speed that children experience something called a *mixed state*. During a mixed state, a child may experience feelings of mania and depression at the same time. While this is difficult to imagine, the child in a mixed state may appear energetic and irritable while simultaneously feeling useless, inadequate, and hopeless. This experience is much less common in adults because they do not cycle rapidly. The *DSM-IV* does provide a diagnosis called Bipolar Disorder–Not Otherwise Specified, which is designed to include any presentation of symptoms that does not fully meet the diagnostic criteria for the disorder but is exhibiting bipolar features. Presently, many children are diagnosed with Bipolar Disorder–Not Otherwise Specified (NOS); the nonspecific, catch-all quality of this diagnosis fails to provide the type of symptom information a more specific diagnosis of Bipolar Disorder I or II would describe. This vague diagnosis does not accurately describe the disorder as children experience it, and it may in fact substantiate the notion that children do not experience true bipolar disorder.

For years, children with bipolar disorder have failed to meet the diagnostic criteria. As a result, clinicians have been encouraged to use the FIND (frequency, intensity, number, and duration) strategy to determine if the child's symptoms have reached a clinical threshold. The recommendation is that symptoms occur most days in a week, are severe enough to cause severe disruption in one area of life or moderate disruption in two or more areas, occur three to four times a day, and last for four hours—but need not be in succession (Kowatch et al., 2005). In addition, the behavior should be incongruent with the context in which it is occurring; that is, an overreaction or out of proportion, inappropriate response to what is happening.

As a result of poorly articulated definitions for the condition, it is believed that children with bipolar disorder are often misdiagnosed with disorders that have similar symptoms, such as attention-deficit/hyperactivity disorder (ADHD), obsessive compulsive disorder (OCD), generalized anxiety disorder (GAD), conduct disorder (CD), oppositional defiant disorder (ODD), depression, and Tourette's syndrome. Boys are more prone to act out their aggression toward others and destroy property to get their feelings out, behaviors which are frequently associated with CD or ODD. Girls may also express anger towards others, especially caregivers, but they are more likely than boys to turn their feelings inward, which results in self-injurious behavior, such as cutting, which can lead to a misdiagnosis of borderline personality disorder or depression.

In fact, there is further confusion in the field over whether these psychopathological conditions occur alongside bipolar disorder and are thus considered comorbid, or if they are simply the way that symptoms present in the course of childhood development of the disorder and are not actually separate diagnoses but all part of the larger picture of bipolar disorder in childhood. While some children may truly have multiple diagnoses, others may just be exhibiting early signs of bipolar disorder. A consensus has not yet been reached on this issue; however, there is movement toward untangling these questions and finding the answers in the upcoming revision of the *DSM*. The brief case study below illustrates some of the diagnostic concerns.

Confusion and Controversy

Jacob, age 6, was diagnosed with PDD-NOS, ADHD, and OCD by age four. His mother still feels desperate for answers. None of the symptoms of his diagnoses seemed quite to match her son's behavior. He threw long, violent tantrums when denied access to a toy or prompted to clean up. His tantrums went on for hours and often included a combination of crying, screaming, throwing his body to the ground, destroying household objects, and hitting and kicking. He typically slept for short periods of about 3 to 4 hours some nights, and for 8 to 10 hours other nights. The day after a short sleep cycle, Jacob was as energetic as on those nights when he got much more sleep, and he never crashed from exhaustion. When awake in the middle of the night, Jacob laughed endlessly and sometimes ran around the house. One night he ventured outside. Luckily, his mother woke when the screen door slammed shut and was able to usher him back inside before he was hurt or lost. Jacob can concentrate for hours on end when playing with his preferred toys, but he cannot tolerate his play time being interrupted for meals. He frequently asks his mother to enact elaborate imaginative sequences that would be impossible to have happen in real life, and then becomes upset when she can't. He becomes obsessed with eating certain foods in specific order and out of specific serving dishes or cups. The slightest change in these routines can set him off on a tantrum. Without any apparent reason, Jacob frequently breaks windows, smashes breakable objects, and dumps over gallons of milk and containers of flour. At home he becomes so overheated that he frequently strips down to his underwear, and his nose, ears, and cheeks are visibly flushed. During calmer moments he is very affectionate and loving with his mother, often hugging and kissing her.

Jacob attends an applied behavior analysis (ABA) focused classroom and partial-inclusion mainstream classroom to support his needs. The specialized classroom serves children with autism spectrum disorder who have similar difficulties with changes in routines and who are prone to tantrums and outbursts. At school he is well-behaved and responds well to the structure and routine his classroom provides. However, Jacob has difficulty focusing, appears disinterested, and displays a very low level of alertness, except when he is allowed to play in the sensory room. There he bounces on the trampoline and crawls repeatedly through the tunnels while giggling excessively. He attends therapy with a social worker at a community clinic, where he also is seen by a psychiatrist and prescribed medication. The number of medications Jacob has tried in his short life is three pages in length. Until recently, he was simultaneously taking an antipsychotic and stimulant, but his mother weaned him off all medication. He had gained over 50 pounds in the past year, and she is not convinced that the medicines work well enough to warrant the health risk. His mother suspects that Jacob might be suffering from a mood disorder and had read a couple of books on the topic, but she is still unsure. Exhausted by his behavior, she sought in-home support; after a few visits, the behavioral consultant suggested that he may suffer from a mood disorder. Feeling validated, Jacob's mother booked an appointment with a noted psychiatrist who specializes in mood disorder in young children.

During the writing of this book, the American Psychiatric Association (APA) made public its proposed changes for the upcoming fifth version of the *DSM*. The APA expressed concern about the enormous increase in the number of children being diagnosed with BPD over the last 15 years, and their new diagnostic guidelines reflect that concern. Widespread diagnostic confusion about pediatric bipolar disorder is one of the reasons for the documented increase, and the proposal suggests both that definitions of the children's symptoms be more specific to the context of expected developmental stages and that the symptoms be considered clinical if they are emblematic of a noticeable change in behavior from that which is considered typical for the individual child. In addition, many children and adults fall short of the criteria for Bipolar I and II, mainly because of manic episodes shorter in duration than the *DSM-IV* criteria of four days. The proposed changes define more specifically how the duration of an episode is calculated as well as adjust the current criteria to include shorter durations to decrease inappropriate use of the nondescript BPD-NOS diagnosis.

Of particular importance is a proposed change that challenges the belief that ongoing and acute irritability is a developmental presentation of mania in children. To differentiate this kind of irritability from true mania, the *DSM* committee may introduce a new, completely separate childhood diagnosis called temper dysregulation disorder with dysphoria (TDD), which would fall in the Mood Disorders section of the *DSM-V*. TDD purports to clearly identify those children who exhibit negative mood and clinically significant levels of irritability characterized by angry outbursts. It is the severity of behavioral impairment and the added mood disorder component that differentiate TDD from other disorders of childhood.

Presently, children with these symptoms are being misdiagnosed with Bi-polar Disorder for lack of any other diagnostic category that speaks to a mood disorder aspect of their symptomology. Treatment of TDD would differ from current treatment modalities for BPD, which means that children will receive the interventions most appropriate to their specific clinical needs, but, like current treatment of BPD, it will probably include a pharmacological component.

Differential diagnosis is problematic, as the definition and understanding of childhood BPD is currently evolving. As of this publication, the most common overlap of symptoms occurs between bipolar disorder and ADHD. Both include manifestations of inattention, impulsivity, and hyperactivity and deficits in areas of executive functioning, so on the surface they may be difficult to distinguish. However, there are subtle differences that help define them. Children with ADHD throw temper tantrums that may last 30 minutes and be disruptive, but they are generally manageable. The child with bipolar disorder will tantrum or feel angry for hours at a time and be so intense that it will be difficult to ignore. Children with bipolar disorder are upset by limit-setting and being told, "no," but children with ADHD tend to react more to sensory or emotional overstimulation. Children with ADHD tend to break things while playing carelessly; children with bipolar disorder destroy property in anger. Children with ADHD are quick to wake up and get out of bed in the morning, but children with bipolar disorder drag their feet and are slow to become alert. These are just a few of the nuances that help distinguish these two very similar sets of symptoms.

It is important to ferret out the distinctions between ADHD and bipolar disorder because treatment of one disorder may adversely affect the other. For example, ADHD is typically treated with stimulants, but stimulants may worsen the symptoms of bipolar disorder. If the child with bipolar disorder also has ADHD, medication for the bipolar disorder must be stabilized before stimulants are tried. Generally, children with a diagnosis of bipolar disorder have 57 percent to 98 percent comorbidity with ADHD, whereas children with a diagnosis of ADHD have only 11 percent to 22 percent comorbidity with bipolar disorder. An added diagnostic category of TDD might decrease the confusion between ADHD and BPD in the future, or that confusion may just shift from ADHD to TDD and BPD.

Since there is a long list of medical conditions that can mimic the symptoms of bipolar disorder and must be ruled out during diagnosis, psychiatrists must have accurate information. Families can assist in the diagnostic process and clarify their own understanding of their child's behavior by charting the child's moods and symptoms on a daily chart and then bringing it to doctor visits. Behaviors to chart should include sleep, anger, energy, mood, and responses to any medications the child takes. Unfortunately, psychiatric visits are generally brief and rushed, thus limiting the likelihood that a full and comprehensive sense of the child and family's experience could emerge. Moreover, overreliance on the parents' report could skew the clinician's understanding of the child's condition if the parents are overwhelmed and poorly equipped to manage a difficult child.

Since treatment for BPD involves powerful psychotropic medication, clinicians and parents must be concerned with false positive identification, that is, children who exhibit symptoms of the condition but for whom the medication is not helpful and potentially harmful. The opposite concern, false negatives, are children who have the disorder but may go unrecognized or treated for something else that may exacerbate the underlying condition. Diagnosis of the disorder in childhood is clearly a controversial issue on several levels. On the one hand, the importance of an accurate diagnosis cannot be stressed enough. Currently, true cases of bipolar disorder are underdiagnosed and often go untreated in both children and adults. For children there is frequently a 10-year delay between the appearance of symptoms and treatment. That delay can interfere with many aspects of the child's life, including the mastery of developmental tasks, social relationships, academic and later job performance, and may even be a precursor to substance abuse and difficulties with the law. Delay can also cause families to live for years with a child that they not only do not understand and have difficulty parenting, but with anxiety and concern about their child's unnamed condition. Knowledge alone can go a long way to providing families with reassurance and understanding. Since this disorder's symptoms overlap with symptoms of a variety of other disorders, children are frequently misdiagnosed.

Misdiagnosis also delays proper treatment and can even elevate symptoms to a psychotic state when the wrong treatments are applied. Improperly treated bipolar disorder can lead to hospitalization, substance abuse, and injury. A child's developing neurological system can become sensitized to the cycles of the mood disorder, and pathways in the central nervous system become reinforced, causing episodes of depression and mania to occur on their own with increasing frequency. With a suicide attempt rate of 15 percent to 25 percent, bipolar disorder poses a real threat of lethality if not properly diagnosed and treated.

While accurate diagnosis is vital, preemptive diagnosis can have its own ramifications. Current diagnostic criteria allow for children to be diagnosed with bipolar disorder as early as age six. Some pediatricians and psychiatrists are reticent to diagnose such a severe disorder in really young children. Mental disorders such as bipolar disorder can create a stigma for the child, essentially labeling her early on, which may adversely affect the course of her school and social life. The threat of stigma combined with an unwieldy list of possible symptoms that frequently overlaps or mirrors other disorders makes some doctors wary of diagnosis until the symptoms elicit a clearer differential diagnosis. Lack of consensus on the set of symptoms and lack of information and conclusive research on bipolar disorder in children generally lead professionals to act with caution. Furthermore, the *DSM-IV* does not distinguish these differences in children, and since every treatment provider uses its guidelines to make diagnoses, they may not feel they can diagnose outside of these parameters. Given the large set of unknowns, many would prefer to err on the side of caution and are conservative in their approach to such a serious disorder. On the other hand, the U.S. heath-care system requires a diagnosis for continued treatment and reimbursements; therefore, numerous physicians gravitate to the vague BPD-NOS diagnosis and prescribe medications in the hope that they will do the child some good and provide some hope and relief to the distraught parent.

Treatment for bipolar disorder typically starts with medication. While lithium is the most common medication used to treat bipolar disorder, there is an array of medications available, and frequently more than one medication is prescribed. Mood stabilizers, antipsychotics, and antidepressants are just a few classes of medications that treat the symptoms of bipolar disorder. Finding the right combination of medications can be a long and involved process, which may be difficult for both child and family. Finding a qualified and conscientious child psychiatrist is crucial.

Both treatment providers and families may have valid concerns about giving children such strong and potentially dangerous medications. The use of powerful psychiatric prescription medication to treat childhood disorders has long been a controversial issue. Many of the pharmaceuticals being prescribed to children at an early age may have negative long-term outcomes or side effects. For the most part those medications have not been trialed in children, nor have their effects been studied over time, and their long-term effects are largely unknown. What is clear thus far is that common side effects may be difficult for children to bear and can even cause other health concerns. For example, many of the antipsychotic medications cause weight gain, which can lead to high blood pressure, diabetes, and added social stigmas. Still, from 1994 to 2003 the prescription of BPD medication for children in the United States increased 40 fold, (Moreno, et.al., 2007). The diagnostic concerns are further clouded by a number of financial improprieties and conflict of interest scandals that were uncovered in recent years by a congressional investigation headed by Senator Charles E. Grassley of Iowa. Senator Grassley's panel found that the most well-respected psychiatrists and experts in the field of childhood bipolar disorder have been underreporting large sums they have received in consulting fees—$1.6 million in one case—by the very pharmaceutical companies that funded their research. Further evidence demonstrated intent to provide pharmaceutical companies with proof that these medications were both safe and effective in children under age 10 and to develop new uses for their already existing medications. In the course of their investigations, the *Wall Street Journal* (Armstrong, 2009) reported that Dr. Joseph Biederman and colleagues incurred at least six breaches of the preschool research protocol. These are the very same research scientists who proclaimed the virtues of the use of antipsychotic medications like Risperdal in children as young as four and advocated that even younger children could be diagnosed with BPD. In 2009, the *New York Times* (Harris, 2009) reported that Dr. Biederman, as director of the Johnson & Johnson Center for Pediatric Psychopathology Research at Massachusetts General Hospital in Boston was in the middle of two controversies: one involving the use of antipsychotic drugs in children, and the other related to conflicts of interest in medicine. Beyond the breaches of protocol and questionable practices unearthed by Senator Grassley, the ethical problems in pharmaceutical research are far from solved. Most prestigious universities and medical research centers across the country still vie for funding from pharmaceutical companies to conduct drug studies; dependence on corporate funding for pharmaceutical research has in fact increased as federal funds have dwindled.

Children with Bipolar Disorder: Family Life

Callie, age 11, is visiting a psychiatrist for a second opinion. Her primary psychiatrist recently diagnosed her with bipolar disorder, and her mother wants to be sure the diagnosis is accurate. She reports that Callie is responding well to the antipsychotic medication she was recently prescribed. When asked about her history, her mother describes long periods of depression interrupted by short spurts of extreme energy. When depressed, Callie wanted to sleep all day and experienced great difficulty transitioning from a sleeping to a waking state, and when energized, she didn't need to sleep at all and talked incessantly about how she was the best soccer player on the planet. Callie reported in the interview that she believed she could win a match against Mia Hamm if given the chance, and said very seriously, "I'm the most awesome soccer player ever." Her mother explained that Callie was sometimes difficult to understand— she spoke quickly and could not be slowed down. When her mother told her she could not go to soccer camp in Colorado this year, Callie hit her mother and broke her nose. When her father confronted her about her behavior, she ran out of the house and into traffic without any regard for her safety. Callie attends a mainstream classroom and is currently in the sixth grade. At school Callie is frequently in trouble for mouthing off to her teachers, pinching classmates, and making lewd comments. Her teachers report that she has trouble concentrating on work, sitting still, and following directions. She is sweet and often apologizes for her missteps, but does not appear to be learning from them. Callie gets into a lot of fights with her friends and is consistently angry when they don't do what she wants them to do. She has a reputation for daring other kids to take risks and then demonstrating them herself when they refuse.

Since she began taking the antipsychotic medication, her mother reports that she has not shown any signs of physical aggression, and although she can still be overly energetic at times, she is able to sleep for a few hours. She is in less trouble at school, is maintaining friendships, and has exhibited less-risky behavior. However, her mother is concerned that this may just be a phase that Callie is going through. Since she is prepubertal and may be experiencing hormone shifts, her mother feels she may just be moody and, like all teens, she will eventually learn from her mistakes. She now wonders if perhaps the medication is not necessary.

Stabilizing the disorder with medication has traditionally been seen as the first step in treatment, but psychotherapy for the child and family is equally important. Callie responded well to medication, and it is unclear what would be the consequences of discontinuing drug treatment. Her family, like all similarly affected families, will require supports to work with the child, to ensure teamwork among adult partners, and to educate and help siblings negotiate this difficult disorder. Families can also learn how to keep a mood chart and can get the child involved in learning how to chart her behavior. Charting will help the family elicit patterns that can be used to prevent future episodes or explosions. Charts can also help track the efficacy of medications.

Unfortunately, there is almost no literature on alternative treatment modalities and their efficacy in treating bipolar disorder in children. The focus of research in the treatment arena has largely been on medication. However, there are certainly alternatives that may augment and facilitate the health of children and their families. Surely there are some methods in family and individual counseling, behavioral interventions, academic modifications, social skills, art or music therapy, and sensory integration that would benefit and perhaps even prevent some of the extreme symptoms of bipolar disorder in children. Although more research is needed in this area, it is abundantly clear that the intensity of conflicts and challenges present in affected families can be alleviated through ongoing individual and family therapy.

As difficult as it has been to conceptualize this disorder in a way that encompasses the range of children who stand under its umbrella, the largest well of confusion and turmoil reside *within* the individual child with bipolar disorder. One may imagine how scary and bewildering the world must be for a child who is constantly receiving the message, "The way you *are* is unacceptable." That is exactly what happens every time a child with bipolar disorder is disciplined for obsessive persistence to obtain a desired object or the consequent torrential tantrum that ensues when he or she is denied the object. What at first appears to be mere defiance, bossiness, and hyperactivity reaches clinical levels in the child with bipolar disorder. In a typically developing child these behaviors can be modified with a tried and true formula—limits are set, rewards and consequences are consistently doled out, and the behaviors decrease. The child with bipolar disorder responds to those same behavior management techniques in a completely opposite manner and the behavior escalates, much to the utter bewilderment of their families and caregivers.

Bipolar disorder affects the whole family. Siblings grapple with complex feelings about having a brother or sister with bipolar disorder and need support. They may feel, justifiably, that they are held to a different behavioral standard in the home. Siblings may need to grieve the loss of a typical brother or sister, may feel embarrassed or afraid of the actions of the child with bipolar disorder, and may also be resentful that he receives plentiful attention while preventing the family from having certain experiences or visiting locations that trigger the affected child's moodiness. Their possessions may be destroyed in a tantrum, their privacy may be compromised, and they could even be hurt physically by the sibling with the disorder. It is important that parents spend time with siblings, acknowledge and talk through these feelings, and explain the disorder as best they can. Sibling support groups are becoming increasingly accessible and provide a forum for sharing experiences with peers, voicing feelings and concerns in a nonbiased environment, and having a time and space that is explicitly devoted to their experience when so much of their daily family life focuses on the child with BPD.

The high genetic correlation in bipolar disorder—children of a parent with bipolar disorder have a 15 percent to 30 percent risk of inheriting the disorder—sometimes leads parents to blame themselves for the child's disorder. And because the disorder is frequently hereditary, parents coping with their own bipolar symptoms are often parenting children affected by bipolar disorder. It may be difficult for parents with bipolar disorder to make accurate observations and reports on their child's behavior. Research shows that children of parents with mental illness adjust to their parents' needs and pay close attention to how their parent is doing as a predictor for how their parent might behave, which eases the parent-child relationship. Children with bipolar disorder are unable to do so and may have particular difficulty interacting with their affected parent. On the other hand, parents with bipolar disorder can provide invaluable information about their own course of the disorder, medication trials, and previous interventions. They may have first-hand insight on their child's experience and may be better able to understand, empathize, and provide support to the child.

Regardless, all parents will experience a range of emotions that may include denial, fear for the child's future, and anxiety about making it through the day in addition to shame, stress, and grief. It is important to process these feelings so that the child feels acceptance and love from the family despite the difficulties. Parents will find they have to give up traditional parenting methods—that reward-charts and time-outs are not effective. The child may not fear consequences or respect their authority and will, in fact, react explosively to limit-setting and consequences. Parents may need to cut through tense moments with humor to throw off the child's mood cycle, speak in calm tones to avoid triggering a stronger outburst, and avoid threatening statements or situations, which include authoritative, consequence-oriented reactions.

It is imperative that parents teach their children to identify their own feelings and validate the feeling itself. This step alone will go a long way to having the child feel understood and accepted. Parents can then separate the child's behavior from the feelings that triggered it. Helping the child learn to differentiate the feeling from the behavior will make it easier to redirect the behavior. Also when the parent tries to stop or correct the behavior, the child does not feel punished for *who* she is. Providing choices is another powerful tool for allowing the child to feel in control of the situation while still giving parents the ultimate say, as they have determined what the choices will be. Allowing the child some power in the situation will avoid triggering the fight-or-flight response. Parents may have to adjust their own agendas and choose carefully between those things that must be discussed or addressed with the child because they pose a safety issue or are nonnegotiable versus topics that consistently trigger the child or are nonessential.

Living in a world that knows so little about and understands even less of the experience of parenting a child with a disorder of this magnitude is a difficult challenge. Some children may exhibit problematic behaviors in public, making it arduous to take them on ordinary trips, even to the grocery store, without incident. Other adults may look on and wonder what is wrong with the child or why the parents do not get him under control. If a child's behavior escalates and cannot be diffused, parents may need to learn how to use therapeutic holds to keep the child and others safe while the child rages. A safety plan that includes family, neighbors, or other local supports in time of crisis should be developed by the family, should the child ever get out of control. Parents will need the support, education, and clinical insights a therapist can provide in guiding the family through this complex disorder.

It is equally important to be involved with the child's school and provide information about a child's specific needs to the teachers, school psychologist, and administrators there. Children with bipolar disorder may need classroom accommodations and benefit from an environment that reduces distractions, has built-in organizational tools, is child directed, and will reorient the child to task. Creative behavioral interventions, strategies for affect regulation, social skills, and thinking creatively about ways to help the child approach tasks and feel good about the academic experience are keys to unlocking the child's current and future successes. The arts can be particularly helpful to help the child give expression to her internal challenges and social conflicts.

Conclusion

Early onset bipolar disorder is a complex and confusing mental health disorder that is presently being researched and redefined. Although there are many conflicting notions and unknowns about this disorder, awareness of and education about it are increasing in the health professions and in education. Children with BPD struggle with severe mood swings, and daily life poses challenges that transform the simplest activities into an ordeal. Their perceptions, needs, and resulting behavior are only now beginning to be understood by families and the psychological community at large. With understanding comes knowledge and awareness that will serve to alleviate the child and his family of painful misconceptions and harmful misdiagnoses that delay treatment and prolong the child's suffering. It will take a team composed of parents, family members, doctors, therapists, teachers, and other supports to wrap around the child and guide him through an experience that is difficult even for adults to negotiate.

References

Armstrong, David. (2009, March 20). Protocol breach reported in Biederman study of preschoolers. *The Wall Street Journal.* Retrieved from http:blogs.wsj.com/health/2009/03/20protocol-breach-reported-in-Biederman-Study-of-pre schoolers.

Faedda, G. L., & Austin, N. B. (2006). *Parenting a bipolar child: What to do and why.* Oakland, CA: New Harbinger.

Geller, B., & DelBello, M. P. (Eds.). (2003). *Bipolar disorder in childhood and early adolescence.* New York: The Guilford Press.

Hanstock, T. L. (2007). Bipolar affective disorder and dissociation: A potentially lethal combination [Electronic version]. *Clinical Case Studies, 6,* 131–142.

Harris, G. (2009, March 20). Drug maker told studies would aid it, papers say. *The New York Times.* Retrieved August 19, 2010 from http://www.nytimes.com/2009/03/20/us/20psych.html?_r=2&pagewanted=print.

Harris, G., & Carey, B. (2008, June 8). Researchers fail to reveal full drug pay. *The New York Times.* Retrieved August 19, 2010, from http://www.nytimes.com/2008/06/08/us/08conflict.html?sq=dr.jospeh biederman&st=cse.

Hastings Center. (2010, March 21). Broad application of bipolar diagnosis in children may do more harm than good. *Science Daily.* Retrieved August 19, 2010, from http://www.sciencedaily.com/releases/2010/03/100318174723.htm.

Hastings Center (2010, May 19). Proposed diagnostic change not enough to help children currently diagnosed with bipolar disorder, experts say. *Science Daily.* Retrieved August 19, 2010, from http://www.sciencedaily.com/releases/2010/05/100519173055.htm.

Killu, K., & Crundwell, R.M.A. (2008). Understanding and developing academic and behavioral interventions for students with bipolar disorder [Electronic version]. *Intervention in School and Clinic, 43,* 244–251.

Knowles, R. J. (2007). Complexity and comorbidity in a case of early-onset bipolar disorder [Electronic version]. *Clinical Case Studies, 6,* 232–251.

Kowalczyk, L. (2009, March 21). Senator broadens inquiry into psychiatrist: Suggests MGH doctor was biased in research. *The Boston Globe.* Retrieved August 19, 2010, from http://www.boston.com/news/local/massachussetts/articles/2009/03/21/senator_broadens_inquiry.

Kowatch, R.A., Fristad, M., Birmaher, B., Wagner, K.D., Findling, R.L., Hellander, M., et al. (2005). Treatment guidelines for children and adolescents with bipolar disorder: Child psychiatric workgroup on bipolar disorder. *Journal of the American Academy of Child and Adolescent Psychiatry, 44,* 213–235.

Lifespan. (2009, July 29). If bipolar disorder is over-diagnosed, what are the actual diagnoses? *Science Daily.* Retrieved August 19, 2010, from http://www.sciencedaily.com/releases/2009/07/090729100936.htm.

McManamy, J. (2008). The bipolar child: What to look for. In *McMan's Depression and Bipolar Web*. Retrieved October 7, 2008, from http://www.mcmanweb. com/bipolar_child.html.

McNicholas, F., & Baird, G. (2000). Early-onset bipolar disorder and ADHD: Diagnostic confusion due to co-morbidity? [Electronic version]. *Clinical Child Psychology and Psychiatry, 5*, 595–605.

Mordoch, E., & Hall, W. A. (2008). Children's perceptions of living with a parent with a mental illness: Finding the rhythm and maintaining the frame [Electronic version]. *Qualitative Health Research, 18*, 1127–1144.

Moreno C., Laje G., Blanco C., Jiang H., Schmidt A. B., Olfson M. (2007). National trends in the outpatient diagnosis and treatment of bipolar disorder in youth. *Arch Gen Psychiatry 64*(9), 1032–1039.

Olson, P. M., & Pacheco, M. R. (2005). Bipolar disorder in school-age children [Electronic version]. *The Journal of School Nursing, 21*, 152–157.

Papolos, D., & Papolos, J. (1999). *The bipolar child: The definitive and reassuring guide to childhood's most misunderstood disorder* (1st ed.). New York: Broadway Books.

Additional Resources

1. Externalizing Disorders of Childhood (Attention-deficit/Hyperactivity Disorder, Conduct Disorder, Oppositional-Defiant Disorder, Juvenile Bipolar Disorder) (February 14–16, 2007)

Prepared by Michael B. First, MD, *DSM* Consultant to the American Psychiatric Institute for Research and Education (APIRE), a subsidary of the American Psychiatric Association

All papers will appear in a monograph published by American Psychiatric Press, Inc.

http://www.dsm5.org/research/pages/externalizingdisordersofchildhood (attention-deficithyperactivitydisorder,conductdisorder,oppositional-defiant disorder,juven.aspx

2. Issues Pertinent to a Developmental Approach to Bipolar Disorder in DSM-5

http://www.dsm5.org/Proposed%20Revision%20Attachments/APA%20Developmental%20Approaches%20to%20Bipolar%20Disorder.pdf

3. Justification for Temper Dysregulation Disorder with Dysphoria

DSM-5 Childhood and Adolescent Disorders Work Group

From www.DSM5.org

CHAPTER 4

Persistent Questions about Attention Deficit Hyperactivity Disorder

Dana Freed

Terry was the first to greet me when I entered the room. He was always friendly, except when his medication dosage was too high. He got up out of his seat and ran over to the door to say hello while his teacher rolled her eyes and said, "Sit down, Terry," for what sounded like the hundredth time that morning. He ran back over to his seat, banging the backs of other students' chairs on his way. "Stop it, Terry!" the other kids screamed, but some of them were smiling. Terry was grinning from ear to ear when he finally sat in his seat, which made it easy to see all of his braces at once. "Come help me, please, come help me, come see my new person I made," he asked and waved his hand so high into the air that he slipped out of his seat. "Sit in your seat, Terry, not on the floor," his teacher said immediately. Terry's desktop was covered with doodles and comic strips on white paper. He was a very talented artist and he loved to draw, but that was all he liked to do in class. He could spend hours drawing. His teacher said, "Okay, Terry, that's enough, let's get back to work." Terry continued to ask me to come help him.

Terry was a 12-year-old African American male, and shorter and skinnier than the other boys in his class. He was in the sixth grade when I met him, attending a public school for children exhibiting behavioral problems. Terry was diagnosed with ADHD, attention deficit hyperactivity disorder, when he was seven years old by his pediatrician and had been on and off a variety of stimulant medications since then. The pediatrician had a difficult time adjusting his medication. Too little of the medication left him unable to focus in school and too much made him almost catatonic in the classroom, not an uncommon problem. Terry shared how embarrassing it was when he took higher doses, since saliva often accumulated in the space between his lower lip and teeth, causing him to drool. Other students teased him when this happened. However, without the higher doses of medication, Terry was physically unable to sit in his seat. Terry also had learning difficulties, specifically in reading and writing. Much of the time he could not organize himself to start working in class, which caused him to feel and express frustration.

Attention Deficit Hyperactivity Disorder, more commonly referred to as ADHD, has been intensely researched and it is a syndrome that has a great deal of acceptance within the mental health professions. Yet, there are a number of unresolved questions and issues related to the disorder, perpetuating misconceptions and myths. ADHD is ubiquitous, and the symptoms associated with the disorder are, in fact, behaviors anyone can exhibit, but individuals with pronounced ADHD have chronic and severe impairments that adversely affect their daily functioning in a society that is not fully tolerant of the manifestations of the condition.

ADHD has made its way into our daily vernacular. It is common to hear statements such as, "My child is so ADHD I can't even be around him without feeling like I want to scream. He would lose his wallet in his back pocket." Statements such as these illustrate the negative perceptions associated with this disorder, despite its common presence in our society. We tend to define individuals based on their identified disorders instead of addressing them holistically. This tendency is particularly detrimental to children as their self concepts begin to be defined and confined by their diagnosed disability. Gaining a better understanding of how a child challenged by ADHD receives information and responds to certain stimuli might help to make classrooms more user friendly to different attentional capacities and change how others, including family members, respond to these children emotionally and interpersonally. It is important to note that children with ADHD can attend well to certain information and situations. However, theirs is an inconsistent display of attention. Attention, in and of itself, is a complex neurological activity that fluctuates according to interest level, lifestyle, diet, emotional and mental states, physical health, and unconscious processes.

To attempt to make this societal shift in the perception of the disorder, especially in educational settings, it is important to understand several aspects of this disorder, while keeping in mind that the symptoms differ amongst individuals. Some children might have extreme symptoms, such as those exhibited by Terry. Most common manifestations of the disorder are externalized, meaning symptoms are predominantly hyperactivity-impulsivity, which are more obvious and able to be observed. In contrast, other people have a form of the condition without the overt outward expression. This is referred to as *predominantly inattentive type*; in these cases the difficulty is mainly about poor concentration. This type of presentation is harder to observe since it is more internalized. A child with ADHD inattentive type might often daydream and get lost in thought. These children have more learning difficulties, but may not stand out in a classroom and may not be identified. The more hyperactive children cannot be ignored, and without treatment they are at greater risk of developing symptoms of conduct disorder. Like Terry, many children have challenges, hyperactivity-impulsive behaviors, and poor capacity for focus and concentration. All children with attentional difficulties are challenged every day, trying to adapt to environments that are not always sensitive to their needs. In many situations, their poor adaptation is misinterpreted as volitional, and consequently adults lose patience and sympathy. Questions regarding symptoms, etiology, perceptions, environment, and different treatments will be examined through the lens of Terry's experience. Despite the condition's relatively long association with pediatric psychiatry, there is still lack of agreement amongst professionals regarding the etiological foundations of the disorder and the efficacy of various types of treatment. All experts speak with authority on the subject, but without consensus it is confusing for parents and educators to make informed choices.

Males are diagnosed with ADHD by a ratio of 3:1 to females. Many of Terry's classmates are males exhibiting symptoms of ADHD. Children with severe externalized presentations of ADHD and not responsive to treatment have difficulties in school and/or might be placed in more restricted environments within educational settings. Children with the predominant inattentive type usually spend more time in regular educational settings because symptoms are less noticeable. Children with ADHD have higher chances of exhibiting symptoms of other disorders, thus further complicating the task of diagnosing and implementing appropriate treatment options. Common cooccurring conditions (comorbid) include depression, anxiety disorders, learning disabilities, and oppositional defiant disorder.

According to the National Institute of Mental Health, between 20 and 40 percent of children diagnosed with ADHD will develop conduct disorder. When left untreated, conduct disorder may develop into antisocial personality disorder in adulthood. A characteristic behavior of both conduct disorder and ADHD is noncompliance. Children with these disorders have difficulties behaving in a socially acceptable manner and following rules. The difference between the disorders is intention, as children with conduct disorders are understood to be willfully noncompliant, interfering with the rights of others, and intending to hurt others. For a child with ADHD, noncompliance is the result of poorly regulated behavior rather than lack of empathy or disregard for social rules. The matter of willfulness is harder to ascertain the younger or more developmentally immature a child is. Also, there is an unavoidable interplay between a child having difficulty controlling his impulses and a social and familial context that consistently disapproves of his behavior. The longer this negative interaction persists, the more likely that the child will grow up frustrated and angry.

In ADHD, like in few other childhood disorders, symptom expression and intensity varies; often as a consequence of the nature of the immediate environment. Generally only children with significant impairments are diagnosed, and symptoms overlap with other disorders. If children do not receive adequate interventions to address ADHD symptoms, they are more vulnerable to other emotional and behavior difficulties that are a direct consequence of being misunderstood.

Symptoms of ADHD that often go unaddressed may include difficulties with attention, planning, organization, executive function, and tendencies to display impulsivity and hyperactivity. Linked to the disorder are neurological difficulties in auditory-verbal processing, visual-spatial processing, sensory modulation, and motor planning, all of which can impact attention. Many children with ADHD are sensory underresponsive, meaning that it is harder for them to differentiate amongst stimuli in the environment. Richard Barkley, a well-regarded expert in this disorder, describes ADHD as being constituted by two components: (a) hyperactivity, a problem with behavioral inhibition, and (b) attention problems, that is, deficits in executive function, primarily with a specific type of memory called working memory. Executive functioning involves memory, decision-making, organization, regulating alertness, sustaining effort, managing frustration, modulating emotion, and self-regulation and attention. Inconsistent attention and the aforementioned symptoms are not conducive to success in a regular classroom. Children with ADHD often experience failure in school and little positive feelings about the self. ADHD has been described as primarily a disorder that aversely affects school life, but it also poses significant problems at home and in the community.

Typical learning in a classroom consists of scheduled, content-driven periods that require children to consistently attend to presented information for a certain period of time, complete assignments, sit in one seat for an extended period of time, and control behaviors and responses. Part of fulfilling the role of the student is adjusting one's behavior to meet the expectations and routines in the environment. However, these expectations often do not make adequate allowances for children like Terry, who cannot physically and psychologically conform to those expectations. Unsurprisingly, Terry was unable to perform within this structure from an early age.

An unfortunate outcome for children with ADHD is that their behaviors are often misconstrued. In school Terry could not follow the rules, finish his assignments, learn the curriculum or necessary skills, or relate well with his peers. Terry was the child unable to sit still and meet the expectations in his environment. He would complain, "Sitting in the seat hurts," and proceed to stand up and walk around the room, which usually frustrated his teachers. The discomfort of sitting and difficulty paying attention to his teacher and classmates made it nearly impossible for Terry to learn in the classroom.

Terry's attentional difficulties were not limited to the classroom. Since he could not attend to one point at a time, listening and engaging in conversations was challenging and affected Terry's ability to make friends.

While socializing, he tended to interrupt, was unable to follow the conversation, and would forget what he was talking about. His way of interacting with his peers often resulted in grabbing and aggression. Another symptom of his ADHD was having difficulty navigating through physical space, causing him to be considered messy by his teachers. His aunt, who was his guardian, noted that he regularly loses his belongings and is not able to understand his personal space and others while interacting.

Throughout his elementary education, his teachers did not know how to help Terry, often punishing him for not following the rules. In most cases, Terry's teachers tried to work with him, but may have found themselves exasperated and unable to change the environment to better meet his needs. Instead of addressing the behaviors associated with his ADHD, he was often penalized for not functioning like his better-behaved peers. Terry usually responded defensively to his teachers and classmates, further exacerbating situations and leading him into more trouble at school. This pattern also deflected attention from his considerable academic difficulties and deepened his learned helplessness and sense of personal failing. The constant attention to Terry's behavior was negative and derogatory: "What's wrong with you? Why can't you be like everyone else?" His teacher's exasperation made him feel hopeless and that there was something unfixable with his brain, but he protested that he was not a bad kid.

Often when a child is diagnosed as ADHD, teachers and school staff feel absolved from taking responsibility for the child's behaviors. It is true that something is affecting the child's behavior, but other contextual factors that affect a child cannot be dismissed. The common belief is that once a child carries a specific label, the problem is perceived as residing within the child as opposed to the child responding to the environment. Approaching the child with this belief system is a disservice, as the diagnosis defines the child and limits understanding of individual needs. Although a child may be properly identified as manifesting ADHD traits, the best way to help her is by organizing and adapting the social and learning environment.

Schooling was a source of frustration, and Terry expressed his distress in the classroom. It is common for children with ADHD to underachieve. Many children with ADHD have similar experiences, eventually attending schools for children with behavioral problems, where academic learning is less emphasized and changing the students' behavior becomes the primary focus. Many children who suffer from ADHD are placed in self-contained classrooms or struggle in regular education classrooms. Some researchers estimate that seven percent of children in the United States show symptoms of ADHD, which invariably affect behavioral compliance and academic performance.

Some symptoms, mostly inattention, do not disappear over time, as was once believed. Seven out of 10 adults diagnosed as children do not outgrow the attentional aspect of the disorder and continue to experience forgetfulness, disorganization, and difficulty concentrating. Hyperactivity is often internalized and described as "inner restlessness." Knowing that this way of functioning is typical for many children and adults, shifting the perception of the disorder to something different as opposed to wrong could potentially break the negative feedback cycle. There are people in our culture who are praised for behaviors consistent with ADHD. Famous comedians have been known to talk excessively, have high activity levels, appear distracted, and switch topics abruptly. In general, the comedians had a hard time in school. So, in a different context, ADHD behaviors are more acceptable and even praised. Some children living with ADHD do clown around in school. Similarly, many prominent sports figures, artists, and inventors are known to have the disorder and to have shown promise in those fields in their school years—even though they may have struggled with school routines.

Symptoms associated with what is now called ADHD are not new. Impulsivity and inattention were traits noted in some children and described in legends, folktales, and stories, such as Icarus, the impulsive son of Daedalus in Greek mythology, and Jack of "Jack and the Beanstalk," the English boy who traded the cow before getting to market and did not think twice before climbing up to the sky on the unnatural vines growing outside his window. However, it was not until 1902, when the condition was first described by George Still, that ADHD gained recognition as a mental disorder. Since that first documentation of this curious disorder, efforts to understand it have caused it to be linked to encephalitis and minimal brain damage, among other things. It has had many names such as minimal brain dysfunction (MBD), hyperkinetic reaction disorder of childhood, and more recently, Attention Deficit Disorder. The focus of the disorder has shifted between inattention and hyperactivity; but now the diagnostic criteria include all symptoms. The etiology of the disorder remains somewhat clouded in mystery. As researchers have tried to make sense of ADHD-like behaviors, there have been many myths and controversies associated with the disorder; and many still endure.

Myths and Controversies

Perhaps the most harmful myth to children with ADHD is that it is not a real disorder. Some have argued that pharmaceutical companies and psychiatric communities invented the condition as a way to generate business. It has also been described as a fictional disorder to explain why some children do not perform well in school. This hypothesis implies that schools fail to be accountable for all children's learning. Those critics posit that ADHD is a contrived condition and a reflection of narrow social values. They argue that parents, teachers, and administrators hold inflexible educational expectations and narrowly proscribed social behaviors for children. Consequently, they believe that the diagnosis of ADHD was constructed for children who were unable to fulfill schools' behavioral codes and norms; through the assignment of the label, in effect, they blame the children for not learning.

Those who see ADHD strictly as neurological disorder propose that children should be treated following a medical model, implying that the condition should be treated and managed as a problem residing within the child's body. On the other hand, those who question whether ADHD is a real disorder suggest that emphasis should be on changing attitudes and increasing tolerance of differences in behaviors. Since there is yet no definitive neurological test to diagnose the disorder, critics of psychiatric approaches still have some sway. Contemporary neuro-imaging studies suggest that new methods may soon be routinely used in diagnosis; but without a clear marker and less-than-rigorous qualifying criteria, many children are erroneously labeled. ADHD is the most commonly diagnosed disorder in childhood. In order to treat children appropriately, beyond medicating them, the disorder needs to be better understood psychologically and medically. A more reasoned approach to this debate considers the interplay between neurology and environment and rejects arguments that consider one without the other. Educational policy needs to refocus on providing accommodations for diverse learners—whether diagnosed or not. The identification of individual cases and courses of treatment should also take into account child and contexts in equal measure.

Perhaps because its origins are not fully understood, ADHD has engendered many folk beliefs and false remedies. A current faddish belief is that too much junk food and sugar intake causes ADHD. This has been proven to be untrue in multiple empirical studies, but the notion persists, particularly among health-food and nutrition enthusiasts. The fact is that food additives and large quantities of sugar tend to elevate activity levels for brief periods of time in all children, with and without ADHD. But activity levels soon return to the children's norm when the effect wears off.

During the 1970s, Dr. Benjamin Feingold developed a natural diet with the premise that food additives and preservatives caused hyperactivity in children, but it was found to be ineffective. Yet, diet continues to be a concern; recent studies show that some children are sensitive to food additives and could benefit from restricted diets. Some nutritionists believe that eating more protein, complex carbohydrates, and Omega-3 fatty acids (e.g., fish, flax) and eating less simple carbohydrates (e.g., candy, corn syrup) can help improve brain functioning and relieve ADHD symptoms. Other dieticians and homeopathic doctors recommend more restrictive hypoallergenic diets that include only organic foods. Parents are advised that processed foods, sugar, processed meats, dairy, and gluten cause hyperactivity. These restrictive types of diets, expensive to maintain, continue to be popular in upper-middle-class communities, even without empirical support.

Another common misconception is that poor parenting causes ADHD. Current thinking suggests that certain parenting characteristics, such as poor disciplining and disorganization, can exacerbate symptoms of

ADHD, but it is not a causal factor. Still, raising a child who displays symptoms of ADHD can be very challenging and taxing on a family. Parents and/or guardians often blame themselves for not being able to control their children's behaviors, and teachers might also be quick to blame the parents. True to this popular misconception, Terry's aunt blamed herself and Terry's biological parents for his behavior.

Prevalence rates vary, but it is commonly assumed that ADHD is over-diagnosed. According to professional publications, incidence of the disorder is estimated anywhere from two percent to nine percent. Given that wide margin, it is impossible to know what is the expected number of children affected and how many actually have diagnosable ADHD. Estimations vary based on demographic factors, such as socioeconomic status and contexts. There are many opinions as to the prevalence of the disorder and the consequences of treatment. The classification criteria for the disorder have changed over time and children now need to present six out of nine symptoms of hyperactivity or inattention. Inattention symptoms include:

> often does not give close attention to details or makes careless mistakes in schoolwork, work, or other activities;
> often has trouble keeping attention on tasks or play activities;
> often does not seem to listen when spoken to directly;
> often does not follow through on instructions and fails to finish schoolwork, chores, or duties in the workplace; often has trouble organizing activities;
> often avoids, dislikes, or doesn't want to do things that take a lot of mental effort for a long period of time;
> often loses things needed for tasks and activities; and is often easily distracted and forgetful in daily activities.

Hyperactivity symptoms include:

> often fidgets with hands or feet or squirms in seat when sitting still is expected;
> often gets up from seat when remaining in seat is expected;
> often excessively runs about or climbs when and where it is not appropriate;
> often has trouble playing or doing leisure activities quietly;
> is often on the go or often acts as if driven by a motor; and
> often talks excessively.

Because *often* is a term left to a parent to assess, one can clearly see that an impatient or frustrated parent will be quicker to identify her child as having the condition. It is interesting to note that incident rates are lower in the UK, where diagnostic criteria are more restrictive than in the United States.

Some mental heath professionals see recent changes in diagnostic criteria as an improvement, while others think these are two separate categories because hyperactivity is prevalent in many disorders. Combining the two sets of identifying criteria could lead to more confusion regarding the diagnosis of ADHD. The diagnosis is being updated in the *DSM-V*, and there is a possibility that hyperactivity and inattention will be treated as two separate categories. High rates of comorbidity, which is the term used to describe the presence of multiple disorders, complicate the issue even more. Symptoms such as inattention and impulsivity are common in other childhood disorders, so it is difficult to rule out ADHD. Children with depression or anxiety and medical conditions such as head injuries, seizures, or lead toxicity might exhibit inattention, hyperactivity, and/or impulsivity. When a child exhibits these symptoms, some parents and teachers are quick to identify them as ADHD and medicate accordingly, while the other disorders are overlooked.

Overdiagnosis has also been linked to the relationship between pharmaceutical companies, physicians, and corporate-sponsored parent support groups. A positive correlation does exist between the number of children diagnosed and the rate of children on medication. Even if there is mostly circumstantial evidence to support this relationship, we need to ask ourselves why children in the United States are 20 times more likely to be diagnosed with ADHD than are children in other industrialized countries. Rates of ADHD mediation consumptions have increased steadily over the past decades, and the drug market is expanding as more Americans are diagnosed in adulthood. It should be noted, however, that through media exposure, Internet use, and online support, there is an emerging universal view of ADHD and, consequently, a more widespread acceptance of the disorder. Psychostimulants are now widely available in countries where ADHD was, until recently, not known.

A critical factor that contributes to uncertainty regarding prevalence rates is how children are diagnosed. Children can be given the diagnosis by pediatricians, psychiatrists, neuropsychologists, and psychologists. Although it is recommended that psychiatrists diagnose the disorder, it is not a requirement. Unfortunately, due to health insurance or lack thereof, a limited numbers of pediatrically trained psychiatrists are available to parents in various geographic locations. Some disorders need to be assessed by a skilled medical professional, yet it is easy for a parent to see a pediatrician, describe the child's symptoms, and leave the office with an ADHD diagnosis and a prescription. Only the parents' description of symptoms is sufficient for diagnosis in American medical practice. Some physicians see little harm in trying medication on a trial basis while considering a diagnosis, others are more cautious in abiding to diagnostic markers. The American Medical Association has promulgated new guidelines, and pediatricians now have to follow more stringent criteria for diagnosing ADHD than were used in the past. Teachers and parents usually complete rating scales, but some practitioners might bypass the assessment process. Adding to these issues in diagnosing, the *DSM-IV*, the *Diagnostic and Statistical Manual of Mental Disorders, Fourth Edition*, does not specify what are abnormal levels for ADHD symptoms, thus relying too much on subjectivity in the diagnostic process. Diagnosis is based on the severity and number of symptoms that cause significant impairments in two major settings. Severity of symptoms is open to interpretation and based on perceptions and opinions. For example, teachers and parents often disagree about symptom severity. Sometimes teachers have different behavioral expectations than parents, and vice versa. Teachers are in positions to make judgments about a child's performance in school. Children in more unstructured classrooms may exhibit more severe symptoms, so teaching style and classroom and school culture can influence a diagnosis.

Etiology

Many of the myths and misconceptions about ADHD are the result of lack of understanding of what causes the disorder. Without a clear cause, anyone can propose an explanation. It has been hypothesized that ADHD originates in genetic, neurochemical, neuroanatomical, neuropsychological, and environmental factors, including prenatal conditions. Most accepted among professionals are the genetic and neurological perspectives, but all areas are continuously being explored.

ADHD is now considered a heritable disorder, with estimates of transmission ranging from 60 percent to 80 percent of parents who had childhood ADHD. If we think of Terry, there is a substantial chance that a close relative exhibited similar symptoms. Current research has focused on the genetic component, and it is believed that many genes are involved. There are lower levels of dopamine, a neurotransmitter associated with attention, movement, learning, and the brain's pleasure and reward system, in individuals with ADHD. Lower dopamine receptor levels occur in the frontal lobe, which is the area associated with attention and focusing. Additionally, it is believed that people with ADHD have less blood flow to the frontal lobes and that stimulant medication increases blood flow to that area, consequently decreasing inattention, distractibility, overactivity, and impulsivity. Stimulant medications increase the release or block the reabsorption of two neurotransmitters in the brain: dopamine and norepinephrine. The most common stimulant medications are Ritalin, Adderall, and Dexedrine. Today, brain imaging shows that children with ADHD have delayed development in the frontal lobe and a faster rate of maturation in an area of the brain that controls movement, explaining higher activity levels and restlessness.

Environmental factors also might play a role in the development of ADHD. Some researchers still believe that ADHD might be a result of brain injury rather than a genetically inherited disorder. There is evidence that prematurity, low birth weight, prenatal exposure to alcohol and tobacco, and postnatal injury to the prefrontal areas of the brain cause symptoms of ADHD. There was limited information about Terry's prenatal care and delivery to trace these causal factors, although it is likely that his prenatal care was substandard.

The psychodynamic perspective links ADHD to an individual's traumatic experiences, overstimulation, and situations that may cause depression and anxiety. Empirical evidence shows that post-traumatic stress disorder leads to poor concentration and memory problems, symptoms of ADHD. It is believed that during infancy and early childhood, there may be a connection between inattention and interactive patterns between caregiver and infant. Instead of long and stable chains of interaction, faster back-and-forth emotional signaling and gesturing and more chaotic family environments are thought to contribute to ADHD symptoms. While not advancing a single psychological etiology of ADHD, most psychologists are likely to consider the nature of the child's temperament in relation to the caregivers', the history of attachment, the level of organization and structure in the home environment, the approach to disciplining, and the capacity for self-regulation. Because ADHD is a behavior disorder, psychologists typically seek the roots of troubling or maladaptive behavior in the child's history, stressors and in family interactions.

Treatment

Common treatments for children with ADHD include medication, parent training, behavior therapy, psychosocial interventions, and classroom-based behavior modification. Professionals would address Terry's symptoms differently depending on their area of training and interest. Multimodal treatments, which are various treatments given simultaneously, are recommended. Psychiatrists and pediatricians prefer medication, as it is the most common treatment to address symptoms of ADHD. However, medication alone is not the answer, especially when children and adults with ADHD need to develop adaptive strategies and skills. Consistent, long-term treatment is more effective with a combination of pharmacological and behavioral therapies.

Terry's pediatrician managed his stimulant medication, although he never visited the school setting and saw him infrequently. Empirical evidence supports the therapeutic efficacy of stimulant drugs to improve learning ability and behavior. However, there is little data to support the effectiveness of long-term stimulant medication use. It has not been found to improve psychosocial, academic, and family functioning in adolescents who had been on long-term medication. There is evidence that stimulant medications, if given to children in preschool, can stunt their growth and disrupt sleep patterns. Even though Terry needed some kind of stimulant medication, his pediatrician was unable to manage the medication at a therapeutic level. It was either too little or too much, causing Terry to experience undesirable side effects.

Terry's experience with stimulant medications was not uncommon, even though they are the most empirically supported intervention and considered first-line treatment. Having a child take medication for an indeterminate amount of time is an emotionally charged decision. Contentious relationships with schools may follow when parents refuse to medicate their children. In Terry's situation, school staff preferred that Terry be sleepy rather than running around the classroom. More recent medications last longer in a child's bloodstream, but medication is only effective for short periods and does not alleviate all symptoms. Once the medication is out of a child's system, symptoms return to their usual intensity, or worse. This is usually the case in the evening, after a school day. Parents report that children's behaviors coming off of stimulants worsen, and that they become very irritable. A medicated child is not free from the drugs' side effects, which include insomnia, decreased appetite, weight loss, irritability, mood changes, stomachaches, and headaches. There are arguments for and against drug holidays, which are intervals of time when children discontinue medication. People who argue against drug holidays believe that symptoms should always be addressed and compare ADHD to a medical illness, such as diabetes. Taking a break from stimulant drugs, others claim, gives children an opportunity to grow, because medication slows down development. It also provides a break from the side effects.

Past beliefs about stimulant medication have changed. It was falsely believed that stimulant medication would paradoxically calm down children with ADHD and excite children without ADHD. Another false belief was that if a child did not respond to stimulant medication the disorder could be ruled out. However, studies indicate that 8 percent to 25 percent of children diagnosed with ADHD do not fully respond to stimulant medication. Low doses of stimulant medication given to all children—with or without ADHD—tend to improve attention and slow down motor activity.

There are many concerns about stimulant medication that are given to children to treat ADHD. One common controversy is that commonly prescribed psychostimulant medications have a chemical structure similar to cocaine, and that early use of Ritalin will predispose children to future drug use. Studies suggest that some children who have taken Ritalin long term were less likely to abuse drugs. Although, illegal trade and use of ADHD medications is a growing concern among adolescents and college students. Some use it to prepare for exams and write papers; others snort it to get high. Dr. Peter Breggin, a prominent psychiatrist and outspoken critic of psychopharmacology, believes that use of stimulant drugs by students without ADHD is a response to the normalization of stimulant medication in our culture. These students may perceive these drugs to be safe and nonharmful due to witnessing their friends with ADHD use medication daily for long periods of time or on an as-needed basis—like studying for a test. What seems to be true is that children with untreated ADHD are at greater risks for substance abuse in adolescence.

Without interventions to help Terry develop compensatory strategies and skills, he may struggle with these issues for most of his life. ADHD is a lifelong disorder. Less than 10 years ago, it was unclear if symptoms were discrete or continuous. Given this information, treatment needs to be ongoing. For example, Terry would need to develop appropriate skills in order to gain more control of his environment. A school psychologist would develop a plan that includes weekly individual and group counseling sessions so that Terry could learn coping, communication, and organizational strategies. Terry should also receive counseling outside of school, but this is not always possible, given insurance costs and/or waiting lists. In addition to counseling, schools are required by law to develop and implement functional behavioral assessments and behavior intervention plans to address behaviors that impede learning. This process shifts the focus from the internal aspects of the disorder to an ecological approach. The goal is to identify environmental factors that reinforce and maintain behaviors. It often requires school staff to change how they interact with children and positively reinforce more appropriate behavior. Behavioral interventions should be adapted as children develop. More positive experiences with school staff, along with consistent counseling, would help Terry to feel more effective and in control of himself within any given environment.

Studies suggest that psychosocial and psychological interventions are effective for brief periods and that individuals with ADHD have difficulties generalizing new behaviors to other contexts outside of treatment. All interventions need to be reinforced at home and in the classroom as well as maintained over long periods of time; this type of treatment is not feasible without Terry's aunt, who should be included in every part of his treatment.

An important aspect of Terry's treatment is educating Terry and his aunt about ADHD. One way to involve a parent is through parent training programs, which have proven to be effective because they provide information about ADHD and support and teach parents new skills, which is what a behavioral specialist or a behavioral psychologist would suggest. Parents need to learn about developmental challenges for children with ADHD. Some parent training curricula includes training on developing positive parent attention skills, how to implement a token economy, how to use time-out techniques, and how to manage a child's behavior in and out of the home. Parent training programs use concepts of behavior therapy, which should be used at home and school. Techniques such as positive reinforcement, token economies, time-out, and response costs are useful when providing structure and teaching a child with ADHD more appropriate behaviors. ADHD is thought to be a genetic disorder, so the chances are low that all parents will adhere to treatment or be consistent.

Local and national support groups are available for parents of children with ADHD. One in particular is Children and Adults with Attention Deficit Disorder, also known as CHADD, a nonprofit organization started by a small group of parents in 1987, which has since grown to 20,000 members in 43 states. The organization purports to educate and support families and individuals with ADHD. There has been controversy regarding the organization's funding. It has been known to receive large contributions from the pharmaceutical companies that manufacture ADHD medications and advocate for less-stringent guidelines for prescribing them. The CHADD Web site states the following: "CHADD does not endorse, recommend, or make representations with respect to the research, services, medication, treatments or products on the Web site." Given the many controversies with ADHD, parents should research organizations prior to joining as support and advocate groups can provide support and useful information.

Currently, education emphasizes differentiated instruction, acknowledging that each student learns differently. Teachers need training in order to understand behaviors of children with ADHD and instruct them accordingly. Because children with ADHD have the ability to hyperfocus on areas of interest, curricula can be specialized to these interests. Anybody might find it difficult to sit in class and learn about something uninteresting, but it can be nearly impossible for a child with ADHD to do so. Terry described trying to sit in his seat and listen as being physically painful. With all of Terry's behavioral problems, it was difficult to identify his strengths. Most people in school were fed up with him, so to they did not adjust instruction to his needs. Given new information about the neurological aspects of the disorder and the lower levels of dopamine and faster maturation in the activity areas in the brain, Terry needs many opportunities to be physically active throughout the day.

Dr. James A. Levine, doctor and professor at the Mayo Clinic, a nonprofit organization and medical practice and research group, supports the idea of an activity-permissive classroom. Current studies are exploring the use of adjustable-height school desks, so that children will not have to sit down all day to learn. To encourage activity, classrooms could provide exercise balls in designated areas for students with ADHD. Unfortunately, most children do have to remain seated most of the day. Chair yoga is another method for bringing movement into the classroom. Students are taught yoga poses in the chair and can do them throughout the day to release energy without disrupting other students. Children with ADHD would also benefit from breathing exercises like yoga, progressive muscle relaxation, and guided imagery. These are strategies that can be used with an entire class. Other examples include incorporating movement into lessons. Children can stand up when answering a question, reading, and reciting phonemes, depending on age level. Creating more interesting classroom environments with music, cooperative learning, technology, and aesthetic spaces would benefit all students, not just students with ADHD.

Many issues and questions remain about ADHD. Coming to agreement about the causal factors of the disorder might help to answer questions about treatment and establish treatment consensus amongst professionals.

Currently, too many opinions make it difficult for parents to make informed decisions. If there is more emphasis on brain injury and prenatal factors contributing to the disorder, then treatment needs to be preventative as well. Because there is evidence to support the positive effects of medication, it should not be dismissed. However, given that this disorder affects a child's social and psychological development, medication should not be on the front line of treatment alone.

As with any psychological condition, we need to reframe the conversation to address individual characteristics and behaviors, learning styles, and strengths of children with ADHD. Schools need to be more tolerant of differences in children's behaviors, especially in classroom learning activities. A child like Terry needs to be building skills and learning about his strengths rather than being fixated on suppressing his disruptive behaviors.

Fortunately, Terry did have an opportunity to learn new skills and build upon his artistic strengths. The principal hired a new art teacher, and she developed a relationship with Terry. Eventually, Terry's reward for engaging in lessons for brief periods was to spend more time in the art room, which was something he enjoyed. The art teacher found an art scholarship for an art class at the local museum. His pediatrician continued trying to adjust his medication to therapeutic levels. His aunt was able to receive services outside of the school to learn ways to manage Terry's behaviors at home, but the services were not consistent. Terry's academic performance improved, but he continued to need support from his aunt, teachers, and pediatrician.

In summary, more attention needs to be focused on making accommodations and providing consistent, long-term support and encouragement for children with ADHD. As we know, symptoms have been known for a long time, but many people have experienced them and were never diagnosed. Symptoms are challenging, but it does not mean a child cannot learn strategies to modulate his behaviors and eventually gain greater capacity for attention, self-control, and progressively use his strengths to achieve meaningful life goals. Parents and educators can provide the best supportive environment by working together.

References

Armstrong, T. (1999). *ADD/ADHD alternatives in the classroom.* Retrieved from http://www.scribd.com/doc/24782895/ADD-ADHD-Alternatives-in-the-Classroom.

Barkley, R. A. (2006). *Attention-deficit hyperactivity disorder: A handbook for diagnosis and treatment* (3rd ed.). New York: Guildford Press.

Castellanos, F. X. (2008, November). *Report of the DSM-V ADHD and disruptive behavior disorders work group.* Retrieved from the American Psychiatric Association Web site: http://www.psych.org/MainMenu/Research/DSMIV/DSMV/DSMRevisionActivities/DSMVWorkGroupReports/ADHDandDisruptiveBehaviorDisordersWorkGroupReport.aspx.

Charach, A., Shachar, R. J., & Thiruchelvam, D. (2001). Moderators and mediators of long-term adherence to stimulant treatment in children with ADHD. *Journal of American Academy of Child and Adolescent Psychiatry, 40*(8), 922–928.

Cohen, D., Lloyd, G., & Stead, J. (2006). Critical new perspectives on ADHD. New York: Routledge.

Foy, M., & Neufeld, P. (2006). Historical reflections of the ascendance of ADHD in North America, 1980–2005. *British Journal of Educational Studies, 54*(4), 449–470.

Julien, R. M., Advokat, C. D., & Comaty, J. E. (2008). *A primer of drug action: A comprehensive guide to the actions, uses, and side effects of psychoactive drugs.* New York: Worth.

Kristjansson, K. (2009). Medicalised pupils: The case of ADD/ADHD. *Oxford Review of Education, 35*(1), 111–127.

National Institute of Mental Health. (2008). *Attention deficit hyperactivity disorder (ADHD).* Retrieved from http://www.nimh.nih.gov/health/publications/ attention-deficit-hyperactivity-disorder/index.shtml.

PDM Task Force. (2006). *Psychodynamic diagnostic manual.* Silver Springs, MD: Alliance of Psychoanalytic Organizations.

Pfiffner, L. (2003). *Psychosocial treatment for ADHD-inattentive type.* ADHD Report, *11*(5), 1–8.

Posner, M. D. (2007, February 3). Attention deficit disorder—conceptions and misconceptions. Retrieved from http://www.americanchronicle.com/articles/ view/20172.

Sauly, S. (2009, February 24). Students stand when called upon, and when not. *New York Times,* p. A1. Retrieved from http://www.nytimes.com/2009/02/25/ us/25desks.html.

Schlachter, S. (2008). Diagnosis, treatment, and educational implications for students with attention deficit/hyperactivity disorder in the United States, Australia, and the United Kingdom. *Peabody Journal of Education, 83,* 154–169.

Schmitt, A., & Wodrich, D. (2006). *Patterns of learning disorders.* New York: Guilford Press.

University of Michigan Health System. (2005, October). *Attention-deficit hyperactivity disorder.* Retrieved from http://www.guidelinecentral.com/Custom ContentRetrieve.aspx?ID=1825442&A=SearchResult&SearchID=1078803& ObjectID=1825442&ObjectType=35.

Wagner, M. J. (2009). *Shake it up, baby: Managing ADHD with movement.* Retrieved from www.adhdchildrentoday.com/ADHDSessionThreeHandouts.pdf.

Weyandt, L. L. (2001). *Attention deficit hyperactivity disorder: An ADHD primer.* Boston: Allyn and Bacon.

Woodard, R. (2006). The diagnosis and medical treatment of ADHD in children and adolescents in primary care: A practical guide. *Pediatric Nursing, 32*(4), 363–370.

Internet Resources—ORGS for Parents and Teachers

http://www.cdc.gov/ncbddd/adhd/diagnosis.html
http://www.bhcmhmr.org/poc/view_doc.php?type=doc&id=13852&cn=3
http://www.chadd.org/Content/CHADD/AboutCHADD/Mission/ default.htm

http://playattention.com/attention-deficit/articles/neurofeedback-adhd-and-medication/

http://www.help4adhd.org/

http://school.familyeducation.com/learning-disabilities/add-and-adhd/34474.html

http://www.adhdnews.com/states.htm

CHAPTER 5

Autism Spectrum Disorders: Current Thinking on Etiology and Diagnosis

Jeanne Angus

Introduction

Entering the bright and cheery classroom, the principal sees kindergartners working industriously, practicing printing the letter A. *From the back of the room comes a low rumbling and muttering of words. The teacher approaches and does not pause before launching into a diatribe beginning with, "You have to get him out of here before he hurts someone, I mean really hurts someone! I don't know why they even think he should be here, he doesn't belong!" Away from the children focused on the letter* A *is a pleasant-appearing boy, fully engaged with his multilevel Lego castle sitting atop an intricately detailed treasure map he has made. He is actively immersed in some audible monologue and seems totally content until a peer comes up to join him and is abruptly pushed to the ground. "No dragons in my kingdom!" he shouts.*

"There's really nothing wrong with my son; he can do all those things at home once I show him. His teacher just doesn't understand him. He's really like every other kid; it's just that he's special. You should see how quickly he can find his way on the subway; he knows all the routes and stops. We never had to teach him. Ask him some facts about hurricanes or when and where the presidents were born. He can even tell you what day of the week you were born, and he'll always remember your birthday. He learned to do that on his own. But he does have a hard time staying in his seat and doing what the class is doing. He's not interested in what they are doing. He says he's bored and doesn't want to have to do the same old things over and over."

Variations of the above narratives are commonly heard from exasperated teachers and from parents seeking help for their child who is struggling to get through each day at school. Some days, the parents report, the child is adjusting and things seem to go pretty well. Then there are the days when nothing seems to go right; something set him off, and he just can't let go of it and move on. He has a hard day all day long, getting into fights, shouting at the teacher, pushing people away who are trying to help, making growling noises to keep everyone in abeyance.

Health professionals, educators, and the general public are increasingly aware of autism and Asperger syndrome. These disorders are receiving much media attention and many anxious parents often seek answers on the Internet and in printed media. Autism spectrum disorders (ASD) includes a range of puzzling behaviors and atypical developmental patterns that leave children socially isolated and seemingly unable to connect emotionally with peers and family members. Although ASD is often used as an umbrella term to describe a wide range of children who have autistic-like features, *pervasive developmental disorder–not otherwise specified* (PDD–NOS) is another term that clinicians may use early in the diagnostic process. Even though the terms are frequently used interchangeably, there are significant differences. A clear diagnostic understanding implies sorting through great amounts of information, a process that can be daunting and confusing, especially for the parent seeking to understand her child's condition. For some parents and individuals with these challenges, one diagnosis can be seen as more socially or personally acceptable than another. They may also be informed there are better services and supports for one diagnosis than for another. Any discussion of autism needs to include a clarification of the meaning of the various diagnostic labels in use, a process complicated by the fact that within the mental health field some of those labels are still contested.

Defining Asperger Syndrome and Pervasive Developmental Disorders

Consideration of autism spectrum disorder and Asperger syndrome (AS) in particular has to take into account the nature of emerging understandings over the past decade during which there has been much productive work on brain function and neurophysiology. Yet, despite considerable advances, many questions and concerns still remain for parents of children with ASD or Asperger syndrome. Autism spectrum disorders, also referred to as *pervasive developmental disorders* (PDD), are neurobiological or neurodevelopmental disorders. Current understanding suggests that there are distinct structural alterations in the brain that result in differences in processing and functioning of affected individuals as they develop. The ASD-PDD spectrum covers a broad continuum of social and behavioral functioning and cognitive skills, with varying degrees of three common diagnostic characteristics: (1) a lack or delay in functional language development and use, (2) a lack or significant compromise in the development of social relatedness with others (especially peers), and (3) significant repetitive behaviors or narrow areas of interest. A notable number of children also manifest some degree of sensory problems (i.e., intense sensitivity to noise, light, smells, touch and texture, or even to food). An ASD diagnosis implies a lifelong psychological disability. But like other disabilities, significant improvements may be achieved with appropriate interventions as families and caregivers learn to understand the challenges, and the children learn to accommodate and compensate for the areas of challenge and/or deficit.

Basic Definitions

Pervasive Developmental Disorders (PDD): These disorders are characterized by deficits in areas of social interaction and communication abilities. This diagnostic category may include autistic disorder, Rhett's disorder, childhood disintegrative disorder, Asperger syndrome (disorder), and pervasive developmental disorder–not otherwise specified—including atypical autism.

Asperger Syndrome (AS): The most commonly used diagnostic criteria from both the *DSM-IV* and ICD-10 include qualitative impairment in social interaction; circumscribed and restricted interests; restricted, repetitive, and stereotypical behavior and activities; and the absence of a clinically significant general delay in language. Social communication deficiencies are perceived as the dominant area of deficit.

Early interest in letters, reading, numbers, and development of a pedantic style of speaking can appear as gifted and precocious and lead to highly specialized and intensely absorbing areas of interest, which can interfere with attentiveness and actual learning. These precocious verbal skills can mask social interaction struggles that initially may not seem significant until the child is exposed to a group of typically developing children and cannot navigate the nonverbal and socially based conventions of relating and communicating.

Autism Disorder: This condition is defined by marked impairment in social interaction, including the lack of social or emotional reciprocity, sharing of mutual enjoyment or interests with others, and a failure to develop peer relationships. The impairment of communication is manifest by lack of speech or developmental delay that includes stereotyped and repetitive and/or idiosyncratic language. Delayed or abnormal developmental functioning is noted within the first three years of life in respect to social interactions, language of social communication, and symbolic or imaginative play. Restricted, repetitive, and stereotyped patterns of behavior and activities are also noted with a rigid adherence to specific and nonfunctional routines. In addition, these children often demonstrate obsessive preoccupations with narrow areas of interest or with objects or parts of objects. Repetitive stereotyped motor mannerisms are also common.

High Functioning Autism (HFA): Although this is an informal term and not found in the psychiatric diagnostic manuals, many clinicians use it to describe individuals with the characteristics of autism who may demonstrate more adaptive skills. They typically have average or above average intellectual capabilities while maintaining the detached social interactions, restrictive, and respective stereotyped patterns of behavior and preoccupations associated with autism. They may excel in particular narrow areas or topics of their interest. They often develop the ability to use scripted social interactions and limited independent living functions as adults without the benefit of intensive, long-term interventions. There is much discussion among experts as to whether this is a category overlapping with AS, a form of AS, or a separate condition.

Pervasive Developmental Disorder–Not Otherwise Specified (PDD–NOS): The majority of children diagnosed on the spectrum are initially given a PDD–NOS diagnosis. Typically, these children show poor social interactions or little interests in others and exhibit unusual sensitivities—for example, toward the sound of a vacuum, to florescent lights, or sunlight. They are severe in their presentation and often inconsistent in their skills. Developmentally, their language is delayed and they have odd and unusual types of behaviors but do not meet all the criteria for Autism and lack the more advanced skills of the child with AS. Frequently they are referred to as "mild autism."

Early identification of PDD–NOS may be a provisional diagnosis that tends to change as the child develops. Some children begin to demonstrate more functional language, social awareness and interest in others while continuing to be absorbed by details and focused interests, or they may progressively show characteristics typical of AS. Other children may begin to stagnate or revert in their development and meet more fully the criteria of a child with autism. There are exceptional instances where children have, over time, developed language, cognitive capacities, socially appropriate skills, and relationships with peers, and consideration has been given to removing the diagnostic label completely.

Incidence and Etiology

In 2007, the Centers for Disease Control and Prevention in the United States reported the incidence of ASD to be 1 child out of every 150, and generally there appear to be three to five times as many boys as girls identified with these disorders. The incidence for PDD–NOS has been reported to be 1 in every 200 children. Asperger syndrome is reported to be much more common among boys, by a factor of five to one, but recently attention has been given to girls who may not be properly identified. Girls with AS typically present as shy, socially observant but removed, with intense interests in fantasy and focused on specific interests.

The much-debated question in medicine, public health, and among the general population is whether there is a growing incidence of ASD among children or whether the higher figures are a function of changing diagnostic practices. There is no clear answer to that question. Certainly the dramatically increased public awareness and increased awareness among professionals about the diagnostic guidelines and the broadening of the spectrum definitions have contributed to the increases reported. Some claim that the rates have not changed but that many affected individuals were not recognized as exhibiting ASD symptoms and were not properly diagnosed. Consideration must also include substantial numbers of older individuals who have been excluded from the records because they were either undiagnosed or may have been misidentified as suffering from ADHD, learning disability, schizoid personality disorder, or other conditions. Due to the mobility of our population and complexity of our health systems record-keeping practices, there are no firm indications whether there is a net increase in the actual incidence of ASD. While the search for answers continues, multiple theories have proliferated linking autism to exposure to noxious substances, environmental hazards, diet, genetic mutations, or other causes.

What causes ASD? Originally, in the 1950s and 1960s, Leo Kanner and Bruno Bettelheim (1967) attributed the cause of autism to be the psychological outcome of rejection from an inadequate, rigid, and emotionally cold *refrigerator mother*. Today there is empirical evidence of neurological impairment where specific structures of the brain do not function as we typically anticipate (Bauman & Kemper, 2003). Studies comparing identical twins and fraternal (nonidentical twins) found significantly concurrent rates of autism (70%–90%) among identical twins versus the nonidentical twins. Co-occurrence among fraternal twins yields low rates (0%–5%). Additional studies that investigated the family history of members who have a number of characteristics of one of the spectrum disorders have revealed a significant genetic component in the makeup from these family members. These genetic commonalities are particularly salient for Asperger syndrome. These genetic studies have supported the notion of heritability, but rather than single gene mutations, they postulate a number of chromosomal variations or interactions among a number of genes. Numerous large research centers throughout the United States and internationally have established cooperative studies investigating chromosomal structures and the DNA of extended family members to continue research into ASD genetics.

Other areas that have been investigated include metabolism of gluten and casein (Elder et al., 2006), which has led to the promotion of gluten-casein free diets. Parents have expressed mixed results with these nutrition-based programs. Studies that focused on viral infections during pregnancy and early childhood have been carried out with inconclusive results due to small sample sizes and lack of methodological controls. The most discussed hypothesis in the media and promoted by activists has been the role of immunizations in triggering autism. The use of the preservative thermisol (mercury) in vaccinations for infants and young children has been the main focus of concern. A review of studies conducted in multiple countries found no consistent link between immunizations and the development of autism (Honda, Shimizu, & Rutter, 2005).

History

The identification of autism and Asperger syndrome originated at approximately the same time on opposite sides of the Atlantic Ocean. In 1943, at Johns Hopkins Medical Center, Leo Kanner, a European physician, identified a group of boys with characteristics of severe social and communication abnormalities with social isolation and repetitive behaviors. Early in 1944, in Vienna, Dr. Hans von Asperger wrote of a group of four boys with social peculiarities and isolation but who differed with average development of language and normal cognitive ability and some motor skill delay or clumsiness. Both men used the term *autis psychopathy* to identify their findings. The work of Dr. Kanner was published in the United States and established the use of the term *autism*, which entered into the *DSM-II* in 1980. It was not until the 1980s that Dr. Lorna Wing recovered the writings of Dr. von Asperger while trying to identify a group of young boys presenting with similar characteristics including lack of empathy, inappropriate one-sided interaction, little to no ability to form friendships, pedantic and repetitive speech, poor nonverbal communication, intense absorption in certain subjects, and clumsy stereotypic motor movements. Wing also reported differences from Asperger's observations, noting delays and deviations in child development that she contended could be detected within the first two years of life.

Subsequently, other professionals contributed to the discussion and debate about identification and description of these individuals, presenting similar but often qualitatively different details of their findings of characteristics. As the debate continued, Wing gathered support to have Asperger syndrome recognized and entered into the *DSM-IV* in 1994 as part of the PDD spectrum, and differentiated from Kanner's classical autism. Prior to the *DSM-IV* classification, many of the clinicians working with these individuals had proposed a variety of detailed diagnostic criteria that they felt reflected their clinical experience. As a result, the definitive criteria used for AS has continued to vary and the standardization of research has often been compromised. Consider the work of two noted PDD researchers who together studied one group of higher functioning individuals to determine whether an appreciable difference between AS and HFA could be established. They used two different assessment approaches that resulted in their reporting two diametrically opposed outcomes and interpretations.

Prominent researchers and experts still debate the validity of Asperger syndrome as a diagnostic category separate and discernable from the higher functional levels of pervasive developmental disorders. Some contend that there is no difference between AS and HFA. The continued attempts to validate Asperger syndrome as a distinct category focusing on impaired social communication skills, a drive to be socially interactive with a friend, and intellectual functioning have not resulted in consistent findings. This was reflected in the diagnostic revisions of the *DSM-IV-TR* (text revised in 2000), where details of criteria for Autism and PDD–NOS have been broadened and expanded to be more inclusive. Children are now first evaluated to ascertain if they meet autism and/or PDD–NOS criteria; individuals who do not meet those criteria are then evaluated for AS.

This exclusionary approach to the diagnosis of AS has resulted in challenges for parents of children who meet the criteria for AS. But in light of the proposal to eliminate AS entirely from the *DSM-V*, due to be published and effectively in use in 2012, may create additional hurdles. At issue is whether children who meet the criteria for AS but not for other forms of autism will still qualify for services within health and the special education systems. Individuals diagnosed with AS now qualify for services, because insurance coverage recently mandated by Congress (2009) for individuals diagnosed with ASD includes AS. Yet children with AS may well be excluded from these services if the labeling changes take effect. Because children with AS may show higher levels of language and cognitive development, it does not mean they are not disabled by their condition. Children with AS are likely to face debilitating struggles to be effectively integrated into the society at large without support and specialized guidance.

Psychological Theories

While diagnosis has been based on medical and psychiatric models with defined observable criteria, psychologists have sought to find explanations for the atypical social development and odd behaviors. Why do children with ASD act in particular ways, and what may cause or sustain their interpersonal difficulties and intense focus on specific interests? The initial theory, as previously mentioned, formulated by physicians and psychiatrists proposed the notion of a *refrigerator mother* who was incapable of forming a healthy attachment with her baby. This theory has long been disproved by psychologists who have continued to explore the nature of thinking and processing among children with ASD. A few current and prominent theories will be briefly presented here.

Theory of mind, first presented and extensively expanded upon by Simon Baron-Cohen, refers to a mind blindness in the perception of empathy, intentions, and motivations of others as it impacts on their behavior and anticipation of interactions. It highlights the inability of the child with AS/ASD to put him- or herself into the shoes of another and giving an impression of an egocentric or self-centered orientation to social interactions. Although it can be challenged because very young children who have not experienced complex social interactions can have evident lack of empathy, even as babies, theory of mind has offered a clearer understanding of the nature of the psychological deficit and helped develop approaches to help children compensate as they develop (Attwood, 2006).

Central coherence weakness, introduced by Frith and Happe (1994) referred to the typical focus children with AS/ASD have for details and their inability to generalize to the larger picture (i.e., *He cannot see the forest for the trees!*) Sometimes called *telescopic thinking,* it contrasts with the more typical child's broader cognitive perspective. This insight into the mind of a child with ASD can help teachers understand that the focus to detail can appear inattentive and will often prevent completion of work assignments in a timely manner (Schoolz et al., 2006).

Executive dysfunction refers to problems in the area of organization and planning, working memory, inhibition and impulse control, time management and prioritizing, problem solving, and using new approaches (Pennington & Ozonoff, 1996; Yerys, Hepburn, & Pennington, 2007). In the early years, these children are impulsive and have difficulties limiting inappropriate responses at home and at school. They also have working memory deficiencies (i.e., holding onto to new information) and encounter difficulties when asked to use new strategies or techniques in social or learning situations. With adequate guidance the child may progress and begin to show more control, but stress and confusion will bring earlier immature reactions, as can the stress of growing responsibility for independence skills.

Extensive research by Nancy Menshew, a neurologist working with this population, and her colleagues, has highlighted another explanation for the developmental difficulties and cognitive functioning patterns observed in ASD. Starting from a developmental disorder orientation, as opposed to a specific, or core, deficit with one area of focus, her team studied the common domains of neuropsychological functioning simultaneously with a population of high-functioning children, adolescents, and adults with ASD. After several well-designed studies, her findings suggested a pattern never seen with other diseases before. The relative impairments were found in higher levels of brain perception of sensory input (e.g., skilled motor movements, memory for complex material, higher order language, and concept formation). They were demonstrated across domains of function with increasing complexity of information processing. Perhaps the most crucial finding was that acquisition of information was intact across all age groups. But the individual's capacity for information processing was reduced or compromised when demands were high or the situation was stressful. It seems that despite intact abilities at a concrete level, the individual facing increasingly complex demands fails because of limitations in working memory. *Working memory* refers to the capacity to retain information while processing it for a more complex application than simple recall. In stressful situations, like interpersonal exchanges, children and individuals with ASD often fail to reach the next higher levels of information processing. Consider the mother in the introduction to this chapter, who repeatedly said she knew her son could do the work, yet her son just did not want to be at school—perhaps the expectations of behavior and performance or simply being in the hectic classroom environment was overwhelming and compromised his ability to attend to and act upon the required tasks.

The second significant finding was that across the common domains, the predominance of symptoms was directly relevant to the complexity of the information-processing demands. There appeared to be a mechanism that was generalized to the development of the brain structures and not confined to the three areas defined in the diagnostic grouping of social, language, and reasoning (Minshew & Williams, 2008).

This generalization across brain structures may contribute to the resistance for change and push for known routines and repetitive behaviors. Impairment in concept formations is prominent in adults with AS and is frequently reported as memory deficiency. Adult clients in therapy often report "I have no memory" or "I cannot remember things about my childhood like other people." Timothy said "I could not pick up my laundry because I forgot that it was Wednesday—that is the day I get my laundry. I will have to remember this week." This young man's rigid routines seem to serve the purpose of reducing the need for improvisation and therefore limit the neurological overload that accompanies new decisions. The work of Minshew and Williams (2008) may open new pathways to studies that can contribute new understanding, perhaps lead to significant changes in diagnostic approaches, and help develop more innovative and effective interventions.

Diagnosis and Assessment

The initial concern about AS or ASD may be voiced by a pediatrician, speech–language pathologist, school psychologist, occupational therapist, or by the parents themselves. Other professionals or a screening referral from preschool or elementary school may raise the question as well. What is the next step? Initial assessments are usually brief and considered the starting point. Parents can become distressed about having the label applied to their child; yet, the diagnosis of ASD can provide access to services and the beginning of a comprehensive assessment. If the child is young, the initial identification will provide access to some intervention services, and then parents will be encouraged to have the child start more intensive services. One of the most critical considerations about interventions is that the sooner they begin, the better the long-term outcomes. Parents typically engage in the process of arranging for an evaluation, leading to diagnosis and a comprehensive assessment. After such a comprehensive evaluation and review of results, a determination of diagnosis interventions options can be addressed.

There is no single recommended way to proceed with an evaluation, because there are so many different systems and programs in place across the country, with substantial variations from state to state and across school systems and districts. Parents must seek a qualified professional or team for an expert level of evaluation. University-based and medical research centers are the most common referrals given where an expert team may evaluate the child for ASD, but these appointments can take time. Upon seeking an evaluation at a medical facility conducting research, parents should inquire about the institution's sources of funding and the nature of the studies under way. Children with ASD may present initially as moody or anxious and could be inappropriately treated with medication for early onset bipolar disorder or antianxiety medication. Before consenting to a drug treatment program, parents should seek another opinion.

Optimally, the outcome of an evaluation will be a well-crafted Individualized Family Service Plan (IFSP) for young children, or an Individualized Education Program (IEP) for school-age children, that will address the needs of the child in a collaborative way with the appropriate agencies and the school system. From this information derived in the assessment an effective plan can be established with appropriate annual and long-term goals. The plan must include information detailing the individualized needs of the child at that time—focusing on present level of functioning, areas of strengths and needs, and specific interventions to address those needs.

The team evaluation or assessment should include:

1. A detailed developmental history. Parents are usually asked to fill out forms documenting development of the child. Baby books or other pertinent mementos could aid in filling in details of the child's development.
2. A psychological evaluation will include an assessment of the child's intellectual and present levels of performance, this aspect of the evaluation also focuses on adaptive functions, that is, how well the child is able to grasp concepts and knowledge and apply them to real-world situations.
3. The speech–language evaluation consists of an assessment of articulation and language development, levels of communication skills, and pragmatic skills—the effective use of purposeful language and its social applications.
4. Occupational therapy and/or physical therapy assessments focus on fine and gross motor skill development and application, including daily living skills (e.g., toileting, dressing, personal care).

5. A diagnostic instrument is normally administered to assess cognitive and behavioral levels of functioning within the ASD criteria. The diagnostic tests for Autism most commonly used include:

Autism Diagnostic Interview–Revised [ADI-R] (Rutter, LeCouteur & Lord, 2003). This instrument involves interviewing parents about the child's history and development to verify the diagnosis; it can be used with children over two years old.

Autism Diagnostic Observation Schedule [ADOS] (Lord, Rutter, Dilavore & Risi, 1999). This protocol assesses the child for behavior and cognitive abilities across a broad span for autistic characteristics.

Childhood Autism Rating Scale [CARS] (Schopler, Reicher, & Rennner, 1988). Usually used as a screening tool, this instrument identifies typical autistic behaviors and estimates their severity.

Gilliam Autism Rating Scales, Second Edition [GARS-2] (Gilliam, 2006). Structured interview for ages 3–s22. This structured interview scale identifies behavior patterns and can contribute useful information for crafting IEP goals.

Diagnostic Tests for Asperger Syndrome

Autism Spectrum Screening Questionnaire [ASSQ] (Ehlers, Gilberg, & Wing, 1999). This screening instrument contains 27 descriptive items rated on a three-point scale by a parent and/or teacher. Scores of 13 or greater indicate possibility of AS and need for additional evaluation

Asperger Syndrome Diagnostic Scale [ASDA] (Myles, Bock, & Simpson, 2001). This rating scale is typically completed by someone familiar with the student; it is used more often to monitor changes in development than for diagnostic purposes.

Gilliam Asperger's Disorder Scale [GADS] (Gilliam, 2001). This normed reference scale is also usually completed by someone familiar with student. It is generally used to monitor development and, less frequently, for diagnosis.

As noted in the previous comments, none of the scales presently available for the diagnosis of AS are properly validated instruments. Diagnosis is primarily based upon levels of cognitive functioning, language use, and difficulties that are evident with social communication skills and interactions with peers. Parents and individual practitioners are cautioned not to use the evaluation based solely upon the experience in the one-on-one environment in an evaluator's office or on family reports of behavior at home, which can be dramatically different from a natural peer-based environment. Medical-center and university-based team assessments will usually have contact with the school for additional information. An on-site observation within the student's own environment and with his peers by an experienced AS evaluator, who can provide a definitive assessment of the student's functioning levels and challenges, are probably the strongest contribution for a diagnostic confirmation. It is this natural setting that the magnitude of the issues and the nature of the stressors become more acutely apparent.

The final outcome of a comprehensive assessment should be compiled into a report that can be clearly understood, including detailed reporting of instruments and procedures used, examples and sources of evidence, a clear diagnosis, and specific recommendations. This detailed report with specific examples and recommendations can form the basis for development of an IFSP or IEP with concrete, attainable goals.

Parent Concerns

Parenting children with AS can be a distinctly different experience from that of parenting children with HFA or PDD–NOS. Children with AS usually demonstrate ability to learn in their areas of interest and read (decode words) at young ages. There is, however, an inconsistency to their performance and an uneven pathway of skill development: *"He can read Greek, but he can't tie his shoes."*

Often, parents of children with AS report that, despite some concern for their child's lack of friends in preschool, their parenting experience during the early infant–childhood years is relatively normal, with their children responding to them and smiling. There is a sense of a delay in the symptom presentation, but with extensive questioning, parents will frequently acknowledge that there were differences. Parents may say things such as "not like other children in the way he played, repeatedly lined his toys up," "liked being alone," "liked things done in the certain way," "would only talk about things that interested him," or "liked collecting eclectic items like hubcaps."

As the chapter has highlighted, there are no simple answers or pathways that lead to the ultimate cure; this is a complex disorder with complex issues for parents to identify and contend with. It can begin with confusion of the diagnosis when it is not clear. Various professionals may present a diagnosis that focuses on their particular area of expertise: *Semantic-pragmatic disorder,* by the speech pathologist; a *nonverbal learning disability* by the neuropsychologist or *right-brain syndrome* by the neurologist. While each of these professionals identifies characteristics, it is only a beginning, not an informative or definitive diagnosis to include across all domains of function. The family that suspected a problem might feel immediate relief with the application of a label, but the underlying concerns linger until a proper diagnosis is identified. Yet, even with a diagnosis, parents need help to understand that AS and ASD present uneven and unusual courses of development, across multiple domains.

These are attractive children who do not stand out with obvious physical disabilities and who appear typically normal with an invisible disability. A mother of a six-year-old with AS once described her son as *"the perfect counterfeit; he looks perfect until it's time to perform."* These invisible discrepancies can lead to creation of performance expectations the child is not prepared to meet.

Perhaps one of the major challenges for parents is knowing how to contend with the behavioral issues: major tantrums (meltdowns) that can happen anywhere and be triggered by the simplest of things; disruptions of church services or rides on the bus; indiscriminate approaches to strangers; and loud, intrusive, inappropriate comments. Simple daily activities and tasks can become monumental events with silent (sometimes not) observers criticizing the parenting skills: *If he were my child, he would never be allowed to do that!*

Seeking professionals and appropriate treatments and therapy can be equally challenging. Because of the complexity of the disorder, which impacts multiple domains, different professionals promote their approaches for working with the child. A professional from a different discipline can urge the use of a conflicting treatment. Parents can become torn when trying to make the best choice. Instead, the focus should be to find professionals who will work collaboratively together and include the parents as active participants. A variety of approaches can be appropriate at different times, when different issues need to be addressed.

There are positive steps that can be taken to help overcome these common issues, which otherwise can bring about serious family disruptions and undermine progress. Parents have a unique perspective of their child's development, idiosyncrasies, likes/dislikes, pleasures, and so on. Parents can become effective advocates and seek to work collaboratively with a team of professionals who provide guidance rather than dictates. The professionals can guide parents to, or offer resources and choices for, effective interventions and services. Every step forward should actively involve the whole family in the decision-making process.

References

American Psychiatric Association. (1994). *Diagnostic and statistical manual of mental disorders* (4th ed.). Washington, DC: Author.

American Psychiatric Association. (2000). *Diagnostic and statistical manual of mental disorders* (4th ed., text rev.). Washington DC: Author.

Asperger, H. (1944). Die autistichen psychopathen: Im kindersalter. *Archive fur Psychiatrie und Nervenkrankheiten, 117,* 76–136. Reprinted (in part) in U. Frith (Ed.), (1991), *Autism and Asperger syndrome.* Cambridge, UK: Cambridge University Press.

Attwood, T. (2006). *The complete guide to Asperger's syndrome.* Philadelphia, PA: Jessica Kingsley.

Attwood, T. (2008). An overview of autism spectrum disorders. In K. D. Buron & P. Wolfberg (Eds.), *Learners on the autism spectrum: Preparing highly qualified educators* (pp. 66–85). Shawnee Mission, KA: Autism Asperger Publishing Company.

Bailey, A., LeCouteur, A., Gottesman, I., Bolton, P. Simonoff, F., Yuzda, R., et al. (1995). Autism as a strongly genetic disorder: Evidence from a British twin study. *Psychological Medicine, 25,* 63–77.

Baron-Cohen, S. (1995). *Mind blindness: An essay on autism and theory of mind.* Cambridge, MA: MIT Press.

Bauman, M., & Kemper, T. L. (2003). The neuropathology of the autism spectrum disorders: What have we learned? *Novartis Foundation Symposium, 251,* 112–122.

Bettelheim, B. (1967). *The empty fortress.* Toronto, CA: Collier-Macmillan.

Buron, K. D., & Wolfberg, P. (Eds.). (2008). *Learners on the autism spectrum: Preparing highly qualified educators.* Shawnee Mission, KA: Autism Asperger Publishing Company.

Centers for Disease Control. (2007). Retrieved from http://www.cdc.gov//Diseases Conditions/az/a.html.

Elder, J., Shankar, M., Shuster, J., Theriaque, D., Burns, S., & Sherrill, L. (2006). The gluten-free, casein-free diet in autism: Results of a preliminary double blind clinical trial. *Journal of Autism and Developmental Disorders, 36*(3), 413–420.

Frith, U., & Happe, F. (1994). Autism: Beyond "theory of mind." *Cognition, 59,* 115–132.

Honda, H., Shimizu, Y., & Rutter, M. (2005). No effect of MMR withdrawal on the incidence of autism: A total population study. *Journal of Child Psychiatry and Psychology, 46*(6), 572–579.

Kanner, L. (1943). Autistic disturbances of affective contact. *Nervous Child, 2,* 217–250.

Koppe, S., & Gilberg, C. (1992). Girls with social deficits and learning problems: Autism, atypical Asperger syndrome or a variant of these conditions. *European Child and Adolescent Psychiatry, 1*(2), 89–99.

Miller, J., & Ozonoff, S. (2000). The external validity of Asperger disorder: Lack of evidence from the domain of neuropsychology. *Journal of Abnormal Psychology, 109*(2), 227–238.

Minshew, N. J., & Williams, D. L. (2008). Brain-behavior connections in autism. In K. D. Buron & P. Wolfberg (Eds.), *Learners on the autism spectrum: Preparing highly qualified educators.* (pp. 44–65). Shawnee Mission, KA: Autism Asperger Publishing Company.

Ozonoff, S., South, M., & Miller, J. (2000). DSM-IV defined Asperger syndrome: Cognitive, behavioral and early history differentiation from high-functioning autism. *Autism, 4,* 29–46.

Pennington, B. F., & Ozonoff, S. (1996). Executive functions and developmental psychopathy. *Journal of Child Psychology and Psychiatry, 37,* 51–83.

Schoolz, W., Hullstijn, W., van den Broek, P., van der Pijlll, A., Gabreels, F., van der Gaag, R., et al. (2006). Fragmented visuospatial processing in children with pervasive developmental disorder. *Journal of Autism and Developmental Disorders, 36*(8), 1025–1037.

Volkmar, F. R., & Wiesner, L. A. (2009). *A practical guide to autism: What every parent, family member and teacher needs to know.* Hoboken, NJ: Wiley.

Wing, L. (1981). Asperger's syndrome: A clinical account. *Psychological Medicine, 11*(1), 115–129.

Wing, L. (2001). *The autistic spectrum: A parent's guide to understanding and helping your child.* Berkeley, CA: Ulysses Press.

World Health Organization. (1992). *International classification of diseases and related health problems* (10th ed.). Geneva: Author.

Yerys, B., Hepburn, S., & Pennington, B. (2007). Executive function in preschoolers with autism: Evidence consistent with a secondary deficit. *Journal of Autism and Developmental Disorders, 37*(6), 1068–1079.

CHAPTER 6

Nurturing Development: Treating Young Children with Autism Spectrum Disorder

Carol Korn-Bursztyn

"We were in the playground and I was leaning against the slide for a moment watching as Jason was just running around, running around in circles near where the other kids were playing. I was just standing there and watching him, and suddenly, I had this eureka moment—what Jason really needs is a best friend. Maybe that would make a difference; maybe that's what he really needs. I remember how important it was to me growing up—to have a best friend, and Jason doesn't have that. Yeah, I'd really like him to have a best friend."

Case Vignette

Jason, flushed with excitement after playing a game of tag with his father and another child his dad had recruited, was now running circles in the playground, alone, while the other children played in loosely organized groups. This father takes an active role in supporting his six-year-old son's play with others, initiating games and joining in the play alongside his son. A critical role that Jason's dad plays here is scaffolding the social experience of play for Jason, creating a structure in which Jason can comfortably participate, such as running an obstacle course, or hunting for hidden objects in a small section of the playground. Another crucial role that this father plays is in keeping the play going. He makes changes to the script when the children's attention seems to flag, or when he sees his son begin to pull back from the game as the stress of interacting with peers mounts.

Neighborhood children like to play with Jason's dad and are quick to join in play that he initiates. Jason participates in the games that his father leads and happily climbs obstacle courses alongside the other children, but when the organized game dissolves, he runs circles alone, near where his peers cluster for spontaneous play. Cheeks flushed with excitement, Jason appears happy. He returns to his father and spontaneously hugs him, pulling mischievously on his shirt to re-engage him in play. Jason does not look longingly at the other children with whom he has just played for the past 30 minutes. He appears satisfied with the afternoon's activity, happy to be at the playground with his dad, seemingly oblivious to the other children. While Jason gives no indication of feeling lonely without the company of his peers, his father aches for what he experiences as the potential emptiness in his son's life. Seeing himself reflected in his child's eyes, Jason's father wishes for a best friend for his child, a foundational experience in his own life but one that his child does not yet long for.

Overexcited by the play with his father and the children, Jason briefly engages in repetitive, motoric activity (running circles), which serves a self-regulatory function. Calmer, he returns to his father, to whom he is deeply attached and with whom he shares an affinity for shared laughter. They can often be seen laughing together; defying stereotypes of children with ASD, Jason gazes lovingly at his dad, pulling on his shirt to signal his desire for more playful engagement. Jason's ability to transfer this relational pattern to interactions with peers has not yet fully emerged independently of the active scaffolding of an adult who can organize and join in play, keeping the play going. This is especially the case when play turns from large motor activity to pretend play. It should be noted, though, that recently Jason has begun to initiate talk with other children and enjoys telling knock-knock jokes to other children and adults.

Jason, like many other able children with autism spectrum disorder (ASD), is capable of symbolic function; he has language and can make requests and can engage in rudimentary symbolic play with toys. His ability to engage in symbolic activity, though, is emerging; he is far more comfortable with simple motoric activities than with symbolic play, which he avoids and often energetically protests against. He and his younger sister engage in play routines at home that are largely constructed around physical activities, including a fair amount of jumping, sliding, and running. Jason's reluctance to expand his repertoire to include novel activities or events is now developing as a significant difference from his typically developing sibling.

His sister soon tires of these play routines but meets with her older brother's frantic opposition when she introduces a new idea for play, one not constructed solely of large motor activity. This has become a source of friction between the siblings. Not yet four, Jason's sister grasps that her older brother's opposition, mounting anxiety, and upset in the face of this challenge to routine is a weakness she can exploit. The child with ASD, for whom affect regulation, or the ability to regulate emotional reactions, is an emerging skill, is often at a loss as to how to deal with the fluctuating power relations that inhere in children's interactions with each other.

Introduction

Social skills development in early childhood is marked by young children's increasing capacity to share power in play relationships. This is expressed in an incorporation of the initiatives, ideas, and words that individual players contribute. When children fail to negotiate the subtle balance of power in play activities, play typically falls apart, and interactions can end in anger and tears. Teasing, which in young children can take the form of repeating words or phrases, may be upsetting to the child with ASD, who may protest this sign of another child's dominance and become overwhelmed by negative emotion. This dynamic is a fairly common phenomenon when play between children with ASD and their typically developing siblings begins to fall apart, especially if the typically developing sibling is younger but more sophisticated socially than the sibling with ASD. Lack of flexibility in children with ASD often gets expressed in insistence on continuation of routine interactions. Changes to an established interpersonal dynamic or transaction between children can be temporarily emotionally destabilizing to the child with ASD, resulting in protests or tantrum behavior and parental exasperation.

In the playground vignette that opens this chapter, the parent wishes for a best friend for his child and perhaps for assurance that his child will have opportunities for a full personal life. Parental concern about their children with ASD goes beyond their children's learning scripts of acceptable behavior. Parents worry about the impact of atypical neurodevelopment on their child's ability to have lasting relationships with others and to be loved by others for who they are—and for how they are, too. Having a best friend speaks to a child's capacity to draw upon and move beyond the bonds of parental love and anticipates a time when the grown child will create intimate ties with others. It looks towards a time when the center of gravity of a child's emotional life will shift from family to peers in anticipation of developing adult relationships.

The quote cited above refers not only to parental desire for children to have full, emotionally satisfying lives but also points to controversies in the field around the aims of treatment with regard to the emotional lives of children with ASD. This parent's concern raises the question of what treatment of children with ASD should be about. Should treatment focus exclusively on the reduction of self-stimulating behaviors? Should it focus on the development of activities of daily living and of skills implicated in the mechanics of social exchange, such as how one makes a polite request and deploys *please* and *thank you*? Or should treatment focus on building complex relational patterns of interaction? And, if so, how can children with ASD learn to recognize and consider the subjective states of others, including their feelings, ideas, and desires, when their own inner states are so opaque? Learning to appreciate the subjectivity of another, referred to in the professional literature as *theory of mind,* suggests a growing awareness of one's own internal state as well as the internal states or feelings of others. It is a prerequisite for developing the kinds of reciprocal relationships that are a hallmark of friendship but that can present a challenge for children with ASD.

Embedded within the controversy around what constitutes social development is a second, related controversy that speaks directly to the identity of the child with ASD. Should the aim of treatment be to normalize children with ASD—to make them appear, at least superficially in their presentation of self, similar to their typically developing peers? Or should treatment respect the differences that children with autism spectrum disorder present, while helping them to develop emotional intelligence, or the ability to understand their own emotions and the emotional and motivational states of others? A third controversy acknowledges the relationship between treatment and education. This suggests that education itself represents a form of treatment for children with autism spectrum disorder. What then should education for children with ASD look like? Like the controversy over treatment, the question about education takes up the debate of discrete skill development as contrasted with an emphasis on the development of the whole child, i.e. the child's social, emotional, cognitive and physical development. Related questions ask about the role of play in classrooms for children with ASD; what are the play needs of children with ASD, and how much of the curriculum should be devoted to play? The arts present another curricular question; what should be the place of the arts in classrooms for children with ASD? What curricula areas can best stimulate interest and provoke curiosity? The multiple roles of adults—parents and teachers—in the lives of children with ASD are salient here. What kinds of adult supports and teacher activity can help children with ASD make gains?

This chapter provides an overview of the major contemporary approaches to the treatment of autism spectrum disorder, together with their underlying conceptual frameworks. Rather than an exhaustive overview of all treatment options that families often turn to, the sections that follow will address Ivar Lovaas's behavioral approach, including applied behavioral analysis (ABA), and Stanley Greenspan's developmental, individual-difference, relationship-based (DIR) model, commonly referred to as the "floortime" approach. Included is a discussion of the role of attachment in the treatment of children with ASD, its role in developing capacity for human relatedness, and its function in furthering cognitive growth.

Discrete Trial Training or Traditional Behavioral Approach

The traditional behavioral approach, also referred to as discrete trial training, relies on a highly repetitive individualized approach in which skills are taught through repeated drill and practice format. Ivar Lovaas, a Norwegian psychologist, pioneered this approach in the late 1970s and early 1980s, based on an operant behavioral model, demonstrated that children with ASD could be taught new skills through teaching that was based on the principles of an operant behavioral model—careful, systematic, and repeated or massed trials, and practice within a framework of deliberate reinforcement schedule. This approach had wide applicability; its principles were applied to sequences of motor abilities required for self-help skills—including reduction in self-injurious and/or self-stimulating behavior—as well as for skills involved with receptive and expressive language.

Lovaas's early work demonstrated that less capable children with ASD could make good progress in mastering skills required for the rudiments of independent living and communication. Children with ASD, though, were viewed as lacking the ability to learn in the natural environments of typical family and school routines as a result of their pronounced learning and attention difficulties. The operant behavioral, or discrete trial, approach took place outside of the natural environment, as typical everyday life was not viewed as an appropriate structure for the highly intensive individual training, repeated practice, and systematic reinforcement required by this approach.

Challenges to the Discrete Trial—Traditional Behavioral Approach

Critiques of this approach came from the fields of developmental psychology, psycholinguistics, and speech and language pathology, whose researchers and practitioners questioned whether operant models provided the best explanations for how typically and atypically developing children develop language and the ability to communicate effectively. In the early 1980s, Prizant; Fay, and Schuler raised concerns about whether traditional behavioral approaches, which are entirely adult initiated and directed, were actually hindering the ability of children with ASD to develop spontaneous language. In behavioral approaches, children are trained to respond to prompts from their adult instructors rather than initiate interaction, including verbal communication. They argued that children are therefore positioned as passive learners, while their teachers control the highly structured interactions.

Advancements in the field of developmental pragmatics, which concerns itself with the social contexts of language and communication development, began, in the 1980s and 1990s, to impact on the fields of speech and language pathology and later on special education. In their review of the developmental pragmatics movement, Prizant, Wetherby, and Rydell enumerated the ways in which the developmental pragmatics movement began to change the conversation about teaching children with ASD. Developmental pragmatics maintains that the social environment, primarily the naturally occurring interactions of family and peers, is the major way in which communication and language develop in children, with and without disabilities. This is in stark contrast to the expressed belief of the traditional behavioral movement that children's natural environment is inadequate or even detrimental to implementation of a rigorous (behavioral) program.

The developmental pragmatics movement maintains that the child is viewed as an active learner rather than a respondent to behavioral trials and reinforcement schedules. This underlying philosophical approach places developmental pragmatics squarely within a tradition of high-quality early childhood education, which follows the principles of developmentally appropriate practice (DAP), as formulated by the National Association for the Education of Young Children. A fuller discussion of early childhood principles as they relate to treatment of young children with ASD is included in discussion of Stanley Greenspan's DIR model. Following this emphasis on the naturally occurring social environment of home and community, developmental pragmatics looks closely at the role of caregivers in creating the contexts, structure, and interactive exchanges in which language development occurs and in which children develop capacity for emotional regulation. The developmental pragmatics movement, like best practices in early childhood education, maintains that communication strategies and goals must be individually determined based on the child's needs and strengths, rather than on a standard protocol.

Concerns that the approach itself might actually preclude the development of initiative and the social skills required to keep communication and interaction going were soon raised. Lovaas himself, in 1977, raised questions about whether the training regime implicit to behavioral approaches might have the unintended consequence of restricting verbalization and even advocated for training in spontaneity to compensate for the children's lack of initiative. The irony of invoking an oxymoron such as spontaneity training, in order to correct the sequelae of training in the first place, went unremarked, though communications specialists were quick to distance themselves from the behavioral approach in favor of the emerging pragmatics movement.

A disturbing outcome of the traditional behavioral approach was the lack of generalizability of the skills in which children were trained. Children who had undergone extensive training through traditional behavioral methods of drill, reinforcement and practice were unable to transfer these skills to situations and environments outside of the training trials. This led to development of the traditional behavioral approach, of which the applied behavioral analysis (ABA), also known as intensive behavioral therapy, or Lovaas technique or therapy.

Applied Behavioral Analysis

Applied behavioral analysis, also known as intensive behavioral Intervention (IBI), and early intensive behavioral intervention (EIBI), or Lovaas technique, is an approach to intervention in behavioral disorders that seeks to control and to predict behavior. Devised by Ivar Lovaas, the technique draws on his earlier work and seeks to control and to predict behavior.

ABA focuses on observing and assessing the relationship between the target behavior and the environment, with the aim of behavior change. It is best known for treating children with developmental disabilities, especially ASD, though the approach is not limited to this. Based on the premise that all behavior serves a function, ABA employs a functional assessment of behavior (FBA) protocol consisting of observing, recording, and gathering of information with the aim of generating hypotheses about the environmental events that trigger the problem behaviors.

ABA is a highly structured program that is home-based, though the treatment occurs outside of the ordinary routines of family life. It employs discrete trial training that begins in early childhood and can last from two to six years. Each year of treatment has its own goals; these become increasingly sophisticated over time, beginning with an early focus on reducing self-stimulating behaviors or *stimming,* teaching imitation and appropriate play with toys in the first year; early language and socialization skills in the second year; and emotional expression, early reading, and math skills in the third year.

The family is integrated into the work in the first year; the program aims to include the community in the child's treatment over time in order to reduce the potential stigmatization that the child might experience. Given the high cost of the program, integration of family and community members serves the dual purpose of providing communicators or therapists to provide individual work on a voluntary basis with the child, as well as building personal investment in the program on the parts of family and involved members of the community.

The Lovaas technique is intensive in nature. The treatment regimen calls for 35 to 40 hours a week—five to seven hours a day, five to seven days a week. Each day's session is divided into trials, with frequent breaks, according to when the trainer feels the child's attention begin to lag. During each trial, the trainer provides verbal or gestural prompts to which the child must correctly respond. A prompter sits behind the child and nudges or touches the child if she fails to respond, physically guiding the child's hand to complete the prompt. Correct responses are reinforced with food, time with a toy, or praise. While ABA relies largely on positive reinforcement of desired behavior, the Lovaas technique is also known for the use of aversive methods including hitting, shouting, and even electric shocks. Aversives are much less common today, a response to its highly controversial nature.

For children who lack functional communication, sessions often include work with the picture exchange communication system (PECS), which was designed to be used in conjunction with applied behavioral analysis. Developed by Andy Bondy and Lori Frost, PECS is an augmentative/alternative communication system that was designed to teach children to initiate communication, with an aim to developing spontaneous speech. In this method, children exchange pictures for items that they want, and later arrange pictures into simple sentences indicating what they want. At its most advanced level, the goal of PECS is for children to be able to respond to simple questions such as "What do you see?" with simple responses, such as "I see a ball."

Contemporary approaches to ABA have shifted from an exclusive focus on the trainer as the sole source of control of the interaction with the child, to greater willingness to follow the child's lead in activity and conversation in order to encourage initiative, rather than passivity. This is substantively different from Lovaas's early injunction against shared control of the interaction. In its more recent tilt towards a more interactive approach in which the trainer rewards initiative, ABA appears to be inching closer to professionally sanctioned early childhood pedagogy.

Treatment Approaches and Early Childhood Education

Best practice in early childhood education, referred to as developmentally appropriate practice, calls for nurturing children's interests, supporting their initiative, and facilitating expression of emotions. Developmentally appropriate practice further calls for matching teacher activity to children's individual developmental needs and for scaffolding teacher response to promote children's growth, within the personal developmental range within which each child presents. It calls for teachers who are highly responsive to and who deliberately encourage children's communications, whether these are spontaneous comments, activities, or gestures. They encourage expression of emotions, and provide multiple opportunities for children to make meaning of their experiences through play and the arts. Developmentally appropriate educational settings for young children also provide many occasions for spontaneous interactions with peers, with teachers providing the supports that individual children require.

Though contemporary approaches to ABA provide more room for reciprocal interactions between adult and child, as a pedagogic approach it offers a far more restricted range of activities—especially of an expressive nature—than developmentally appropriate early childhood education. It offers significantly fewer opportunities for spontaneous interactions with peers or adults than is called for in early childhood pedagogy. While the highly structured, adult dominated routines associated with behavioral approaches are demonstrably effective in reducing the rate of self-injurious and self-stimulating behavior among many children with pronounced symptoms, these same routines may result in underpreparation of able children for spontaneous interactions with peers and adults, thereby exacerbating already existing conditions of social awkwardness.

In contrast to the behavioral approaches to treatment of children with ASD, Stanley Greenspan's developmental approach, the developmental, individual-difference, relationship-based (DIR) model, which will be described in greater detail later, draws on principles of early childhood practice and is compatible with a view of development as arising out of human relationships. DIR is also referred to as "floortime" approach; individual work with young children with ASD largely takes place on the floor in this approach, allowing for close proximity to, and interaction between child and adult, mimicking typical play scenarios of young children (with and without disabilities) in family settings. This contrasts with the format of behavioral approaches in which the trainer typically sits directly across from child at a table. The structure of each treatment approach speaks directly to the aims of each method.

When child and adult trainer are seated opposite each other at a table, this signals that the focus of the interaction is on the discrete skill to be developed, rather than the relationship between child and adult. In the behavioral approach, physical proximity functions as a distraction to learning rather than an avenue for developing children's capacity for spontaneity and initiative. For typically developing young children, most learning takes place informally, in interaction with responsive caregivers and with other children. High-quality programs for typically developing toddlers and preschool-aged children involve lots of opportunities for children to seek physical proximity to their caregivers, a hallmark of attachment behavior. Storybook reading with very young children, for example, is best conducted individually or with a few children seated in close proximity to or, even, if the child desires, on the caregiver's lap. Seeking physical proximity is a key indicator of attachment, or bond between child and other.

Attachment and Children with ASD

Attachment emerges first in interactions between children and their parents; it is formed out of ties of love that bind children to adults and serves the function of helping children anticipate their parents' reactions, particularly when they are in need of soothing. Secure attachment, which rests on the expectation that parents will be available for—and can effectively sooth—is central to children's ability to self-regulate negative emotions in stressful situation. Children who are securely attached also evidence greater exploratory behavior; they are curious about their surroundings and explore and manipulate toys and other objects. Exploratory behavior in early childhood leads to developing an attitude of curiosity and engagement, which in turn results in increased learning.

In contrast, behavioral approaches to treating children with ASD, which take up the greater part of the child's waking hours, take place primarily in situations that preclude opportunity for physical proximity between young children and caregivers. There may be fewer opportunities for young children with ASD who are involved in long-term behavioral protocols, such as ABA, to develop key attachment behaviors that are stimulated by warm, playful engagement, including proximity seeking and mutual interactions.

Despite their well-documented difficulties with social interaction, researchers in the 1990s including Dissanayake and Crossley, and Rogers and colleagues, suggested that children with ASD demonstrate patterns of secure attachment behavior with their parents. This supports observations among numerous earlier researchers, including Bernabei et al., Buitelaar et al., Sigman and Mundy, that children with autism, like their peers without autism, seek closeness to their parent following a separation.

However, when attachment was looked at more closely, a finer gradation in quality of attachment relationships between children and parents began to emerge. Research conducted in 2004 by Rutgers and her colleagues at Leiden University in the Netherlands looked at attachment patterns of children with autism in comparison with typically developing children and with children who presented with intellectual disability and communication disorders. Following a contemporary trend that returns researchers to naturalistic settings in which to observe children and families, the researchers deployed an instrument developed by Waters, in 1987, called the Q-set. Unlike Ainsworth's earlier procedure, the Strange Situation, in which attachment is measured in a laboratory setting, the Q-set involves observation in a naturalistic setting, such as the home. Both procedures were developed for and are used with infants and toddlers only. Their results suggested that when the quality of attachment behaviors is assessed, children with ASD present as significantly less securely attached than children without ASD.

Based on their observations, Rutgers and her colleagues concluded that less secure attachment in children with autism might be related to a less flexible style of interaction between parents and children. They noted that the parents of children with ASD appeared to interact less flexibly with their children, and were less attuned to their children's needs, which were often exceedingly difficult to read. This resulted in less matching or synchronic interactions between parents and children. Rutgers et al. hypothesized that the weaker attunement of parents to their children might be tracked to the social impairments that children with ASD typically present—the greater the social impairments, the greater the challenges to developing smooth, synchronous interactions between parents and children.

As a result of social impairments that are typical of children with autism, Rutgers and her colleagues concluded, it may be more difficult for parents to correctly read their children's attachment needs and signals. This may lead to more insecure patterns of attachment when compared with typically developing children or with children who present other clinical conditions, such as intellectual disability or language disorders. Level of cognitive functioning turned out to be an important variable here, too. Children with stronger cognitive functioning or, what researchers refer to as mental development (as contrasted with chronological age), tend to be more securely attached to their parents than children with ASD and intellectual disability. Children with ASD and intellectual disability, in turn, are less securely attached than children who present with intellectual disability, but without autism. What emerges from the attachment research with typically and atypically developing children is the connection between facility of social interaction and the establishment of secure attachment. Children, who do not easily engage with others, can present challenges to developing the kinds of reciprocal interactions that lead to patterns of secure attachment.

While attachment patterns first emerge in infancy, these are not fixed and immutable. Rather, with facilitating therapeutic and educational experiences, children can develop more secure and confident relational patterns. Secure attachment brings benefits that are both social/emotional and cognitive; for this reason alone it is a critical area of development for children with ASD. The approach described below, Stanley Greenspan's DIR model, takes up the concern for the development of children's capacity for human relations and presents a model for developing relational capacity for humanistic reasons and also for its instrumental value in furthering language and communication, cognition, and social/emotional development.

Developmental, Individual-Difference, Relationship-based Model

Stanley Greenspan's DIR model assumes that all children, whether or not they present with clinical conditions, have emotional needs for connection to others, even when they present with pronounced difficulties in social interaction. DIR is a functional, developmental approach to treating children with developmental disorders, including ASD. Like good early childhood practice, this model engages children at their identified level of functioning. Each child's functioning is assessed across a spectrum of capacities; intensive interactive experiences within the context of ongoing relationships are then designed to engage the child in order to help her master new capacities. DIR addresses what are referred to as the functional emotional processes that underlie social skills, such as turn-taking, making requests, or sitting quietly. This is an important distinction between DIR and behavioral approaches, which aim to entrain social-skill behaviors but which do not address underlying emotional processes.

Greenspan and Weider tracked the emergence of functional emotional processes to early emotional interactions between children and their parents. They identified three components that impact the child's ability to master these functional emotional milestones: (a) the child's biology, including neurological potential or challenges; (b) the child's interactive patterns with her parents, teachers, other significant people; and (c) the child's family, culture, social, and physical environment. Greenspan and Weider's work in functional emotional processes anticipated the contemporary emphasis in attachment research on the reciprocal impact of child and parent on the development of attachment as well as the impact of culture and environment on attachment patterns.

They theorized that a deficit in critical social capacities that involve reciprocal, positive emotional exchanges is a reaction to underlying biological based sensory difficulties, rather than a primary deficit. This suggests that the capacity for warm relatedness with others, marked by reciprocal emotional exchanges including smiling, laughing, imitating, gesturing, and sequences of pleasurable interactions, can emerge under social and environmental conditions that take into account children's individual needs and sensory deficits.

Even the most competent parents, Greenspan and Weider noted, can easily become confused and frustrated by a child who looks away or withdraws, a common experience for parents of children with ASD. This may set in motion an interactive pattern in which parents can lose engagement with their children, who might then withdraw more deeply into their own idiosyncratic worlds. In the second year of life, Greenspan and Weider observed, typically developing children begin to display intentionality in problem solving and to develop meaningful language based on connecting their intentions to their actions and to their growing capacity to use symbols. Their behavior becomes increasingly goal oriented, with motoric efforts typically directed at the desired object, interesting phenomenon, or appealing person in their surroundings. Greenspan and Weider hypothesized that when critical connections between affect and intention (or what Adam Phillips, following Freud, refers to as desire) are not created, children become more likely to engage in aimlessly repetitive behavior and language, rather than develop increasingly intentional behavior, including language.

Greenspan's DIR model is based on the premise developed by Reuven Feuerstein et al. that affective or emotional interactions that are positive in nature, warm and encouraging of children's initiative, and can promote cognitive and emotional growth. Intentionality lies at the core of DIR; its goal is to help children create a sense of themselves as intentional, social beings, capable of interacting with others. Cognitive growth and language ability flow from this growing sense of intentionality, which is stimulated by the heavily interactive treatment program. The DIR approach emphasizes the child's emotions, intent, and relationships and takes into account each child's developmental level, as well as individual differences in motor, sensory, affective, cognitive and language functioning.

Interactive experiences at home, referred to as *floortime*, range from two to five hours a day. Consultation with and support for family is an integral part of the program. Additionally, the program includes interactive speech-language therapy (three to five times a week), and occupational therapy (two to five times a week). For preschool children, an inclusive preschool (one quarter of the class consisting of children with disabilities and three quarters of the class, children without disabilities) with specially trained, warm, and responsive teachers is recommended. The DIR model fits well within the tradition of high-quality early childhood and pragmatic speech-language therapy practices. It is consistent with developmentally appropriate early childhood practice and follows the guidelines of the National Association for the Education of Young Children.

Greenspan identified six core functional developmental levels that guide the design of each individually tailored treatment approach. The developmental points or levels at which each child's development went off-track are identified; by providing corrective developmental experiences, the DIR model helps children become more emotionally connected, spontaneous, and intentional in their actions and words. The key developmental levels follow.

1. The ability to take interest and pleasure in the sights, sounds, and sensations of the world, and, importantly, to calm oneself (i.e., self-regulation).
2. The ability to engage in relationships with other people, including evidencing preference for and pleasure in being with a parent or caregiver.
3. The ability to engage in two-way communication with gestures, including imitating.
4. The ability to create complex gestures or communications. These involve organizing what Greenspan refers to as chains of two-way communication, or opening and closing circles of communication, with the aim of increasing the number of consecutive opening and closing communication circles.
5. The ability to create ideas, including symbolizing emotional experience in pretend play or language.
6. The ability to build bridges between ideas to make them reality based and logical. This capacity is implicated in reality testing, impulse control, stable mood, and logical planning.

These six developmental levels serve as a basis for assessment, planning, and revision of treatment goals as children make progress. Development is viewed as dynamic and, in most cases, responsive to intervention. As children make progress and become increasingly curious about the world, receptive to and interested in human relationships, treatment goals are reset. The therapist attends to each child's regulatory profile, noting overreactivity or underreactive to sensations in various sensory modalities, including sound, sight, touch, movement, auditory processing visuospatial processing, motor planning, and sequencing. Additionally, the therapist attends to the interactive patterns between the child and family members and caregivers, noting how well they understand the child's sensory and motor needs and sensitivities as well as their patterns of interaction with the child.

Therapists working in the DIR model employ key characteristics of high-quality early childhood pedagogy, which include following children's initiative and lead, and creating new experiences tailored to children's individual needs, sensitivities and developmental levels. Through the use of developmentally appropriate interactions, the therapist works with the child and family to draw on the child's emotional or affective range, broadening the child's experience and capacity at each developmental level.

The program involves three components. The first is spontaneous, in which the therapist and family engage the child by following the child's lead. The second involves a focus on semistructured problem solving in which challenges are introduced so that the child learns something new, and the third involves sensorimotor, sensory integration, visuospatial, and perceptual motor activities. Play with peers is introduced once the child is fully engaged and interactive. DIR is an interdisciplinary model; in addition to home-based intervention sessions, it also includes speech-language, sensory integration, occupational therapy, or physical therapy. When children can interact and imitate gestures and words, and engage in nonverbal problem solving, attendance in an inclusion program or in a general education preschool program with an additional teacher or aide is recommended.

Conclusions

[O]ne of the most painful things I went through was I assumed that each professional saw my child as a whole person and they didn't. In the early years I felt like I was Kimberly's contractor and I sub-contracted out parts of her to professionals. The information is so contradictory.

The quote above, by a mother of a young girl, raises the dual issues of intensive but often fragmented treatment of young children with ASD as well as the complex task of researching competing theories and approaches that already burdened parents face. It implies the key role that parents have in developing understanding of different approaches and their theoretical underpinnings as well as orchestrating their child's treatment. Parenting a young child with ASD requires of parents that they master the particulars of treatment approaches, and become lead figures in their children's treatment.

In this chapter, key approaches to treatment of children with ASD, including applied behavioral analysis and the developmental, individual-difference, relationship-based model are presented. Attachment theory is presented as a link between development of discrete skills and their underlying processes. Review of the characteristics of high-quality early childhood experiences serves the purpose of demonstrating how treatment for young children with ASD can draw upon high-quality pedagogic approaches for young children that promote social development and capacity for human relatedness, and that nurture initiative and its developmental expression in curiosity and learning about the environment.

References

Ainsworth, M.D.S., Blehar, M.C., Waters, E., & Wall, S. (1978). *Patterns of attachment*. Hillsdale, NJ: Erlbaum.

Bernabei, P., Camaioni, L., & Levi, G. (1998). An evaluation of early development in children with autism and pervasive developmental disorders from home movies: Preliminary findings. *Autism, 2*, 243–258.

Bondy, A.S., and Frost, L. (1994). The picture exchange communication system. *Focus on Autistic Behavior, 9*(3), 1–19.

Buitelaar, J. (1995). Attachment and social withdrawal in autism: Hypotheses and findings. *Behaviour, 132*, 319–350.

Dissanayake, C., & Crossley, S.A. (1996). Proximity and sociable behaviours in autism: Evidence for attachment. *Journal of Child Psychology and Psychiatry, 37*, 149–156.

Dissanayake, C., & Crossley, S.A. (1997). Autistic children's responses to separation and reunion with their mothers. *Journal of Autism and Developmental Disorders, 27*, 295–312.

Fay, W.H., & Schuler, L. (Vol. Eds.). (1980). *Emerging language in autistic children*. In R.L. Schiefelbusch (Series Ed.), *Language intervention series* (Vol. 5). Baltimore: University Park Press.

Feuerstein, R., Miller, R., Hoffman, M., Rand, Y., Mintsker, Y., Morgens, R. et al. (1981). Cognitive modifiability in adolescence: Cognitive structure and the effects of intervention. *Journal of Special Education, 150*, 269–287.

Greenspan, S.I. (1979). *Psychopathology and adaptation in infancy and early childhood: Principles of clinical diagnosis and preventive intervention*. In ZERO-TO-THREE: National Center for Clinical infant Programs (Ed.), *Clinical Infant Reports* (Vol.1). Madison, CT: International Universities Press.

Greenspan, S.I. (1989). *The development of the ego: Implications for personality theory, psychopathology, and the psychotherapeutic process*. Madison, CT: International Universities Press.

Greenspan, S.I. (1992). *Infancy and early childhood: The practice of clinical assessment and intervention with emotional and developmental challenges*. Madison, CT: International Universities Press.

Greenspan, S.I. (1997). *The growth of the mind and the endangered origins of intelligence*. Reading, MA: Addison Wesley Longman.

Greenspan, S.I., I Wieder, S. (2000). A developmental approach to difficulties in relating and communicating in autism spectrum disorders and related syndromes. In A. M. Wetherby & B.M. Prizant (Vol. Eds.). *Autism spectrum disorders: a transactional developmental perspective* (Vol. 9). Baltimore: Brookes.

Lovaas, O.I. (1977). *The autistic child: Language development through behavior modification*. New York: Irvington Press.

Lovaas, O.I. (1987). Behavioral treatment and normal educational and intellectual functioning in young autistic children. *Journal of Consulting and Clinical Psychology, 55*, 3–9.

Phillips, A. (1998). *The beast in the nursery: On curiosity and other appetites*. New York: Vintage Books.

Prizant, B.M. (1983). Language acquisition and communicative behavior in autism: Toward an understanding of the "whole" of it. *Journal of Speech and Hearing Disorders, 48*, 296–307.

Prizant, B.M., Wetherby, A. M. & Rydell, P.J. (2000). *Communication intervention issues for children with autism spectrum disorders.* In A.M. Wetherby & B.M. Prizant (Vol. Eds.), *Autism spectrum disorder* (Vol. 9). Baltimore: Brooks.

Rogers, S.J., Ozonoff, S., & Maslin-Cole, C. (1993). Developmental aspects of attachment behaviour in young children with pervasive developmental disorders. *Journal of the American Academy of Child and Adolescent Psychiatry, 32,* 1274–1282.

Rutgers, A.H., van Ijzendoon, H., Bakermans-Kranenburg, M.J., Swinkels, S.H.N., Van Daalen, E., Dietz, Cl., et al. (2007). Autism, attachment and parenting: A comparison of children with autism spectrum disorder, mental retardation, language disorder, and non-clinical children, *Journal of Abnormal Child Psychology, 35,* 859–870.

Sigman, M., & Mundy, P. (1989). Social attachments in autistic children. *Journal of the American Academy of Child and Adolescent Psychiatry, 28,* 74–81.

Waters, E. (1987). *Attachment behavior Q-set* (Version 3.0). State University of New York at Stony Brook, Stony Brook, NY (Unpublished instrument).

Waters, E. (1995). The attachment Q-set. In E. Waters, B.E. Vaughn, G. Posada, & K. Kondo-Ikemura (Eds.), Caregiving, cultural, and cognitive perspectives on secure-base behavior and working models. *Monographs of the Society for Research in Child Development, 60,* 247–254.

CHAPTER 7

Who Is the Real Emotionally Disturbed Child?

Harold Golubtchik

Philip is a 17-year-old African American teenager, living in a group home, and has been placed in special education classes since the fourth grade. His Individualized Education Program indicates that he is emotionally disturbed, and he is now attending a self-contained school for severely disturbed students. Almost six-feet tall, Philip is proud of his hard body, due to his daily weightlifting routine. He is concerned about the way he looks, especially his sneakers and baseball cap. On days when he claims he did not have time to do his hair, he will refuse to remove his cap. Philip earned only 4 of the required 44 Carnegie units and will most likely not earn a high school diploma. He reads and writes on a fourth-grade level, but his math scores are two years higher. His initial response to his teachers' directions and requests is to ignore them. Sometimes he responds on his own terms, and other times he continues to ignore. He challenges his classmates frequently and gets in their face to assert his power. Interestingly, his actions rarely result in fights. Teachers are not sure if he can control these behaviors or not. Philip likes to have conversations with adults, and the topics of discussion usually focus on his complaints about school. He refuses to have a notebook and flips through magazines while teachers conduct lessons, although, at times, he seems to listen attentively. When asked what he wants to do after high school, Philip says that it really doesn't matter because most of his homeboys are dead before they reach the age of 30.

During my first few weeks as the new principal of this urban special education high school, I walked into classes with my assistant principal, dean, and several counselors and asked students to share their concerns or ask questions about the school. Philip's comments stood out:

> You guys only do your job for the paycheck. You don't respect us. You don't give a damn about us.
>
> You lie to us about getting out of this place. You say that if we work hard we can go back to regular schools, but I been here for three years and I ain't seen nobody leave. I'm not out of control like I was in the third grade, so why am I in special ed? Man, being here is like serving a life sentence.
>
> The point system program you got here don't make no sense. You really think I'm going to change the way I am for some lame prizes? We're way too cool for that.

Antonio, a 15-year-old Latino, is also labeled emotionally/behaviorally disturbed (E/BD). He lives with his mother and grandmother and has no siblings. He is slightly overweight and does not care about the way he looks. Often he wears the same clothes two or three days in a row. His behaviors are significantly different from those of Philip, even though they are both in the same class. Antonio's favorite position in class is one where he puts his head down and rests it on his desk. Sometimes he places his head on his folded hands, and sometimes directly on a large book. He seems lethargic and speaks in a slow, monotone tempo. He uses the phrase "I don't care" often, even when offered choices. He has no close friends in the class and often rejects overtures by other students to have a conversation. Philip reads and writes on an eighth-grade level and follows directions to begin his class work, although he rarely completes assignments. He does not like to talk to adults, even to his guidance counselor who sees him for 45 minutes every day. Several months ago, on his birthday, Antonio brought a realistic looking plastic gun to school. He confessed to his counselor that he intended to point the gun at a policeman after school in the hope that the officer would shoot him. After six weeks in an adolescent psychiatric center and new medications, Antonio returned to school.

I was the principal of the school that Philip and Antonio attended, and their descriptions have not been embellished or exaggerated. It may be difficult to comprehend how two youngsters who demonstrate such divergent behaviors could both wear the same label. Yet, they and 379 additional teenagers were under the same E/BD classification, in the same school. Each and every child fits within the continuum of internalizing and externalizing behaviors—from depression, anxiety, and withdrawal from social interaction to aggression, defiance, and a lack of self-control—behaviors that affected the student with the disorder and behaviors that had direct or indirect effects on other people.

As I reflect on my many years as a teacher, staff developer, and principal working with troubled youth, I have come to the conclusion that the common denominator among all those labeled as emotionally/behaviorally disturbed (E/BD) is that there is no single, clear common denominator.

In fact, I would argue that each E/BD student is unique. Unlike physical disabilities such as blindness that are clearly defined and measureable, emotional disturbance is much more complex and subjective. This leads to a lack of correspondence between the E/BD definitions as seen through the eyes of the psychiatric community and school law. Heward (2009) argued that a clear definition is lacking because disordered behavior is a social construct and no clear agreement exists about what constitutes good mental health. In fact, our common sense acknowledges that all children behave inappropriately at times and may have minor social, emotional, or behavioral difficulties, particularly during times of unusual stress.

Two additional factors make it difficult for mental health professionals to reach consensus on a clear definition. First, expectations and norms for appropriate behavior are often quite different across ethnic and cultural groups. Second, emotional and behavioral disorders often occur in conjunction with other disabilities, making it difficult to determine whether one condition is an outcome of the other.

The Student with E/BD

The causes of emotional disturbance have not been adequately determined. Although various factors such as heredity, brain disorder, diet, stress, and family functioning have been suggested as possible causes, research has not shown any of these factors to be the direct cause of behavior or emotional disturbance (Turnbull, Turnbull, Shank, & Smith, 2004). It is interesting to note that while some children exhibit E/BD symptoms as early as preschool, other children with a genetic predisposition for emotional or behavioral disorders exhibit few, if any, signs of a problem until adolescence.

Some of the characteristics and behaviors seen in children who have emotional disturbance include hyperactivity (short attention span, impulsiveness); aggression/self-injurious behaviors (acting out, fighting); withdrawal (failure to initiate interaction with others; retreat from exchange of social interactions, excessive fear or anxiety); immaturity (inappropriate crying, temper tantrums, poor coping skills); and learning difficulties (academically performing below grade level) (Turnbull et al., 2004).

The symptoms of emotional and behavioral disorders are often divided into two broad categories. The first is externalizing behaviors that have direct or indirect effects on other people. Examples include aggression, defiance, disobedience, lying, stealing, and lack of self-control. The second is internalizing behaviors that primarily affect the student with the disorder. Examples include anxiety, depression, withdrawal from social interaction, eating disorders, and suicidal tendencies (Ormrod, 2003). Although students with externalizing behaviors are those whom teachers are more likely to refer for evaluation and special services, students with internalizing behaviors are often at just as much at risk for school failure.

Students with E/BD who exhibit extreme externalizing behaviors are a major concern of schools. Practitioners, both teachers and clinicians, generally agree that these students' lack of school success is due to two intersecting forces: these students' capacity for compliance and the adults' expectation for compliance. These problems are often due to a lack of skills in the domains of flexibility, adaptability, frustration tolerance, and problem solving. More specifically, students with E/BD tend to lack the capacity to defer or delay their own goals in response to the imposed standards of those with authority. This would seem to be a powerful explanation for failure. But additional descriptors exist in the E/BD profile that lead to further frustrations and inappropriate behaviors. Researchers have found that many of these youngsters have difficulty expressing thoughts, needs, and concerns in words. They tend to misread social cues, especially nonverbal ones. Students with E/BD often lack basic social skills—how to start a conversation, how to enter a group and how to connect with people, as examples. And finally, they have a poor sense of how they are being perceived by others or to what extent their behavior is affecting others.

The Student with E/BD: Demographics and Prognosis

During the 2005–2006 school year, 471,306 children and youth labeled E/BD, ages 6 to 21 years, received special education and related services in public schools in the United States (U.S. Department of Education, 2007). This number represents approximately one percent of the school-age population. A 2001 U.S. Surgeon General report estimated that the true prevalence is probably three to six times greater and that only about one in five children and youth with emotional disturbance receive mental health or special education services. Reasons for underidentification include economic factors, concerns about a stigmatizing label, and a vague definition.

Youngsters identified as emotionally disturbed present a grim reality and prognosis. They are at risk for academic problems due to their pervasive behavioral issues and documented resistance to instructional efforts. They are less likely to graduate from high school than students with other types of disabilities. The Individuals with Disabilities Education Act (IDEA, 2004) required that all children with disabilities, to the maximum extent possible, be educated with children who are not disabled. Yet, more students with E/BD remain in separate classes when compared to all other students with other handicapping conditions listed in the IDEA.

The transition from school to adult life is very difficult for many adolescents and young adults who are diagnosed as having a serious emotional disturbance. As many as 64 percent of these youth fail to complete high school, and after leaving high school they are less likely than their peers to be employed and less able to participate in adult learning or continuing education. The failure to complete school increases the likelihood of imprisonment or trouble with the law, along with greatly reduced earnings over a lifetime. Of the students who do graduate high school, relatively few complete, or even pursue, postsecondary education. Furthermore, workers with emotional/behavioral disorders experience lower employment rates as compared to people with no disabilities and those with other disabilities. In addition, individuals with E/BD are more likely to be employed part time rather than full time and earn less than individuals without disabilities or those with other disabilities.

The E/BD Definition Conundrum

A major challenge in the identification of students as ED involves a decision regarding whether emotional and/or behavioral difficulties constitute a disability. That is, when does a behavior problem become an "emotional disturbance?" When does social withdrawal and shyness become an anxiety disorder? When does sadness and loneliness become a major depressive disorder? When do overactivity, impulsivity, and inattention become an attention deficit/hyperactivity disorder? The answer to these questions is not straightforward and ultimately involves some degree of subjective judgment. The category of Emotional Disturbance describes a group of students whose behavior differs from their peers more in terms of *degree* rather than *kind*. (Gresham, 2005, p. 329)

The Individuals with Disabilities Education Act defines emotional disturbance in detail:

Emotional disturbance means a condition exhibiting one or more of the following characteristics over a long period of time and to a marked degree that adversely affects a child's educational performance:

  (i)   An inability to learn that cannot be explained by intellectual, sensory, or health factors.
  (ii) An inability to build or maintain satisfactory interpersonal relationships with peers and teachers.
  (iii) Inappropriate types of behavior or feelings under normal circumstances.
  (iv) A general pervasive mood of unhappiness or depression.
  (v)   A tendency to develop physical symptoms or fears associated with personal or school problems.

The term includes schizophrenia but does not apply to children who are socially maladjusted, unless it is determined that they have an emotional disturbance.

[Code of Federal Regulations, Title 34,
Section 300.7(c)(4)(i–ii)]

J.M. Kauffman, a leading expert in the field of emotional disturbance, outlined the importance of a clear definition of emotional and behavioral disorders. First, a definition that is accepted reflects the manner in which the problem is conceptualized and therefore what interventions are considered appropriate. Second, a definition specifies what population is to be served and as a result has a powerful effect on who receives services and how they are served. Third, decisions of legislators, courts, and school administrators concerning the appropriation of funds, and training and employment of personnel are guided by the definition (Kauffman, 2001).

In considering Kaufman's concerns about the importance of a clear definition of E/BD, the IDEA definition of E/BD is troubling. Foremost, it is conspicuously vague, as the description of E/BD behaviors can apply to many at-risk students as well. Because the definition is vague and does not focus on the degrees of severity or rate of occurrence, clinicians and evaluators are not provided with guidelines as they evaluate students for possible special education referrals. The definition also ignores aggressive or even noncompliant or acting-out aspects that are evident in most students' behaviors in classes for E/BD. Finally, there is no explanation as to the research or framework that was the basis for this definition.

The IDEA definition has been one of the major reasons that children with emotional disturbance are underidentified and underserved in the public schools when compared to the number of children experiencing social/emotional problems. The U.S. Department of Health and Human Services (1999) estimated that 11 percent of the student population experience severe functional social, emotional, and/or behavioral impairments. Such children typically experience mood disorders, anxiety disorders, conduct disorders, ADHD, and other psychiatric disorders. However, the national rate of students identified as E/BD has been less than one percent (U.S. Department of Education, 2004).

An additional concern with the IDEA definition is its three limiting criteria for classifying emotional disturbance: the condition exists (1) over a long period of time, (2) to a marked degree, and (3) adversely affects educational performance. However, no operational definition for each criterion is provided. The phrase "which adversely affects educational performance" has received additional criticism. It is argued that this phrase is narrowly interpreted, limiting educational performance to academics, and that a broader interpretation should be used to include affective, vocational, and social domains of performance. On the other side of the spectrum, there are many children who exhibit E/BD behaviors but who demonstrate adequate and even superior academic performance. Those students may not qualify for E/BD services.

Finally, the IDEA definition of emotional and behavioral disturbance does not specify the severity of the disturbance. For example, the New York State Education Department uses the IDEA definition to describe all students with E/BD, those who are labeled as demonstrating moderate as well as severe disturbance. The determination of *severe* versus *moderate* is left to the discretion of the local school-based evaluation teams.

The law excludes from entitlement to services those students who are socially maladjusted, yet no definition or description of behaviors is offered to clarify the differences between students who are emotionally disturbed and those who are socially maladjusted. The *Diagnostic and Statistical Manual of*

Mental Disorders, Fourth Edition, Text Revision (DSM-IV-TR) (2000) applies the term *socially maladjusted* to children who exhibit various patterns and degrees of aggressive, antisocial, noncompliant, and disruptive behaviors. It generally involves volitional behaviors that are deemed inappropriate by society and which cause conflicts with others. Two assumptions seem to apply to the child who is socially maladjusted: (1) These children make conscious decisions to behave inappropriately, and (2) these children have a lack of guilt or remorse for their problematic behavior.

Not everyone agrees with these assumptions. Current research shows that the problems associated with externalizing, antisocial behaviors result from a complex interplay of predisposing, biological, family, community, and cultural factors and go beyond simple choice (Lahey, Waldman, & McBurnett, 1999; Shaw, Bell, & Gillion, 2000). One study found strong evidence indicating approximately 50 percent of the variance for antisocial behavior can be attributed to heredity (Mason & Frick, 1994).

The assumption that lack of remorse exists is also problematic. Genuine feelings of guilt or lack of remorse are difficult emotional states to empirically demonstrate. There are no direct tests for remorse or guilt and their presence or absence is generally inferred by verbal behavior of the student (Olympia et al., 2004).

The implications for this lack of clarity between emotional disturbance and social maladjustment are profound. School personnel often misclassify a student who is socially maladjusted as severely emotionally disturbed. Sometimes those errors occur because the behaviors of students who are emotionally disturbed and who are socially maladjusted overlap, and school evaluation teams are unable to make clear and accurate judgments. In fact, the National Association of School Psychologists (2007) reported that the vast majority of school psychologists indicated it is extremely difficult to clearly differentiate between student behaviors that are within the student's control or outside it.

Sometimes the misclassifications are purposeful. For example, students who are socially maladjusted may be classified as emotionally disturbed because of the serious problems they cause for teachers and other students or because no funding is available for classes for students who are socially maladjusted. Some schools may choose to pressure evaluators to find ways that would allow these students to fit into the IDEA definition so that districts would be reimbursed for the educational expenses. Other schools with the same situation may choose to insist that socially maladjusted students not be considered as E/BD because E/BD students cannot, by law, be expelled from school, while others can be expelled.

However, this is not simply a matter of a technical, inappropriate classification. In fact, it raises the question of whether the child with E/BD and child who is socially maladjusted should be in the same classroom. Some argue that students who are socially maladjusted typically do not fare well in special education classes and can be disruptive to emotionally disturbed students in the same class. Gacano and Hughes (2004) claim that children

who are socially maladjusted act in ways that demonstrate a pathological egocentricity and a failure to accept responsibility for their actions.
The authors concluded that students who are socially maladjusted are best
served in separate setting environments with strict behavioral controls and
a clearly defined set of rewards and consequences, a setting not necessarily appropriate for children identified as E/BD.

As a result of the dissatisfaction with the IDEA definition of E/BD, an
alternative definition was proposed by the National Mental Health and
Special Education Coalition (Merrell, 2003). The coalition is made up of
approximately 30 professional mental health and education associations.
The following is the alternative definition:

> (i) The term Emotional or Behavioral Disorder (E/BD) means a dis-
> ability characterized by behavioral or emotional responses in school
> so different from appropriate age, cultural, or ethnic norms that they
> adversely affect educational performance. Educational performance
> included academic, social, vocational, and personal skills. Such a dis-
> ability (a) is in the environment; (b) is consistently exhibited in two
> different settings, at least one of which is school-related; and (c) is un-
> responsive to direct intervention in general education or the child's
> condition is such that general interventions would be insufficient.
> (ii) This category may include children or youth with schizophrenic
> disorders, affective disorders, anxiety disorders, or other sustained
> disturbances of conduct or adjustment when they adversely affect
> educational performance in accordance with section (i).

This alternative definition is important, as it does not deny services to
children and adolescents who are identified as socially maladjusted. Additionally, the definition does not use the term *emotionally disturbed*, a term
that can be stigmatizing because it tends to elicit images of psychiatric
hospitals and highly disturbing behavior. Rather, it substitutes the term
emotional or behavioral disorder for *emotional disturbance.* However, despite
the recommendations for the alternate definition, no changes or modifications in the IDEA definition have been made yet.

Ethical Issues in Special Education

Minority children with disabilities all too often experience inadequate
services, low-quality curriculum and instruction, and unnecessary isolation
from their nondisabled peers. Moreover, inappropriate practices in both
general and special education classrooms have resulted in overrepresentation, misclassification, and hardships for minority students, especially African American children (Losen & Orfield, 2002).

It is clear that minorities are overrepresented in several special education
categories and are underrepresented in programs for gifted and talented
students. Although African American students make up 17 percent of the
student population, they constitute nearly 35 percent of students identified

as having intellectual disability and more than 26 percent of students identified as seriously emotionally disturbed (Donovan & Cross, 2002).

Some argue that poverty is the key variable in the disproportionate placement of minorities in special education classes. But the notion that poverty is the single or even the main cause of overrepresentation is not accurate. Osher, Woodruff, and Sims (2002) noted that African American children are only slightly more likely than Caucasians to have such physical disabilities as visual or hearing impairment. Yet, they are significantly more likely than Caucasians to be labeled *intellectually disabled* and *emotionally disturbed*. It makes no sense that poverty alone would have such an inconsistent impact.

Two additional themes have emerged to explain the overrepresentation of African American children in special education. One is the misinterpretation by educators of students' cultural behaviors. For example, when some African American students, accustomed to a more active, participatory pattern, demonstrate their engagement by providing animated comments and reaction, teachers may interpret such behaviors as rude and disruptive. While researchers generally contend that in most cases there is no conscious intent to discriminate, overrepresentation can be linked to unconscious bias, which can lead to special education placement.

The second theme focuses on the lack of quality intervention for at-risk students in general education classes. Systematic and effective interventions, especially those that support the delivery of quality instruction, have been successful in reducing overall special education referrals and placements. These interventions are relevant for minority students as well. For example, Gravois and Rosenfield (2002) investigated the impact of Instructional Consultation (IC) Teams on the referral and placement of minority students compared to existing prereferral practices in 20 schools. IC Teams provided data-based support to classroom teachers that focused on effective instructional and management practices within the classroom to address specific measurable goals. Each team was composed of administrators, support personnel, and representatives from general and special education. The teacher met with one member of the team who was called a case manager. The entire Instructional Consultation membership remained available to support the case manager and the teacher at any point that assistance was needed or requested. Analysis of special education referral and placement patterns revealed that significantly fewer African American students who were supported by the IC Teams in their schools were referred for evaluation or placed in special education when compared to existing prereferral practices.

For minority communities, the disproportionate representation of their children in special education is only one facet in the denial of access to equal educational opportunity. The denial often begins in regular education classrooms with tracking, rigid discipline, less access to gifted and talented programs, and fewer general education resources. Specifically, African American children with emotional disturbance often receive far fewer hours of counseling and related services than Caucasian students with emotional disturbances. Furthermore, schools with a high concentration of low-income minority children are less likely to have experienced, well-trained teachers.

An additional educational trend that is troubling for minority students involves school discipline. Since the zero-tolerance approach to school code violations began several decades ago, student suspensions have almost doubled. The enactment of new laws mandating referral of children to law-enforcement authorities for a variety of school code violations has also significantly increased suspensions, expulsions, and other consequences that keep students out of schools. Minorities are heavily overrepresented among those punished in schools. Nationally, African American students are 2.6 times as likely to be suspended as Caucasian students. The over-representation of minorities continues in the prison system as well. In fact, the racial disparities within schools and prisons are so similar and glaring that it is almost impossible not to connect them. In fact, advocates and educators have crafted terms such as *school-to-prison pipeline* to describe these parallel trends. Wald and Losen (2003) share some disturbing statistics:

1. 68 percent of inmates in 1997 had not completed high school
2. 70 percent of the juvenile justice population suffer from learning disabilities
3. 33 percent of the juvenile justice population read below the fourth-grade level
4. At the end of the 20th century, 791,000 African American men were in prison or jail, and only 603,000 African American men were in colleges or universities

Schools and the Student with E/BD

Students in crisis or students with disruptive behaviors are not a new phenomenon, nor is the concept of interventions within the educational system. Schools have used many different approaches and methods of intervention with students with emotional problems, but there is a lack of consensus as to which are effective. After conducting a comprehensive study of educational and mental health programs, Richardson and Wubbolding (2001) concluded that the majority of programs for children with emotional and behavioral problems are often little more than a rigid curriculum of control, and that "overuse of simplistic behavioral intervention is contributing to a sense of hopelessness for troubled children and fosters further alienation" (p. 38).

The conventional response to youth violence and inappropriate behaviors has been punishment, a focus on zero tolerance, and placing responsibility for controlling children's behavior on families and others outside the school. Urban schools are obsessed with classroom management at the expense of quality education. Compliance has become the greatest virtue.

Teachers and administrators, frustrated with the job of trying to educate students in an era when schools are under scrutiny for statistical improvements, sometimes resort to interventions that range from ineffective to ethically unsound. Such practices and policies as excessive focus on standardized test preparation, mandated lesson formats, a de-emphasis on the teaching of science and social studies, skyrocketing suspension rates, and the unofficial policy of "getting the disruptive kid out of the classroom at any cost" have not shown documented effectiveness. This trend is antithetical to the beliefs of most advocates for children and youth with E/BD who believe in preventive treatment and individualized and positive educational interventions for misbehavior (Scheuermann & Johns, 2002).

Why is it so difficult for even experienced educators to move beyond the emphasis on control and to choose more effective ways of dealing with inappropriate behaviors? One hypothesis is that it is difficult for adults to give up the mistaken perception that they can control students. When these coercive techniques fail, the common strategy is to increase the level of coercion. The second hypothesis is that adults, in an effort to not give up, often continue with ineffective strategies although they are aware that their strategies are not working. It is also possible they are not certain another approach will work, or perhaps they do not even know that other approaches exist.

Many school psychologists and educators stress the importance of breaking the punitive cycle in which the student acts out and the teacher punishes, the student increases his resistance and the teacher increases the punishment. They argue that what is needed instead of coercion is a great deal of creativity and patience, both of which tend to be in short supply. Specifically, they suggest a focus on internal control as an alternative to the coercive external control paradigm. Many students, including those labeled as E/BD, thrive in a noncoercive culture where the role of the teacher is that of a caring facilitator rather than a change agent. Proponents of the internal control paradigm believe that students, like all human beings, are internally motivated, choose their behaviors, and thus need to be involved in changing them.

The Power of School Culture

Children with emotional and behavioral problems are different from each other and have an assortment of strengths and challenges. Educators and mental health professionals need to find ways to match appropriate approaches that meet the individual needs of these children. Interventions in schools can make significant differences. When children are no longer in schools, interventions are less likely to be effective. Yet, appropriate strategies and interventions are significantly more effective if they are part of a school-wide culture that promotes emotional health.

There is a positive connection between emotional health in children and school functioning and performance (Arnold et al., 1999; Schonkoff &

Phillips, 2000). Investing in the emotional health of children is not only a compassionate, responsible approach to designing educational programs for children in elementary school, but it actually affects children's learning in positive ways. The emotionally healthy school can support general education students, students at risk, as well as students labeled E/BD. In fact, longitudinal studies have found that school connectedness, defined as a student's feeling part of and cared for at school, is linked with lower levels of substance use, violence, suicide attempts, pregnancy, and emotional distress (McNeely et al., 2002).

A study of the New Beginnings Project in Newark, New Jersey, by Kopacsi and Onsongo (2001) documented significantly higher scores in reading and math for children who had spent two years or more in the New Beginnings Project, a child-centered model with a developmental interactive approach to learning and an active commitment to the emotional health and social competency of the students. Children in this program also had significantly higher rates of school attendance than did a control group.

The U.S. Public Health Service Report (2000) explained that the concept of emotional well-being is complex and multifaceted. Essentially, someone who is emotionally healthy understands and adapts to change, copes with stress, has a positive self-image, has the ability to care for others, and can act independently to meet his or her own needs. Emotionally healthy people are able to adjust to and solve problems, and in doing so, help others as well as themselves to get satisfaction out of life. The report focused on the unmet mental health needs of U.S. children and concluded that school-based mental health programs are essential in order to provide for children's well-being and to prevent issues from becoming serious and debilitating later as children grow older. The authors urged elementary school principals to promote positive mental health in their students because as adults these students will need to be able to maintain a stable sense of positive self-worth in order to be productive and have skills to deal with social issues. To emphasize this point, the authors looked at profiles of middle school– and high school–age students who have used guns to shoot others and found patterns of peer isolation and alienation or unhappiness that have often been present since kindergarten.

Often, schools collaborate with school-based mental health clinics that provide mental health services to meet the emotional and psychological needs of students. Yet such external programs cannot succeed if school practices undermine the children's emotional health. These external programs cannot replace an in-house commitment to making the school environment a supportive one. In addition, a wholehearted commitment by school administrators is needed to help schools support the emotional well-being in students. Effective school principals set an interactive positive tone throughout the building, communicate to all staff the importance of emotional well-being as a precursor to learning, and create school-wide policies and practices that support the needs of children and staff.

Emotional health will not be a priority if principals lend only nominal support to this goal. Staff members are generally well attuned to a building administrator and often seek status and approval by mirroring their administrator's vision of school success.

The administrator who runs an emotionally responsive school often articulates a personal vision concerning learning and emotional well-being and uses the authority of the position to make sure that the actual experiences that children have at a school are commensurate with that vision. Because there is no one else with the authority to protect the emotional well-being of students, the extent to which the school functions as an emotionally safe environment depends almost entirely on the administrator's willingness to embrace the authority and enforce standards for how adults at school relate to children and relate to one another. A committed, compassionate principal with a clear vision that focuses on a healing environment is an essential component of success. The principal has the authority and the perspective needed to make the vision for an emotionally healthy school become a reality. This is especially true in schools serving E/BD students (Koplow, 2002).

This focus is especially important in secondary schools, where 40 percent to 60 percent of all students—urban, suburban, and rural—are chronically disengaged from school. Casner-Lotto and Barrington (2006) asked 400 human resource professionals what skills they believed would be necessary for success in the workplace in this century. Of the 20 skills respondents cited most, three of the five rated most important for high school graduates were professionalism/work ethic, teamwork/collaboration, and ethics/social responsibility. A focus on the emotional health of students is an integral part of the formula for achieving or developing these skills.

The Collaborative for Academic, Social, and Emotional Learning (CASEL) at the University of Illinois at Chicago acknowledged that educators are beginning to recognize the centrality of social and emotional competence yet need support in developing programs towards that goal. To help educators, the Collaborative delineated five competency areas for schools to consider: social awareness, self-awareness, self-management, relationship skills, and responsible decision making (CASEL; 2005).

Social awareness skills, such as recognizing what others are thinking and feeling, empathizing with people with differences, and showing compassion, form a basis for community building. The Collaborative concluded that students need a sense of community in order to perform well academically. Self-awareness includes skills in recognizing personal emotions and promoting or identifying personal strengths and positive qualities. Self-management involves managing emotions as well as establishing and working towards goals. Relationship skills and responsible decision making relate to the teamwork and collaboration skills and socially responsible behavior that employers rated as crucial. An example of a relationship skill is the ability to apologize, as taking responsibility for one's behavior—a key component of professionalism and workplace ethics.

School connectedness, or a feeling of belonging in a school, refers to an academic environment in which students believe that adults in the school care about their learning and about them as individuals. Three school characteristics stand out as helping adolescents feel connected to schools while simultaneously encouraging students to achievement academic success and social competence. The first is high academic standards coupled with strong teacher support. The second is an environment in which adult and student relationships are positive and respectful. The third is a physically and emotionally safe school environment. Students who feel connected to school are less likely to use substances, exhibit emotional distress, demonstrate violent and deviant behavior, experience suicidal thoughts or attempt suicide (Lonczak et al., 2002). In addition, when adolescents feel connected to schools, they are less likely to skip school or be involved in fighting, bullying, or vandalism. Students who experience school connectedness like school, feel that they belong, believe that teachers care about them and their learning, believe that education matters, have friends at school, and believe that discipline is fair.

Malley, Beck, and Adorno (2001) advocated for a paradigm for healthy schools that would address the needs of students and society:

> Modern day pedagogy has been based on an industrial paradigm, one that has concerned itself with the mass production of useful citizens to meet the needs of a growing economy. With the rapidly growing population, the breakdown of the nuclear family, and major changes in child rearing practices, a new "ecological" paradigm for education is needed to ensure a healthy, sustainable human community. The impersonality of large, bureaucratic schools; the emphasis on compliance, control, and orderliness; and the preoccupation with grades, competition, and individual success, have all created a social milieu in which all too many children feel alienated, isolated, and rejected. (p. 22)

Theory to Practice

Is it possible that an emotionally healthy school could play a therapeutic role in addressing problems and challenges of students with E/BD? And if so, is there a blueprint for such a school? The experiences of the two teenagers described in the beginning of the chapter provide a hopeful, if guarded, lesson.

Philip was a typical student in our high school that served almost 400 students labeled severely emotionally disturbed—failing academically, somewhat aggressive, defiant and impulsive, demonstrating inappropriate social skills, and frequently making poor choices. Yet, he seemed capable of choosing at least some of his behaviors. His actions, inappropriate as they may have been, were generally not hurtful to others. Does the IDEA definition of emotional disturbance really apply to Philip? Could he have been supported in a general education environment? Philip's troubles in school began at an early age and it may be argued that school experiences not only failed to address his problematic behaviors, they in fact have exacerbated his tendency toward non-compliance and hopelessness. I would submit that are many children like Philip unhappily sitting in special education classes.

Philip's counselor believed that, in fact, he had the capacity to make better choices, but he was hampered by the limited options that existed in his mind. To clarify this notion, he shared a conversation with Philip after he was suspended for fighting. Philip's justification for fighting focused on another student's disrespect of his mother. "He cursed my mother, so I hit him." When the counselor suggested that, perhaps, Philip could have chosen another way to deal with the disrespect, he protested vehemently: "No, he made me hit him. Ever since I was in kindergarten, everyone told me that if anybody curses your mother, you hit him. And you know what? Everyone I know would do the same." When the counselor asked him to consider, theoretically, what he could have done instead of hitting, Philip had a difficult time coming up with alternative answers.

Finally, let us reexamine what Philip actually said when we met him early on in the chapter. He complained that adults didn't care, that a reward system focusing on tangible rewards was demeaning, and that the school does not set up a clear plan for him to succeed. Those were insightful and perceptive comments coming from a long-term E/BD teenager. He was telling us that the school system had failed him and continued to do so.

Antonio, the second student, presented severe negative internalizing behaviors and represented only a small percentage of students in our school. His academic skills were only slightly below grade level, and his depressive behaviors were being addressed through counseling and medication. Would a general education environment have been sufficient to support Antonio? Again, the answer is not clear, but we may also conclude that schooling had not been particularly helpful.

As a new principal, I collaborated with teachers and clinicians of our school for many weeks before deciding on a school-wide philosophy that would be the driving framework for our pedagogical and therapeutic actions. Ultimately, we chose William Glasser's Choice Theory to frame our vision of an emotionally healthy school. Our version of an emotionally healthy school underlined several key principles of Choice Theory. In the following paragraphs I describe how we translated those ideas into practice and to describe how the school changes affected Philip and Antonio.

Central concepts of Glasser's Choice Theory are the notions that all human beings are internally motivated, choose their own behaviors, and thus need to be motivated in changing them. Conversely, external forces, often in the form of reward and punishment, cannot force behavioral responses. Glasser, elaborating on ideas proposed by Maslow, teaches that humans are born with certain genetic needs that are innate, not learned, and that are not limited to a specific race or culture.

These needs are (1) to survive, (2) to be loved and connected to others, (3) to achieve a sense of competence and personal power, (4) to act with a degree of freedom and autonomy, and (5) to experience joy and fun. All human behaviors can be understood as attempts to satisfy these genetic instructions. Misbehavior, according to Choice Theory, is a reaction to not having needs met. Glasser contends that schools have the power to serve as a conduit to help students meet their drives, and when they do, inappropriate behavior will diminish and student success will increase (Glasser, 1998).

How exactly did we translate Glasser's Choice Theory to the realities of relating, teaching, and learning? Let me briefly describe several specific examples.

We abolished surprise quizzes and all tests that would recognize only memorization. We introduced open-book tests, group tests, and projects in lieu of written exams. We created a publishing center where students who produced quality writing, as indicated by a rubric, would have their work bound and become part of the class library. We offered independent study options and other individualized learning opportunities. These changes communicated that school was more interested in student learning than in behavior control and punishments.

We offered positive consequences that focused on the students' basic needs. Based on conversations with our students, we selected consequences that would focus on more freedom and responsibility. For example, they told us that they were humiliated and resentful at having to be accompanied by a paraprofessional when going to the bathroom, a policy that had been in existence for years, with the original rationale no longer remembered. We made sure that the first positive consequence offered for reasonable behavior was to treat them with respect and dignity, in the basic form of going to the bathroom unescorted. Additional effective positive consequences included opportunities to earn a stipend for tutoring general education second graders after school, permission to go outside the school for lunch, and options for part time inclusion in a local general education high school.

Remember Philip's insistence that he had no option but to hit the student who cursed his mother? We realized that many more students had too few options in their behavioral repertoire and decided to develop a program to increase their choices. Several teachers and counselors offered their students the option of creating a video that would focus on confrontations among students that resulted in fights or other unproductive endings. This unusual creative learning opportunity was embraced by the youngsters. Students were asked to describe typical confrontations, create role-plays, and videotape themselves. They were asked to have three different endings to each confrontation. The project took several months, and involved aesthetic and role assignment discussions, learning to edit videos, and experiences to improve social skills such as negotiation and compromise. The completed video included a final section where the students analyzed the pros and cons of each approach to resolve a confrontation. The District Superintendent was so impressed with the project that she offered these students stipends to take the video "on the road" and present it to E/BD students in middle schools.

The school staff learned to change the language and tone used when we spoke to our students. Most notably, we eliminated threats and deterrents; we no longer used "do it because I said so or else" language. We attempted to avoid language that would cause a student or teacher to lose face because we came to understand that many confrontations were rooted in wounded pride or the potential for public humiliation. Administrators encouraged teachers to use phrases such as "Remember, when I ask you to behave appropriately, it is not me against you. It's really you against the rules."

One year after Choice Theory was implemented, suspensions decreased significantly, inclusion was expanding and the school culture was moving towards noncoercion. Students began to graduate in greater numbers and consequently changed the common perception that our school was a dead end. It became clear that a Glasser philosophy focus helped create an emotionally healthier school culture and it was also evident that the students behaved more like average teenagers rather than inmates.

One may ask to what extent our school's success was a validation of Choice Theory. Can we be certain that this theory was the critical reason for the positive changes? We can only reflect on our experience and suggest the need for comparative and longitudinal studies. It is possible that many of our students were not truly E/BD, and, in fact, this model may be less effective for more severely affected E/BD students. There is a need to conduct research of students with E/BD, especially those who demonstrate improvements in their academic and social development and assess how schools can play a therapeutic role. It is also critical to know how school experiences impact students' lives after they leave school. For example, can these young people maintain a job, avoid criminality, and form stable family relationships? This information is needed to provide feedback to schools and point out to educators where they have succeeded and what areas need further attention.

Unfortunately, most principals, teachers, and clinicians in both general and special education schools have not been prepared in their professions to create emotionally healthy schools. In a zeitgeist where standardized tests are a priority, pre-service and in-service training have typically not focused on school cultures and philosophies, or on the implementation of school-wide therapeutic models. Clearly, policy makers need to provide resources and funding to individual schools to create training modules that spell out the unique features of each school. These modules could help each school clarify its own philosophy and vision for meeting the needs of all its students. Collaboration between schools and local universities may focus on creating laboratory schools where different models and approaches are practiced and where staff development focuses on improving emotional outcomes for children with behavioral challenges.

Epilogue

Philip's counselor had mentioned to our assistant principal that Philip shared with him that he enjoyed cooking and had been cooking such items as scrambled eggs and casseroles at his foster home. His foster mom taught him some basic cooking skills, and he was good at it. Here was a perfect opportunity to infuse some of Glasser's basic needs of connectedness, self-worth, freedom, and fun.

Although we had a limited home economics program in the school, we offered Philip extra opportunities to work with the caring home economics teacher and to learn to cook new dishes. In return, he had to demonstrate a minimum level of academic effort and a decrease in his aggressive behavior. Our unofficial contract was purposefully vague, allowing for flexibility and second chances for this motivated youngster. We also videotaped Philip while he was cooking and asked him to describe what he was doing and why. This was a powerful way to let Philip see what others were seeing and to reflect on his actions. We also videotaped scenarios with him and the home economics teacher where we simulated role plays where the teacher was a boss and was making some reasonable, as well as unreasonable, demands. Our transition coordinator searched for a cooking program in general education vocational high schools in the area and found one that was willing to take Philip on a trial basis, part time. Behavior standards and responsibility were looming as potential problems, but with daily communication with the vocational school and visits by our transition coordinator, Philip successfully completed a six-month training program. He was placed in a work environment at a soup kitchen where he was paid a salary. He was a productive worker at the soup kitchen for two years, and then moved on to a better-paying cooking job.

Antonio's story, perhaps not as dramatic, still suggested solid gains. We offered him the opportunity to work in the computer lab with the computer teacher focusing on academic software. He accepted the offer without any show of affect. Since he had reasonable academic skills, he began working toward passing his exit exams and earning credits towards his high school diploma. In an effort to reduce his isolation, we asked him to tutor freshmen students using his strength—academic software. He was reluctant initially, but eventually agreed and was a helpful tutor. His lethargy gradually dissipated; he was less resistant to meet with his counselor; he kept his appointments with out-of-school counseling and took his medication as prescribed—all small but steady victories on a long trail toward healing.

References

American Psychiatric Association. (2000). *Diagnostic and statistical manual of mental disorders* (4th ed., text rev.). Washington, DC: Author.

Arnold, D.H., Ortiz, C., Curry, J.C., Stowe, R.M., Goldstein, N.E., Fisher, P.H., et al. (1999). Promoting academic success and preventing disruptive behavior through community partnership. *Journal of Community Psychology, 5,* 589–598.

Blum, R. W. (2005). A case for school connectedness. *Educational Leadership 62*(7), 16–20.

Carson, R., Sillington, P., & Frank, A. (1995). Young adulthood for individuals with behavior disorders: What does it hold? *Behavioral Disorders, 20,* 127–135.

Casner-Lotto, J., & Barrington, L. (2006). *Are they really ready to work? Employers' perspectives on the basic knowledge and applied skills of new entrants to the 21st century U.S. workplace: Partnership for 21st century skills.* Retrieved April 28, 2007, from www.21stcenturyskills.org/documents/FINAL_REPORT_PDF9-29-06. pdf.

Collaborative for Academic, Social, and Emotional Learning. (2005). *Social emotional learning competencies.* Chicago: Author.

Committee for Children. (1995). School climate and social and emotional learning. Retrieved June 28, 2010, from http://www.cfchildren.org/ss-e-newsletter-april-2010/school-climate-and-sel/.

Conroy, M. A., & Brown, W. H. (2004). Early identification, prevention, and early interventions with young children at risk for emotional and behavioral disorders: Issues, trends, and a call for action. *Behavioral Disorders 29,* 224–236.

Council for Children with Behavioral Disorders. (1990). Position paper on provision of service to children with conduct disorders. *Behavioral Disorders, 15,* 180–189.

DiPaola, M. F., & Moran, M. (2003). The principalship at a crossroads: A study of the conditions and concerns of principals. *NASSP Bulletin, 87*(634), 43–65.

DiPaola, M. F., Tschannen-Moran, M., & Walther-Thomas, C. (2004). School principals and special education: Creating the context for academic success. *Focus on Exceptional Children, 37*(1), 3–10.

Donovan, S., & Cross, C. (Eds.). (2002). *Minority students in special and gifted education.* Washington, DC: National Academy Press.

Education for All Handicapped Children Act of 1975, 20 U.S.C. § 1400–1485.

Forness, S. R., & Kavale, K. (2000). Emotional or behavioral disorders: Background and current status of the E/BD terminology and definition. *Behavioral Disorders, 25,* 264–269.

Gacano, C. B., & Hughes, T. L. (2004). Differentiating emotional disturbance from social maladjustment: Assessing psychopathology in aggressive youth. *Psychology in the Schools, 41,* 849–860.

Glasser, W. (1998). *Choice theory: A new psychology of personal freedom.* New York: HarperCollins.

Gravois, T. A., & Rosenfield, S. A. (2002). A multi-dimensional framework for evaluation of instructional consultation teams. *Journal of Applied School Psychology, 19,* 5–29.

Gravois, T. A., & Rosenfield, S. A. (2006). Impact of instructional consultation teams on the disproportionate referral and placement of minority students in special education. *Remedial and Special Education 27*(1), 42–52.

Gresham, F. M. (2005). Response to intervention: An alternative means of identifying students as emotionally disturbed. *Education & Treatment of Children 28,* 328–344.

Heward, W. L. (2009). *Exceptional children.* Upper Saddle River, NJ: Pearson.

Kauffman, J. M. (2001). *Characteristics of emotional and behavioral disorders.* Upper Saddle River, NJ: Prentice Hall.

Klem, A. M., & Connell, J. P. (2004). Relationship matters: Linking teacher support to student engagement and achievement. *Journal of School Health, 74*(7), 262–273.

Kopacsi, R., & Onsongo, E. (2001). *1999–2000 evaluation update: New Beginnings student outcomes—Cohort and non-cohort comparison.* Newark, NJ: Newark Public Schools, Office of Planning, Evaluation, and Testing.

Koplow, L. (2002). *Creating schools that heal.* New York: Teachers College Press.

Kortering, L.J., Braziel, P.M., & Tomkins, J.R. (2002). The challenge of school completion among youth with behavioral disorders: Another side of the story. *Behavioral Disorders, 27,* 142–145.

Lahey, B.B., Waldman, I.D., & McBurnett, K. (1999). The development of antisocial behavior: An integrative causal model. *Journal of Child Psychology and Psychiatry, 40,* 669–682.

Lonczak, H.S., Abbott, R.D., Hawkins, J.D., Kosterman, R., & Catalano, R. (2002). The effects of the Seattle Social Development Project: Behavior, pregnancy, birth, and sexually transmitted disease outcomes by age 21. *Archives of Pediatric Adolescent Health, 156,* 438–447.

Losen, D., & Orfield, G. (2002). *Racial inequity in special education.* Cambridge, MA: Harvard Publishing Group.

Malley, J., Beck, M., & Adorno, D. (2001). Building an economy for non-violence in schools. *International Journal of Reality Therapy, 21,* 22–26.

Mason, D.A. & Frick, P.J. (1994). The heritability of antisocial behavior: A meta-analysis of twin and adoption studies. *Journal of Psychopathology and Behavioral Assessment. 16,* 301–323.

McNeely, C., Nonnemaker, J., & Blum, R. (2002). Promoting school connectedness: evidence from the national longitudinal study of adolescent health. *Journal of School Health, 72*(4), 138–146.

Merrell, K.W. (2003). *Behavioral, social, and emotional assessment of children and adolescents.* Mahwah, NJ: Erlbaum.

National Association of School Psychologists. (2002). *Position statement on students with emotional and behavioral disorders.* Bethesda, MD: Author.

National Association of School Psychologists. (2007). *Guidelines for assessment of students for emotional and/or behavioral disorders.* Washington, DC: Author.

Olympia, D., Farley, M., Christiansen, E., Pettersson, W. J., & Clark, E. (2004). Social maladjustment and students with behavioral and emotional disorders: Revisiting basic assumptions and assessment issues. *Psychology in the Schools, 41,* 835–846.

Ormrod, J.E. (2003). *Educational psychology: Developing learners.* New York: Prentice Hall.

Osher, D., Woodruff, D., & Sims, A. (2002). Schools make a difference: The overrepresentation of African American youth in special education and the juvenile justice system. In D. Losen & G. Orfield (Eds.), *Racial Inequality in special education* (pp. 3–21). Cambridge, MA: Harvard Publishing Group.

Patton, M.Q. (1990). *Qualitative educational research methods.* Beverly Hills, CA: Sage.

Richardson, B., & Wubbolding, R. (2001). Five interrelating challenges for using reality therapy with challenging students. *Journal of reality therapy, 20,* 35–39.

Scheuermann, B., & Johns, B. (2002). Advocacy for students with emotional or behavioral disorders in the 21st century. *Behavioral Disorders, 28,* 57–68.

Schonkoff, J.P., & Phillips, D.A. (2000). *From neurons to neighborhoods.* Washington, DC: National Academy Press.

Shaw, D.S., Bell, R.Q., & Gilliom, M. (2000). A truly early starter model of antisocial behavior revisited. *Clinical Child and Family Psychology Review, 3*(3), Sept. 2000, pp. 155–172.

Sugai, G., Horner, R. H., & Gresham, F. M. (2002). Behaviorally effective school environments. In M. R. Shinn, H. M. Walker, & G. Stoner (Eds.), *Interventions for academic and behavior problems II: Preventive and remedial approaches* (pp. 315–350). Bethesda, MD: National Association of School Psychologists.

Trout, A. L., Nordness, P. D., Pierce, C. D., & Epstein, M. H. (2003). Research on the academic status of children with emotional and behavioral disorders: A review of the literature from 1961 to 2000. *Journal of Emotional and Behavioral Disorders, 11,* 198–210.

Turnbull, R., Turnbull, A., Shank, M., & Smith, M. J. (2004). *Exceptional lives: Special education in today's schools.* Upper Saddle, NJ: Prentice Hall.

U.S. Department of Education. (1997). *Nineteenth annual report to Congress on the implementation of the Individuals with Disabilities Education Act.* Washington, DC: Author.

U.S. Department of Education. (2002a). No Child Left Behind Act (NCLB), Public Law No. 107–110, 115 Stat.§1425. Retrieved November 12, 2006, from http://www.ed.gov/nclb/landing.jhtml.

U.S. Department of Education. (2002b). *Twenty-fourth annual report to Congress on the implementation of the Individuals with Disabilities Education Act.* Washington, DC: Author.

U.S. Department of Education. (2004). *Twenty-sixth annual report to Congress on the implementation of the Individuals with Disabilities Education Act.* Washington, DC: Author.

U.S. Department of Education, National Center for Education Statistics. (2007). *Dropout rates in the United States 2005.* Washington, DC: Author.

U.S. Department of Education, Office of Special Education Programs (2009). Positive behavioral interventions and supports: Effective schoolwide interventions. Retrieved October 3, 2010 from www.pbis.org.

U.S. Department of Health and Human Services. (1999). *Mental health: A report of the surgeon general.* Washington, DC: Author.

U.S. Public Health Service. (2000). *Report of the surgeon general's conference on children's mental health: A national action agenda.* Washington, DC: Author.

Wald, J. & Losen, D. (2003). Defining and redirecting a school-t-prison pipeline. *New Directions for Youth Development, 2003*(99), 9–15.

Wubbolding, R. (2000). *Reality therapy for the 21st century.* Philadelphia: Taylor & Francis.

CHAPTER 8

When Schools Fail: Alternative Therapeutic and Educational Settings for Youths with Severe Emotional and Behavioral Challenges

Jennifer Foster

Maria is a 10-year-old girl whose family has a history of domestic violence and strife; child protective services have been involved with the family on numerous occasions. At the age of seven, Maria and her siblings were removed from her biological mother's custody as a result of substantiated educational, mental, and medical neglect. Allegations of sexual abuse were noted at the time but were not confirmed. Upon removal form her mother's care, Maria and her siblings were initially placed with their father. However, all three children were removed from their father's custody six months later due to further neglect and were placed into three separate foster-care homes.

Maria lived with a foster family, where she attended elementary school and participated in a general education program with academic supports in basic-skills reading, language arts, and math. As part of her placement in foster care, child protective services arranged for both psychological and psychiatric evaluations. Results from these evaluations indicated that Maria had an adjustment disorder with anxiety, mild intellectual disability, and a learning disorder. In addition, it was reported that Maria was struggling to cope with her removal from her home, disruption of the family, and exposure to mental/emotional and physical neglect. Approximately six months later, an initial school-based evaluation found Maria eligible for special education and related services. Assessment results from the evaluation indicated that Maria's overall cognitive abilities were in the low-average range, with academic abilities in the average range in reading, math, and written language. A speech and language evaluation indicated delays in language development; behavior and personality assessment results suggested higher than average levels of hyperactivity, oppositional and/or dysfunctional behaviors, and feelings of anxiety coupled with dependency needs. Maria was placed in a second grade inclusion classroom, where she received in-class support. As part of recommended services, Maria also received weekly speech therapy and counseling services for approximately 30 minutes each.

During the summer, Maria and her siblings were returned to the custody of their biological father, and Maria was enrolled in a new elementary school. However, prior to beginning school, Maria was placed at a therapeutic partial-day treatment facility from September to January. While at the day treatment facility, Maria received a diagnosis of oppositional defiant disorder, mood disorder, and learning disorder–not otherwise specified (NOS). The program's progress report indicated that Maria had low frustration tolerance and as a result would often shut-down, that she functioned better in a small setting with clear boundaries as well as consistent consequences and rewards, and that she would require a large amount of one-to-one assistance. While progress was reported by the program, concern that Maria would be vulnerable to regression during the transition period back to school was noted. Treatment recommendations for her discharge included a small class, frequent breaks, and a one-to-one personal aid. Upon her return, Maria was classified as multiply disabled and placed in the second grade in a self-contained classroom. At the end of the school year, it was decided that due to her academic progress, Maria would be enrolled in a third grade inclusion classroom the following year.

I crossed paths with Maria in the early months of third grade, in which Maria would endure another tumultuous year. Three months into the school year, Maria had been experienced a gradual decline in her progress and developed numerous emotional and behavioral problems, both at home and in school. I was called in for a behavioral consultation and to assist in developing a behavior intervention plan. In school, Maria's teachers reported challenging behaviors in addition to episodes of withdrawal. Reports from home included behaviors such as extreme aggression, uncontrollable outbursts, and severe mood swings on a daily basis. Maria also began presenting with early stages of self-injurious behaviors. She had been observed picking scabs on her arms excessively and pulling off the skin surrounding her finger nails. On one occasion, her stepmother reported that Maria intentionally cut her eyelashes. Shortly thereafter, Maria locked herself in the bathroom after an argument with her father and proceeded to scratch both sides of her face to the point of breaking the blood vessels in her cheeks. When asked about hurting herself in all these instances, Maria stated, "It doesn't hurt, I don't feel anything." In addition to the turmoil that Maria was experiencing, Maria's father and stepmother also reported having difficulty managing the behavior of Maria's two older, biological siblings. According to Maria's stepmother, a mobile crisis unit has been called to the house on multiple occasions and provides 10 hours a week of counseling to Maria and her brothers. Maria's parents were frustrated and tired of living in a state of chaos. They contacted the child study team and requested that Maria be placed in a residential treatment facility.

Over the last decade, the number of children and adolescents receiving mental-health related diagnoses and services has increased steadily from year to year. In the year 2000, there were more than 130,000 short-term (30 days or less) psychiatric hospitalizations for children and adolescents under the age of 15 where a mental disorder was listed as the primary diagnosis (Best, Hauser, Gralinski-Bakker, Allen, & Crowell, 2004). According to the U.S. Surgeon General, it is estimated that one in five children suffer from a mental illness that is both identifiable and treatable (U.S. Department of Health and Human Services, 1999). In the annual report to Congress by the U.S. Department of Education (2002), in the 2000–2001 year, there were more than 470,000 children and adolescents receiving special education and related services under the classification of emotional disturbance. Across the United States, school districts are reporting annual increases in the number of students diagnosed with emotional and behavioral disorders. According to the U.S. Department of Health and Human Services (1999), in the course of one year, 20 percent of students exhibit mental health symptoms, and 75 percent to 80 percent of these students do not receive appropriate services. These incidence rates are important when one considers the limited availability and capacity of school-based mental health services currently available to students. For a student like Maria, the weekly counseling provided by the school district is simply not enough to make a positive impact in her daily functioning.

Students classified as emotionally disturbed, or identified as at-risk for developing an emotional or behavioral disorder, experience impairments in psychosocial adjustment and school performance that may warrant services through school-district special education departments or through community mental health agencies. However, unless students have been formally classified via special education evaluations, they are not usually seen as eligible for therapeutic services in the school setting (Greenberg, Domitrovich, & Bumbarger, 2000). In relation to educational outcomes, students with severe emotional and/or behavioral problems have the lowest grades and the highest rate of restrictive and out-of-district placements. As a result, these students have the highest drop-out rates compared to both general education and special education students (Eber, Nelson, & Miles, 1997). While emotional and behavioral disturbance only accounts for a relatively small number of children attending school nationwide, it is by far the most costly disorder for school districts and the most disruptive to the educational environment (Eber, Sugai, Smith, & Scott, 2002). A study by Walter, Gouze, and Lim (2006) found that 50 percent of the teachers surveyed felt that disruptive behaviors were the greatest mental health problem within their schools, with a lack of training cited most frequently as a barrier to preventing these problems. The researchers also found that

teachers who indicated they had taught students with mental health related issues also reported that they had minimal mental health training,
did not benefit from consultation with mental health professionals, and
were less confident in their ability to manage mental health problems in
their classrooms (Walter et al., 2006). For Maria, every time she experiences
difficulty in the classroom, she is physically removed from the room and
placed temporarily in an alternative setting; consequently, she often loses
instruction time and opportunity for developing the academic skills necessary for her to meet grade-level requirements.

While, the school setting is often considered an appropriate context to
provide mental health services due to the availability of service providers
such as school psychologists, social workers, crisis staff, counselors, and
intervention specialists (Dryfoos, 1994; Knoff & Batcsche, 1990), these services are largely inadequate for students who experience severe emotional
and behavioral difficulties. Students like Maria need structured learning
environments, independent learning strategies, opportunities for peer-
mediated learning, and teachers with sufficient background in behavior
management skills to assist students in decreasing their disruptive behaviors (Wagner et al., 2006). Routinely, schools have adopted a "wait to fail"
approach whereby warning signs are largely ignored until emotional and
behavioral problems reach a level of disruption that can no longer go un-
attended. Subsequently, students identified with severe emotional and
behavioral disorders may participate in outpatient services, attend day-
treatment programs that are deemed better suited to manage their mental illness, or placed out-of-district in short-term psychiatric hospitals,. In
some cases, when students make sufficient progress and are considered
stable, they are then discharged and returned to school.

Unfortunately, many schools do not have adequate reintegration systems in place that provide different levels of support for these students
(Easterson-Rock, Rosenberg, & Carran, 1994). The result is that students
with severe emotional challenges spend a significant amount of time reac-
climating to the school environment and in the process become frustrated
due to the lack of support. Many of these students begin a downward spi-
ral, and much of what was learned prior to returning to school is lost. Within
months of their return, behavioral and emotional problems can increase
to a point that is perceived as uncontrollable, and the student will most
likely be returned to the out-of-district placement. This circular pattern,
commonly referred to as "the revolving door syndrome," places additional
burdens and strains on the child, family, and school. This situation is all too
common and will generally cost school districts considerably over time in
funding, staff hours, and staff morale. Maria, her parents, and the school
district are currently caught in this cycle. Students like Maria typically need
a longer-term placement in a program with the proper level of support and
family involvement in order for them to make significant progress. When
school districts feel pressured by federal laws to keep students in least restrictive environments, there is a tendency to overlook the needs of the

student in the interest of maintaining compliance. Thus, short-term placements in regular school offer a quick fix to the compliance concern, but long-term consequences may be dire.

Schools, with the support of parents, typically adopt multiple programs that focus on preventing disruptive behaviors, school violence, drug use, sexual behavior, or student drop out (Payton et al., 2000). With the best intentions, many of these programs have been hastily selected and poorly implemented in schools across the nation, creating a wave of staff disinterest and cementing disbelief that any program will effectively address students' needs (Payton et al., 2000). Even though most troubled students' exhibit early signs that they are in need of support, in many cases, due to inadequate coordination of services, lack of staff training, and limited resources, these needs go largely ignored. In addition, the degree to which intervention services are deemed successful largely depends on whether or not the programs were implemented as outlined by individuals other than the consultant (Noell & Witt, 1996; Sheridan & Gutkin, 2000). Researchers often claim that implementation within the school setting continues to be problematic because empirically based procedures for accurate implementation have not been clearly delineated (Noell & Witt, 1996; Sheridan & Gutkin, 2000).

Yet, the realities of school life are such that implementing programs designed elsewhere, even when they are well described, may not be suitable for the local context; moreover, burdened practitioners may find it difficult to adhere to stated guidelines. Other challenges related to successful intervention services include the large number of students being referred annually, poor follow-up at the implementation and evaluation stages, poor treatment fidelity, lack of staff training in managing emotional and behavioral difficulties in the school setting, and time limitations. When these challenges accumulate over time, service providers at the school level become overwhelmed and, as a result, overlook many students in need of services.

In many urban school districts, it is not uncommon that the first intervention services a student receives is the direct result of a major event that triggered the involvement of administrators and school personnel. Even at this stage, an initial event is generally not seen as serious until a blatant pattern of misconduct is apparent. Unfortunately, in most cases, once this pattern forms, it is too late. What is even more crucial to understand is that this group of students only represents those who externalize their emotions and behaviors. Students with more internalized problems like anxiety and depression are virtually invisible and are typically not attended to until there is an emotional breakdown or the threat of suicide.

While students like Maria continue to struggle to function from day to day in the classroom setting, some students may have access to in-district alternative programs or vocational schools that have been developed for students with more severe emotional and behavioral difficulties. However, most public school districts lack adequate resources, even in affluent jurisdictions. Many programs and resources may be listed as available, but they are typically poorly staffed; lack professional guidance; have inadequate structure, supports, and resources; and tend to become a dumping ground for behavioral problems. So what options do parents have beyond the school setting? The following is a discussion of a community-based program followed by three different types of out-of-district programs that may provide parents with alternatives to the generic school-based interventions that historically have not had a significant impact on students with severe emotional and behavioral difficulties.

Community-Based Wraparound Services

In the mid 1980s, the concept known as *a system of care* was developed as a way to provide community-based services that integrated multiple professionals and agencies in a collaborative relationship to serve families in need. This was envisioned as a collaborative, team-based approach that would focus on providing children and families in need with service planning and support needed to meet their goals. The core assumption of a system of care is that if the needs of a child and their family are met, it is likely that they will have a good or at least improved life (Eber, Sugai, et al., 2002). Out of the system of care philosophy emerged the approach known as wraparound, which gained significant attention in the mid 1990s as a way to carry out a system of care. This evidence-based practice was initially seen by researchers as a way to provide comprehensive services to children suffering from severe mental illness. Eber, Sugai et al. described wraparound as a planning process that incorporates a family-centered and strength-based philosophy of care to guide service planning for students with emotional and behavioral disorders and their families. At the core of wraparound, the team consists of the child and family who are then joined by a wraparound facilitator, mental health professionals, educators, representatives from community agencies, other family members and friends. In general, team members are determined by the family through the assistance of the wraparound facilitator and once in place, the team meets regularly to design, implement, and monitor the individualized service plans.

In 1998, a meeting was held at Duke University, where 10 essential features of the wraparound model were identified by a panel of professionals, wraparound trainers, parents, and researchers in an effort to provide a foundation that would increase fidelity and assist in organizing a community's response to children and youth with severe mental health problems (Quinn & Lee, 2007). According to Quinn and Lee, each of these components needs to be in place during the four phases of the wraparound process, otherwise the child and family outcomes may be compromised. These elements include the following:

1. *Voice and Choice:* Youth and family are full and active partners throughout the entire wraparound process.
2. *Youth and Family Team:* Wraparound process is a team approach.

3. *Community-Based Services:* Must be based in the community.
4. *Cultural Competence:* The process must be culturally competent and build on the values, preferences, and strengths of the family.
5. *Individualized and Strength-Based Services:* Services and supports must be individualized and built on the strengths and needs of children and families across life domains.
6. *Natural Supports:* A balance of formal and informal community and family supports.
7. *Continuation of Care:* Must be an unconditional commitment to serve children and their families.
8. *Collaboration:* Plans and services are based on interagency, community-based collaborative process.
9. *Flexible Resources:* Child and family teams have flexible approaches and adequate and flexible funding.
10. *Outcome-Based Services:* Outcomes must be determined and measured for the program, the individual, and the child and family.

Four Phases of Wraparound

Phase One: Engagement and Treatment Preparation (One to Two Weeks)

There are five steps within this initial phase: (1) orient the family, (2) plan crisis response, (3) identify long-term goals, (4) assemble a team, and (5) schedule the initial planning meeting. Prior to the first step, the wraparound facilitator contacts the family and presents the opportunity to participate in the wraparound process. Emphasis during this meeting is given to family voice and choice, sensitivity to culture, and building trust. The process and procedures of wraparound are discussed as well as who will participate and what will be expected from team members. In addition, alternatives to wraparound will be discussed so that families can make informed choices. Once the family agrees to participate, a crisis plan is created to address any immediate crisis concerns. Since the duration of this first phase is between one to two weeks, the purpose of this plan is to alleviate concerns and issues related to safety and basic needs. Next, the facilitator gathers information related to the families strengths, needs, cultural context, and long-term goals; team members are identified; barriers to participation such as transportation and childcare are addressed; and an agenda is set for the initial planning meeting. At this point, the facilitator contacts the individuals who will participate as part of the family team and explains the wraparound process, their roles and responsibilities, asks each member to identify the individual strengths that they bring to the team, and solicits the team member's opinions of the family's strengths and needs. Afterwards, the facilitator generates a report that serves as a starting point for the intervention. In the last step of this phase, the initial planning meeting is scheduled, the initial report is distributed to all team members, and barriers to team member participation are eliminated.

Phase Two: Initial Plan Development (1 to 2 Meetings)

During this phase, a step-by-step planning process begins, in which the child and family's strengths and needs are considered in an ecological context and across all life domains. There are three tasks within this phase: (1) develop the wraparound plan, (2) develop a crisis plan, and (3) plan logistics and information dissemination that focus on intervention priorities and family voice and choice. In the initial meeting of this phase, ground rules are set to guide the operation of the team that include meeting procedures, issues related to confidentiality and the law, and steps to problem solving and conflict resolution. In addition, strengths of the family are agreed upon and a long-term goal to guide the team is determined. The next area identifies and prioritizes the family's needs and determines the desired outcomes and progress indicators for each need. Both formal (evidence based) and informal strategies are then developed to assist the family in meeting their long-term goals. These decisions are primarily based on family fit and the probability that the family team will carry out a particular strategy. Once these strategies are finalized, roles and responsibilities are delineated, with timelines for completion clearly stated.

The next step in this phase is utilized to develop a crisis plan that clearly outlines both prevention and intervention plans to ensure the child and family's safety in the home, school, and community environments. Prevention plans, for example, may consist of behavior modification strategies that are utilized across domains. Crisis intervention plans need to be in place 24 hours a day, seven days a week to deescalate a crisis situation. In some cases, training in this area may be necessary for some team members. All steps of the plan should be indicated and everyone's responsibilities clearly defined. The final step in this phase is to decide on plan logistics (i.e., dates and locations of future meetings, bringing necessary materials to the meetings, between-meeting responsibilities, etc.) and how to disseminate information (i.e., telephone calls, emails) to all team members.

Phase Three: Implementation (Varies)

This phase consists of carrying out the wraparound plan and focuses on four main tasks: (1) implement the plan, (2) monitor and update the plan as needed, (3) build cohesiveness and trust, and (4) organize logistics. Throughout this phase, the facilitator is responsible for following up with team members and documenting plan progress related to each member's responsibilities. The main responsibilities of the team members are to implement the wraparound plan as it was designed. During this phase, emphasis is on tracking individual and group progress, monitoring the fit between needs and supports, and ensuring treatment fidelity for each support that is being utilized. In addition, progress toward desired outcomes will be tracked using the measures outlined in phase two. During this time, the plan is continually modified and adjusted according to the changing needs of the family. Lines of communication must remain open to foster honest dialogue between team members and encourage celebrations of accomplishments. This phase requires full participation by all team members and diligent and reliable documentation and record keeping of process notes, steps taken, team-member involvement, service use, expenditures, and outcome data. The duration of this phase will vary depending on the needs of the child and family.

Phase Four: Transition (Ongoing)

As goals are achieved, there is a time when supports will begin to be gradually withdrawn and the family will be encouraged to operate independently of the wraparound team. Ultimately, transition should occur throughout the wraparound process as goals are met. The main tasks of this phase are (1) to plan cessation of services, (2) to plan and implement closure services, and (3) to remain available to the family. In general, the needs of the family and their progress will largely determine when the transition phase will begin. Supports should be withdrawn while continuing to monitor family outcomes, and all plans should be updated to reflect the family's current status. In addition, potential problems should be identified and addressed and contact should be facilitated with new sources of support. A distinct end point should be identified, reflect the family's cultural views, and celebrate their success. Finally, the team should remain available to the family, check their progress from time to time, and refer them to resources within the community should a new problem arise.

Overall, researchers have reported that wraparound is useful in building positive relationships and supports among students with emotional and behavioral disorders, families, teachers, and other caregivers because it goes beyond the school setting to connect the different contexts of the child's life. Wraparound has also led to improvements in child behavior, increased academic achievement, and social and emotional gains. While the majority of research studies report positive outcomes—including improvement in parent functioning, increased participation in less-restrictive settings, and reduced spending—most of the research conducted on wraparound programs has lacked rigorous experimental designs, and there are few research studies that have done comparative analysis between different wraparound programs (Potter & Mulkern, 2004). Although it is clear that more sound empirical studies need to be conducted to continue exploring the effects of wraparound programs, the initial results are promising. To date, many communities throughout the United States have implemented programs based on this wraparound model. This option offers parents who are struggling with the challenges their child presents with concurrent and comprehensive access to multiple services rather than attempting to access these agencies individually. Further, wraparound programs are generally grant funded and typically operate at no cost to the family, making this a viable option for low-income youth and their families.

Alternative Programs

Parents of youth with severe emotional and behavior difficulties often seek alternative programs outside their school districts that provide highly structured therapeutic and educational programs; the wraparound option is not widely available. While examining options, parents often become overwhelmed with the daunting task of choosing the setting that will best fit their child's needs. One point of confusion begins with understanding the different types of programs available. For example, what differences exist between a therapeutic boarding school and a residential center? In addition, these programs may operate as separate or combined programs (i.e., residential treatment center only or wilderness therapy camp only, or a residential treatment center with a wilderness therapy program). Another area of major concern with these types of programs, particularly for the residential and wilderness therapy programs, are allegations of child abuse and the reported deaths of adolescents in such boot camps and other residential settings. For parents desperate to find treatments that restore balance and harmony in the lives of their children as well as their families, these decisions pose significant dilemmas and add another layer of frustration to a situation that already feels impossible. The following section will attempt to (1) address issues related to the differences among these programs, (2) report of their effectiveness and highlight research outcomes, and (3) provide information related to issues of abuse and the industry's progress toward regulation.

Residential Treatment Centers and Therapeutic Boarding Schools

As the needs of students at greatest risk for the worst outcomes continue to expand, school administrators and personnel are becoming painfully aware that the support services for these students in the school setting are severely inadequate. As a result, residential treatment centers and therapeutic boarding schools have become alternatives that provide parents with long-term treatment options beyond the school setting. The terms *residential center* and *therapeutic school* are often used interchangeably when discussing out-of-district placements for students with severe emotional and behavioral difficulties. While there are many similarities between the two programs, there are some subtle differences that classify them as two separate treatment options.

Residential treatment centers are programs in which students are re-moved from their home environments and provided specialized assistance, requiring clinical-level support in order to facilitate growth in the areas of emotional and behavioral development. Residential environments are gen-erally structured, highly supervised, and therapeutic in nature. Youth in residential facilities struggle with a variety of issues including substance use/abuse, eating disorders, anxiety, depression, oppositional and aggres-sive behaviors, dipolar disorder, and other more severe mental illnesses. While some residential programs are developed to focus on only one of the aforementioned areas, many act as transitional programs for youth exit-ing the school system into the real world; thus addressing several areas si-multaneously. Most residential centers offer intense programs that include individual and group therapy, medication management, structured phys-ical activities, social skills training, educational support, and vocational training for older students. In addition, quality programs also have a fam-ily component that is central to the child's recovery. Residential treatment centers may operate as part of clinical/psychiatric hospital settings as well as home-based environments such as a youth home for troubled boys or girls.

Therapeutic boarding schools are somewhat similar in that they pro-vide structured environments that focus on social, emotional, and be-havioral growth and well as the development of a positive sense of self, improvement in decision-making skills, problem solving, and interper-sonal skills. Unlike residential centers, therapeutic schools provide a strong educational program to assist students with a history of poor academic per-formance, a lack of motivation, and who experience self-esteem issues. As such, therapeutic schools work to change students' negative behaviors while promoting a positive self-perception. Therapeutic schools focus en-ergies on nurturing students through a supportive curriculum that in-cludes individual and group counseling within the academic environment. All students must adhere to school policy and procedures and contribute in positive ways to campus life. For example, at Montana Academy lo-cated in northwestern Montana's Lost Prairie Valley, students may spend time working the land or caring for the animals. Therapeutic schools differ most from residential centers in that the emphasis is more academically driven, the intensity of student difficulties is less severe, and, what is most important, access has typically been limited to students from upper middle-class families who can afford the out-of-pocket costs for tuition. Although loan programs are available, making this an option for middle-class fam-ilies, therapeutic school are for the most part out of financial reach for low-income families. Costs for both placements can be upward of $60,000, depending on a student's treatment plan and length of stay. Unfortunately, school districts and insurance companies typically do not pay for ther-apeutic schools, whereas the cost for residential treatment centers have often been paid for in total by school districts or split between the school,

Medicaid, or the parent's insurance company. In some cases, districts will fund such placements following successful litigation by parents' lawyers.

Although the costs are high for both placement types, treatment outcomes have shown promise. Support for residential centers and private therapeutic schools has grown significantly and has documented the sustainability of outcomes one year posttreatment. Behrens (2006, as cited in Behrens, Santa, and Gass, 2010) conducted treatment and outcome research at nine programs owned/operated by the Aspen Education Group, a company that has developed several therapeutic schools nationwide and in the United Kingdom, where close to a thousand students and their parents reported on their experience in the program. Results, using standardized assessment measures, indicated positive effects for the treatment of depression, anxiety, attention problems, aggression, and oppositional behaviors. Further, increases in overall functioning, higher academic achievement, and the development of improved parent relationships during treatment have also been indicated. These positive effects were maintained 12 months after treatment; by the end of one year, the majority of students had moved from the clinical range to the normal range of behavioral and psychological functioning. Several other studies have been carried out and report similar gains for both residential centers and therapeutic schools (Hong, 2010; Hong & McKinnon, 2009; Hong & Santa, 2007; Leichtman, Leichtman, Barber, & Neese, 2001; Lewis, 2005; Wright & Zakriski, 2003; Zakriski, Wright, & Parad, 2006; Zakriski, Wright & Underwood, 2005).

Wilderness Therapy Programs

Another alternative treatment option for students with severe emotional and behavioral difficulties falls under the umbrella of wilderness experience programs (WEPs). WEPs have been defined as "organizations that conduct outdoor programs in the wilderness or comparable lands for purposes of personal growth, therapy, rehabilitation, education or leadership/organizational development" (Russell, 2001). The beginnings of WEPs date back to 1901, when doctors at the New York Asylum for the Insane relocated its psychiatric patients with tuberculosis to tents set up on hospital grounds as a means to reduce the spread of the disease (Roe, 2009). When patients began to improve, doctors attributed the increase in health to the personalized care they received and exposure to the outdoors. The more intentional use of the outdoors as a therapeutic avenue can be attributed to the creation of Outward Bound, in Wales, in 1941, by Kurt Hahn and Lawrence Holt. The organization was founded to promote what is commonly referred to today as *wilderness therapy* (Roe, 2009). These early programs focused on the character development of sailors in the areas of personal responsibility, kindness, justice, honesty, self-reliance, and independence as well as promoting academic achievement. Outward Bound arrived in the United States in the early 1960s, with the Colorado Outward Bound School, and began to flourish with new charters opening across the nation, such as Outward Bound Discovery, serving adolescents at risk for academic failure, early dropout, and a trajectory toward incarceration, and Outward Bound Urban Centers to service inner-city youth (Roe, 2009). The common setting in which all these programs operate is the wilderness.

As a type of WEP, wilderness therapy involves complete immersion in the wilderness, group living with peers, individual and group therapy sessions, and educational and therapeutic curricula including back-country traveling and wilderness-living skills (Russell & Phillips-Miller, 2002). All of these elements are combined to identify and tackle behavior difficulties while developing personal and social responsibility and emotional growth. These programs have become an alternative to the more traditional offerings of outpatient and inpatient treatment facilities, particularly with adolescents who have not typically responded to these modes of care. Wilderness programs, which can last anywhere from 21 days to 12 months, provide at-risk youth with an opportunity to challenge themselves both physically and emotionally while exploring the maladaptive behaviors that have blocked them from being successful in their academic, social, emotional, and behavioral growth (Russell & Phillips-Miller, 2002). Youth are supervised by trained counselors to look introspectively at their core to begin to break down their operating negative belief system in order to rebuild a more positive and productive self-image.

Wilderness therapy programs are based on a core set of theoretical foundations that include a family systems perspective and emphasis of cognitive behavioral therapy techniques. According to Russell (2001), wilderness therapy programs integrate the therapeutic benefits of the wilderness with a nurturing and intense therapeutic process through which youth are assisted in accessing their feelings and emotion that have been deeply masked by anger, drugs, alcohol, and depression. For example, through the use of natural consequences in wilderness living, support staff can step away from positions of authority and avoid power struggles. In these instances, staff assumes more nurturing, caring, and empathetic roles. Wilderness therapy does not force change; rather, participants are influenced by their surrounding environment. If participants are not ready to embrace change, staff steps back (Russell, 2001). During these times it is believed that the combined forces of being away from family and physical exercise continue to have an impact.

Specific components of wilderness therapy include outdoor adventures under the direction of skilled leaders aimed at targeted behavior change, development of primitive skills, self-reflection, group therapy facilitated by qualified individuals, and evaluation of individual growth and progress. One of two models is often employed: (1) continuous flow programs, where leaders rotate in and out, new participants may be added to existing groups, and a therapist visits weekly; or (2) contained programs, where wilderness leaders and therapists form a treatment team that remains with the same group of participants for the duration of the program

(Russell, 2001). Regardless of the model utilized, there are generally three phases each participant will encounter as they make their way through the wilderness therapy program.

The first phase is referred to the *Cleansing*. During this period, the goal is to address the participants presenting issues and chemical dependencies they may have developed by removing them from their familiar environments and those environments that have sustained their maladaptive behaviors (Russell, 2001). Staples of this phase include a healthy diet, intense physical exercise, teaching of self-help skills, basic survival skills, and the removal of all cultural stimuli such as music, cell phone and computer access, and television. It is during this phase that participants are prepared for the wilderness experience and begin to learn personal responsibility through the natural consequences of their actions. The skills learned at this stage will be built upon during the upcoming stages.

The second phase is referred to as the period of *Personal and Social Responsibility* and occurs in the wilderness. Natural consequences coupled with peer interaction become the major therapeutic influences, where participants learn and accept personal and social responsibility. The goal for participants is to generalize what they have learned through self-care and natural consequences to real life. For example, students who choose not to learn how to make fire will eat cold meals, or those who fail to prepare for rainy weather will get wet. Another component during this phase is wilderness therapy, where participants are placed into social units of approximately six individuals and three leaders (Russell, 2001). During this time, wilderness living conditions make cooperation and communication necessary to the group's safety and comfort. Group leaders model appropriate ways to manage anger, express emotions, and process interpersonal issues within the neutral and safe environment of the group setting. At the same time, therapeutic staff works with the participants' parents and other family members to help them understand their child's problem behaviors and facilitates reconnection between the participant and their family.

Throughout the last phase, labeled *Transition and Aftercare,* participants prepare for their return to their previous environments or to another designated aftercare setting. Staff time is focused on assisting participants in what they have learned and how to use the information in their home environments. This period is spent by participants in intense one-to-one counseling and group sessions with their peers, developing the strategies necessary for them to meet and sustain their goals once they are back home (Russell, 2001). For some, arrangements are made for weekly visits to Alcoholics Anonymous meetings, outpatient counseling, or family therapy. Where appropriate, wilderness staff will work with mental health professionals to ensure that aftercare is accessible.

Outcomes for wilderness programs show progress such as elimination of target behaviors and maintenance of skills over a 12-month period, however, research in the area of wilderness therapy has been limited. Similar to most other fields, research of wilderness programs has encountered many of the same problems, such as the lack of a standard definition, inconsistency of implementation, and sound research methodology that may lead to replication. In addition, while some programs across the United States have sought accreditation by national organizations, such as the National Association of Therapeutic Wilderness Camps (NATWC), as a way to monitor practice, others do not. Further, programs exist along a broad spectrum of wilderness programs that range from the program previously described to more traditional wilderness programs that typically do not offer a therapeutic component such as those commonly referred to as *boot camps*, which adopt a more militaristic approach to behavior management. Parents interested in wilderness therapy programs need to be cautioned that not all programs are created equal, and they should thoroughly research programs they are considering.

Another area of concern that is continually on the minds of parents who have a child suffering from a severe emotional or behavioral problem, or any illness for that matter, is how to finance the services their child desperately needs. With tuition costs ranging from approximately $7,000 to $65,000, school districts will not be likely to deem wilderness therapy as an appropriate mode of treatment without credible evidence that strongly supports its use. Some programs offer financing such a loan programs and payment plans. Most HMO and Medicaid plans typically do not offer any kind of reimbursement for these types of programs, but parents interested in a particular program should contact the admission department of the organization for information about how to obtain insurance coverage. Unfortunately, more often than not, parents typically end up paying tuition fees on their own. Thus, like therapeutic schools, these types of therapy programs remain out of reach for most low-income families.

Controversy with Alternative Programs

Regardless of research results supporting residential treatment centers, therapeutic schools, and wilderness programs as promising treatment approaches for youth with severe emotional and behavioral difficulties, these options have not escaped controversy or criticism by the public. A report released by the U.S. Government Accountability Office (GAO; 2007b)— *Residential Treatment Programs: Concerns Regarding Abuse and Death in Certain Programs for Troubled Youth*—sheds light on a number of incidents that were a direct result of the lack of operational regulations in place, compliance with what little regulations exist, ineffective management, inadequate equipment and training, and overall leadership neglect of program needs. The GAO found that during the period from 1990 to 2007 that there were thousands of allegations of abuse. For example, in 2005 alone, 33 states reported 1,619 staff members at residential facilities were involved in incidents of abuse. In addition, the report also reviewed the deaths of 10 adolescents from 1990 to 2004 and found that ineffective management led to the employment of (1) untrained staff, (2) lack of adequate nourishment, and (3) reckless or negligent operating practices that were directly implicated in each of the deaths (GAO; 2007b). It is important to note that the majority of these deaths occurred while the adolescents were participating in a wilderness therapy program rather than a residential-only or therapeutic school program and that 8 of the 10 programs were ordered to close at the completion of court proceedings.

While all states have required licensing and monitoring procedures in place to regulate the operation of residential facilities and wilderness programs, there appears to be gaps in these assurances. Another report from the GAO in May of 2007, titled *Residential Facilities: Improved Data and Enhanced Oversight Would Help Safeguard the Well-Being of Youth with Behavioral and Emotional Challenges,* indicated that there are many problems with the licensing and regulation of the facilities in which youth are placed. For example, some government and private organizations, such as juvenile justice facilities or boarding schools, are exempt from licensing by law or regulation. Further, some licensing requirements do not adequately address parental concerns such as suicide prevention/response, quality of education programming, and the use of psychotropic medications that may compromise the safety of adolescents (GAO; 2007a). Where these requirements do exist (i.e., suicide prevention plans), various programs may be implementing them differently as well as inconsistently. Other issues are tied to limited state resources, such as the inability to conduct regular on-site evaluations due to fluctuations in the number of state employees available to carry out these visits. The lack of programs having their licenses suspended or revoked was also cited as the result of already having limited services available for displaced youth (GAO; 2007b). This gap perpetuates the notion that it is better to have some place to go, regardless of quality of services, than no place at all. Lastly, interagency coordination of services for the purposes of monitoring that students are receiving appropriate services and specialized services was also lacking. So where does this leave parents in need of securing services for their child?

Parents need to be cautious consumers and need to monitor their child's progress closely. Parents also need to understand what licensing and regulations exist in their state, ask questions pertaining to these areas, and request proof of these requirements when researching programs. In response to these issues, the National Association of Therapeutic Wilderness Camps (NATWC), an organization that seeks high standards in wilderness therapy programs, highlights several questions parents should ask when researching potential program options for their child. These questions cover areas such as the number of years a program has been in operation, licensure requirements, staff credentials and training, admission criteria, appropriateness of program curriculum and structure, and whether or not programs have any lawsuits pending. Interested parents should visit http://nationalyouth.com/wildernessandoutdoor.html for a complete list of recommended questions. Additional questions for parents to ask should focus on the programs response in crisis and emergency situations, implementation of a suicide prevention policy, and procedures to access outside medical attention when needed. It is important to note that while many of these questions are geared toward wilderness programs, they can easily be adapted for residential treatment centers and therapeutic boarding schools.

Parents also need to be cautioned about being lured by programs' promises to resolve their child's issues. Parents of children with severe emotional and behavioral difficulties are easy targets for talk of magic elixirs that boasts returning their children back home problem free. Parents of children with severe emotional and behavioral difficulties are worn down, exhausted, and are most likely in need of healing themselves. Referring back to Maria's case, presented in the beginning of the chapter, her father and stepmother were desperate to find an alternative placement. Maria's parents having experienced enormous disruption to their daily lives may be eager to secure the first placement offered. They may be vulnerable to the opinions of professionals and tempted to find quick relief from the chaos they have been living with for the past several years. Yet Maria's parents will need to be more involved and cautious than ever if they wish to find a placement that will match Maria's needs.

Until parents and school officials can rely more comfortably on the policies and regulations set forth at the federal, state, and local levels, it is recommended that parents take an active role when assessing the quality of alternative programs. Quinn and Rutherford (1998) highlight six components for parents to be acutely aware of when presented with program choices and making placement decisions. Alternative programs should have policies and procedures in place for the following:

1. Conducting functional assessments of academic and nonacademic behavior
2. Providing a flexible curriculum that places emphasis on functional academic, social, and daily living skills
3. Implementing effective and efficient instructional strategies
4. Transition programs that link the alternative program to mainstream educational settings and the larger community
5. Comprehensive systems for providing students with both internal alternative and educational services and external community-based services
6. Hiring and training appropriate staff and securing adequate resources for students with disabilities

References

Behrens, E., Santa, J., & Gass, M. (2010). The evidence base for private therapeutic schools, residential programs, and wilderness therapy programs. *Journal of Therapeutic Schools and Programs, 4*(1), 106–117.

Best, K. M., Hauser, S. T., Gralinski-Bakker, H., Allen, P. J., & Crowell, J. (2004). Adolescent psychiatric hospitalization and mortality, distress levels, and educational attainment. *Pediatrics and Adolescent Medicine, 158,* 749–752.

Dryfoos, J. (1994). *Full service schools: A revolution in health and social services for children, youth, and families.* San Francisco: Jossey-Bass.

Easterson-Rock, E., Rosenberg, M. S., & Carran, D. T. (1994). Variables affecting the reintegration rate of students with emotional disturbance. *Exceptional Children, 61*(3), 254–268.

Eber, L., Nelson, C. M., & Miles, P. (1997). School-based wraparound for students with emotional and behavioral challenges. *Exceptional Children, 63*(4), 539–555.

Eber, L., Sugai, G., Smith, C. R., & Scott, T. M. (2002). Wraparound and positive behavioral interventions and supports in the schools. *Journal of Emotional and Behavioral Disorders, 10*(3), 171–181.

Gable, R. A., Bullock, L. M., & Evans, W. H. (2006). Changing perspectives on alternative schooling for children and adolescents with challenging behavior. *Preventing School Failure, 51*(1), 5–9.

Greenberg, M. T., Domitrovich, C., & Bumbarger, B. (2000). *Preventing mental health disorders in school aged children: A review of the effectiveness of preventions programs.* University Park: PA: Prevention Research Center for the Promotion of Human Development, College of Health and Human Development, Pennsylvania State University.

Hong, N. N. (2010). *A longitudinal study of change in the quality of adolescent relationships.* Symposium presentation at the Annual Meeting of the National Association of Therapeutic Schools and Programs, La Jolla, California.

Hong, N. N., & McKinnon, J. (2009). *Beyond symptomatology: Maturation in adolescents.* Symposium presentation at the Annual Meeting of the National Association of Therapeutic Schools and Programs, Austin, Texas.

Hong, N. N., & Santa, J. (2007). *Family functioning in the lives of adolescents in therapeutic boarding schools.* Symposium presentation at the Annual Meeting of the National Association of Therapeutic Schools and Programs, La Jolla, California.

Knoff, H., & Batcsche, G. (1990). The place of the school in community mental health services for children: A necessary interdependence. *The Journal of Mental Health Administration. 17*(1), 122–131.

Leichtman, M., Leichtman, M. L., Barber, C. C., & Neese, D. T. (2001). Effectiveness of intensive short-term residential treatment with severely disturbed adolescents. *American Journal of Orthopsychiatry, 71*(2), 227–235.

Lewis, R. E. (2005). The effectiveness of Families First services: An experimental study. *Children and Youth Services Review, 27,* 499–509.

Noell, G. H., & Witt, J. C. (1996). A critical re-evaluation of five fundamental assumptions underlying behavioral consultation. *School Psychology Quarterly, 11,* 189–203.

Payton, J. W., Wardlaw, D. M., Graczyk, P. A., Bloodworth, M. R., Tompsett, C. J., & Weissberg, R. P. (2000). Social and emotional learning: A framework for promoting mental health and reducing risk behavior in children and youth. *Journal of School Health, 70*(5), 179–185.

Potter, D., & Mulkern, V. (2004). *Wraparound services.* Cambridge, MA: Human Services Research Institute.

Quinn, K.P., & Lee, V. (2007). The wraparound approach for students with emotional and behavioral disorders: Opportunities for school psychologists. *Psychology in the Schools, 44*(1), 101–111.

Quinn, M. M., & Rutherford, R.B. (1998). *Alternative programs for students with social, emotional, and behavioral problems.* Reston, VA: Council for Children with Behavioral Disorders.

Roe, E. (2009). *Wilderness therapy adolescents: Utilizing nature to effect change in youth.* Retrieved August 27, 2010, from http://natwc.org/journal-of-therapeutic-wilderness-camping/.

Russell, K.C. (2001). What is wilderness therapy? *The Journal of Experiential Education, 24*(2), 70–79.

Russell, K. C., & Phillips-Miller, D. (2002). Perspectives on the wilderness therapy process and its relation to outcome. *Child and Youth Care Forum, 31*(6), 415–437.

Sheridan, S.M., & Gutkin, T.B. (2000). The ecology of school psychology: Examining and changing our paradigm for the 21st century. *School Psychology Review, 29*, 485–502.

U.S. Department of Education. (2002). *Improving learning and literacy in Abbott classrooms.* Retrieved April 3, 2009, from http://www.state.nj.us/education/abbotts/.

U.S. Department of Health and Human Services. (1999). *Mental health: A report of the surgeon general—xecutive summary.* Retrieved July 14, 2010, from http://www.surgeongeneral.gov/library/mentalhealth/home.html.

U.S. Department of Health and Human Services. (2001). *Mental health: Culture, race, and ethnicity—A supplement to mental health: A report of the surgeon general.* Retrieved July 14, 2010, from http://download.ncadi.samhsa.gov/ken/pdf/SMA-01-3613/sma-01-3613.pdf.

U.S. Government Accountability Office. (2007a). *Residential facilities: Improved data and enhanced oversight would help safeguard the well-being of youth with behavioral and emotional challenges.* Retrieved August 27, 2010, from http://www.gao.gov/new.items/d08346.pdf.

U.S. Government Accountability Office. (2007b). *Residential treatment programs: Concerns regarding abuse and death in certain programs for troubled youth.* Retrieved August 27, 2010, from http://www.gao.gov/new.items/d08146t.pdf.

Wagner, M., Friend, M., Bursuck, W.D., Kutash, K., Duchnowski, A.J., Sumi, W.C., & Epstein, M.H. (2006). Educating students with emotional disturbances: A national perspective on school programs and services. *Journal of Emotional and Behavioral Disorders, 14*(1), 12–30.

Walter, H.J., Gouze, K., & Lim, K.G. (2006). Teachers' beliefs about mental health needs in inner city elementary schools. *Journal of the American Academy of Child and Adolescent Psychiatry, 45*(1), 61–68.

Weist, M.D., & Paternite, C.E. (2006). Building interconnected policy-training-practice-research agendas to advance school mental health. *Education and Treatment of Children, 29*, 173–196.

Wilson, S.J., Lipsey, M.W., & Derzon, J.H. (2003). The effects of school-based intervention programs on aggressive behavior: A meta-analysis. *Journal of Consulting and Clinical Psychology, 71*, 139–149.

Wright, J.C., & Zakriski, A.L. (2003). When syndromal similarity obscures functional dissimilarity: Distinctive evoked environments of externalizing and mixed syndrome boys. *Journal of Consulting and Clinical Psychology, 71*(3), 516–527.

Zakriski, A. L., Wright, J. C., & Parad, H. W. (2006). Intensive short-term residential treatment: A contextual evaluation of the "stop-gap" model. *Brown University Child & Adolescent Behavior Letter, 22,* 6.

Zakriski, A. L., Wright, J. C., & Underwood, M. K. (2005). Gender similarities and differences in children's social behavior: Finding personality in contextualized patterns of adaptation. *Journal of Personality and Social Psychology, 88*(5), 844.

CHAPTER 9

The Impact of Food Allergies on Social and Emotional Development

Suzanne Huber

Introduction

After we boarded the plane, the flight attendant announced that there was a small child on board who was severely allergic to peanuts and so they would not be serving peanuts on board. She also requested that we not eat peanut snacks we brought on board ourselves. I was so angry. I am going to write them a letter. That's a violation of my civil rights! (As told to a parent of a toddler with a peanut allergy by her close friend.)

There is increasing discussion about food allergies, especially about children with food allergies. Until recently, many people were unaware of the severity of food allergies, and many adults have no memory of other kids having food allergies when they were growing up. According to the American Academy of Allergy, Asthma and Immunology, the number of children with food allergies increased 18 percent from 1997 to 2007 for children under the age of 18. There are a number of theories about why the rate of food allergies in children is increasing at such an alarming rate; most of the evidence relates back to changes in the environment. The primary theory that explains the increase is known as the *hygiene hypothesis*. A basic explanation of this theory is that the immune system was designed to fight infections, parasites, and bacteria, but because in developed nations there are fewer organisms for the developing immune system to fight, the immune system finds things that would ordinarily be harmless and attacks them, such as food particles. Some scientists speculate that the immune system is sitting idle, looking for other invaders to fight off, resulting in food particles and particles in the air (i.e., pollen, dust, etc.)

to become enemies to the immune system. The rise of vaccines to prevent disease that children previously fought off with their immune systems, the increase use of antibiotics, and the use of antibacterial cleaners and soaps all reduce the number of invaders the immune system has to fight (Sicherer, 2006). There is evidence to support this theory, including the reduced risk of asthma in children who attend day care; older siblings have more allergies than younger siblings possibly because the younger siblings grow up exposed to older sibling's germs; children growing up on farms have a reduced risk of allergies, possibly from the exposure to manure and bacteria; children growing up with pets have fewer allergies to those pets than do children who did not grow up with pets. According to the hygiene hypothesis, future treatment and prevention of allergies may include finding ways to keep the immune system busy to promote a healthy immune response (Sicherer, 2006).

The American's with Disability Act of 1990 (ADA) and the ADA Amendments Act of 2008 give protection to all people with disabilities. *Disability* is defined as a physical or mental impairment that substantially limits one or more major life activity, including but not limited to caring for oneself, seeing, hearing, eating, breathing, walking, learning, reading, and communicating. It also extends to major life functions, which include but again are not limited to the functions of the immune system, normal cell growth, and digestive, bowel, bladder, neurological, brain, respiratory, circulatory, endocrine, and reproductive functions. People with food allergies are protected under the ADA. Section 504 of the Rehabilitation Act of 1973 is a civil rights law that prohibits discrimination in an educational setting based on disability status (see, e.g., Food Allergy Initiative in the Resources section). The Office for Civil Rights, an agency within the U.S. Department of Education, enforces federal civil rights laws. Civil rights laws prohibit discrimination on the basis of race, color, national origin, sex, disability, and age. All schools, colleges, vocational programs, rehabilitation agencies, libraries, and museums that receive funding from the Department of Education must comply with these laws. Children with food allergies may qualify to have a 504 Accommodation Plan if their food allergy affects their respiratory, cardiovascular, or digestive systems or a host of other bodily functions. However, to qualify to have a 504 Accommodation Plan, the family needs to submit medical documentation that shows how the food allergy impairs the child and substantially limits a major life activity. Since anaphylaxis interferes with the major bodily function of breathing, families may argue that their child with food allergies is protected under these laws. Families may seek protection from a 504 Accommodation Plan, but most students begin school without a plan and only apply for one after the school fails to accommodate the child with allergies. For many students an emergency plan for how to handle an allergic reaction and a plan for how the school will keep the child safe are adequate to address their needs during the school day.

For many, disability is something visible. You see a person in a wheel-chair or see a person using sign language. Disabilities that are not visible, such as learning disabilities, diabetes, and severe food allergies may be more difficult to accept as a condition that needs protection under the law. Many families with children with food allergies find roadblocks along the way to keeping their child safe. Some are perceived to be overzealous about food and about their child's safety. Many people who have never witnessed an anaphylactic reaction do not believe that it is truly life threatening. For families who have children with food allergies, the fear of a fatal reaction is with them at all times. The most relaxing and fun family events are laden with fear. A trip to the zoo, amusement park, shopping mall, or a family gathering requires extensive planning to ensure the child's safety. The child's entire development is clouded with the knowledge that a fatal reaction is possible. Fortunately, the actual numbers of deaths from food allergies are relatively low compared to other causes of death. There are approximately 200 deaths, but there are between 50,000 and 125,000 trips to the emergency room each year caused by food-induced anaphylaxis.

Family Life

Many families discover their child has a food allergy by accident. The child is given or takes a food and has a reaction. Families have witnessed their child's face begin to swell up and panic takes hold, and the child is rushed to the hospital, or the parent calls 911. As Patty, the mother of Lauren put it:

I didn't even give her the peanut butter. She was holding the spoon from her big brother's peanut butter. She never put it in her mouth. But she started to swell up anyway. I mean her whole head swelled up. She wasn't saying anything. I threw the kids in the car and went to the emergency room. I was so panicked

Lauren is a two-year-old girl. After her reactions, she received allergy testing and was found to be allergic to peanuts, tree nuts, sesame seeds, eggs, fish, and milk. Often these reactions happen in infancy or toddlerhood, when parents give their children foods for the first time. Sometimes younger children take an older sibling's food and taste it without their parent's knowledge. Many parents have been cautious about introducing peanut butter because of the increases in peanut allergy; however, their children may be exposed to peanut butter in other ways, such as with craft projects. The initial shock of the anaphylactic reaction colors the way parents respond to the diagnosis. If one parent witnesses anaphylaxis and the other sees only the completely recovered child, the parent's reactions will be different. Siblings who witness the reaction might be traumatized, but siblings who do not might have trouble believing that a food could cause so much trouble. The child who has the reactions might be traumatized by the anaphylaxis and the events that surround it. The age of the children and their developmental level at the time of the first anaphylactic reaction and subsequent reactions will impact how they adjust to their diagnosis.

A common way for families to cope with allergies is for the entire family to adopt a diet that excludes the allergens. This can be challenging, especially if other siblings are accustomed to eating the allergens before the diagnosis, and can cause jealousy and resentment. The problems with allowing the foods in the house include increased risk of accidental exposure and the additional work of creating separate meals. As children grow up, they might become angry that other family members can enjoy something they cannot.

> *Charlie, an eight-year-old boy with allergies to peanuts and tree nuts, has a precocious sense of justice. Charlie's mom reports that he will say, "That's not fair. You're not allowed to eat it either." I now hide nuts in my house on a very high shelf, and they are only eaten when he is not home.* (Marshak & Prezant, 2007)

Most families of children with disabilities go through a period of mourning after the initial diagnosis. Mourning is a natural way for parents to come to terms with the disability and eventually to move on; the parents are mourning what they envisioned their child's life would be like. For parents of children with food allergies, the adjustment includes accepting that their child has a potentially life-threatening diagnosis and that they are primarily responsible for making sure their child does not have a life-threatening reaction. For families with children who have other disabilities as well as the food allergy, the adjustment will include fears about how other caretakers will ensure their children's safety. For instance, if the child has a communication disability and cannot tell others about his or her allergies, the parents' responsibility for protecting their child will likely not lessen with age as it may for parents of children with food allergies who have typical development.

When a child is treated in the emergency room or doctor's office, the parents are often given a prescription for a self-injectable epinephrine (with the use of a device such as an EpiPen or Twin-Jet). The EpiPen looks like a fat magic marker that encloses a needle that can be inserted into the child's thigh when the child has an anaphylactic reaction. The Twin-Jet is similar, but it is thinner and has needles on either end so that it is smaller in size and easy to carry. Parents are instructed to carry the epinephrine everywhere they go and are often told to carry two auto-injectors in case the anaphylaxis doesn't respond to medication in the first auto-injector, or in case the first injector's medicine doesn't release. Parents must also provide the self-injectable epinephrine to their child's school (with paperwork completed by the physician about when and how to use it). Parents are also instructed to carry antihistamines, which should always be accessible to the child with food allergies. For some parents, the medicine pack is a reminder of the allergy and instills fear; for others the medicine pack is seen as a tool to protect their child in an emergency and is viewed as a way to continue living as normal a life as possible and include their child in activities typical for his or her age.

Even families that have never experienced anaphylaxis but have a child who has tested positive for food allergies need to have the medicine available when they go out:

> We found out Charlie was allergic to several foods by chance. He had asthmatic symptoms and had environmental allergies, so he underwent blood testing. He tested positive for almost every food, but with skin testing, it was narrowed to three foods. We avoid those foods, and he has an EpiPen at school. We take the EpiPen when we go to a party or a restaurant, but we are not stressed about it in the way we see other families, whose child has suffered anaphylaxis. Our good friends have a son who did go into anaphylactic shock, and they seem more anxious. If that was me, I would be crazed all the time in fear. Since that hasn't happened, and Charlie is already eight, I am confident that his allergy is not severe. However, I would never feed him knowingly a nut or a peanut without a food challenge by a doctor first. I am too afraid of what could happen. When I think about what could happen, I could go crazy.

Having to constantly carry the medicine pack is a source of stress for some families. It can be difficult to keep track of in a busy household; it may be forgotten repeatedly, when the family is still adjusting to the diagnosis. One parent might find it easier to manage than another. One parent may be terrified to an auto-injector Some parents do not feel they adequately understand how to administer epinephrine or when to use it. Many worry they will not recognize an anaphylactic reaction in time. The medicine pack should always be available to the child. That means if the child goes to a friend's home, the medicine pack needs to be there, too. The parents of the child with food allergies must ensure that the other family is willing to keep the medicine pack, learn to use the auto-injector, and learn how to recognize symptoms of anaphylaxis. Children with food allergies often bring their own food to a play date but, depending on their age, might try the other child's food, increasing the possibility of a reaction. Foods at home that are safe might not be safe at another home, even if they look alike. Many parents of children with food allergies buy cookies, cereals, and pastas that look the same as other foods but do not contain allergens. For example, it can be extremely easy for a glass of regular milk to be mixed up with a glass of soy or rice milk.

Parents that do not live together, especially if the relationship is not amicable, might disagree about the severity of the allergy. If the custodial parent keeps a home free of food allergens but the noncustodial parent does not, the chance the child will have a reaction when with the noncustodial parent is higher. Also, medicine packs for both homes must be created and kept updated, which can cause stress between siblings if it prevents visits or outings with the noncustodial parent.

Grandparents are frequently mentioned in discussions among parents of children with food allergies. Grandparents' homes are often more unsafe from allergens than the child's home, making the risk of accidental exposure more likely. Grandparents might feel they know more than the child's parents because they have already raised children. They may have less information about food allergies and not have been exposed to how severe allergies can be. At family gatherings, tensions might rise over traditional food dishes that need to be changed or taken off the menu. Losing the support of members of the extended family can have grave psychological consequences for parents going through the crisis of adjusting to a child's diagnosis of a potentially life-threatening food allergy.

Sonia, the mother of four-year-old Anthony, said in reference to difficulties with relatives:

There was a big family party. I have always been at the center of organizing these events. I spent days preparing food and I made it to accommodate the likes and needs of a lot of people, not just my son with allergies. I was horrified when my sister brought chocolate chip cookies with walnuts and insisted on putting them in easy reach of my preschooler. This has really impacted our family life. I am not the center of parties anymore. That is a huge loss for me. Even more hurtful though is that I know I cannot count on my sister for support. I have to think of a new way to have family parties, or not go. I expected my children would grow up surrounded by cousins and aunts and uncles, and now I see that for my son's safety I may have to give that up.

Marshak and Prezant (2007) reported that many people felt their family did not understand their child's disability, especially when the disability was not visible. They report that the lack of understanding, coupled with denial, minimizes the child's needs as well as the needs of the parents of that child. To cope with living with life-threatening food allergies, families must find support both within and outside of the family. Parents can join support groups and online message boards to decrease the level of isolation they feel. Parents of school-age children can find support from other parents in the school who are also dealing with food allergies. Other parents who have children with food allergies can be resources for tips on managing at home and in school. They might know safer restaurants, safer places to travel, and safer airlines to fly. They might also have a better understanding of school-required paperwork or know about a fantastic allergist. The extended family goes through an adjustment period to the diagnosis, and family members who resist changing their behavior to accommodate the child with allergies realize that by doing so they can cut themselves off from a full relationship with that child. Over the years and through different stages of development, extended family members can become more or less supportive. For families in conflict with the extended family over how seriously to take the allergy, seeking outside support from other parents who have children with food allergies can help get them through very isolating times.

Treatments and Approaches to Managing the Condition

Food allergies are generally diagnosed through blood testing and skin testing by an allergist. Families provide a medical history and a history of observed food reactions and, depending on the age of the child, how foods have been introduced. A food challenge may also be conducted, which involves giving the child tiny amounts of an allergen food, sometimes disguised in other food, under the supervision of a doctor. If there is no reaction, more of the food is given in small increments. This is considered the only way to know for sure that the child is truly allergic. Some children test positive to a food but are able to tolerate it. A food challenge allows the family to know that the child may safely eat that food.

There is no known treatment for a food allergy, only medicine to treat the symptoms of an allergic reaction. For this reason children with food allergies are put on avoidance diets. Avoidance diets remove all food with the allergen, including trace amounts, from the child's diet. Some children are also put on elimination diets to try to pinpoint what they are allergic to. This includes removing all suspected foods and then reintroducing them. Nursing mothers also use elimination diets to try to pinpoint foods causing their infants to have allergic symptoms, such as atopic eczema. Once particular foods are determined to be problematic for the baby, the nursing mother goes on an avoidance diet to keep those foods out of her body and/or puts the baby on a formula that does not contain those allergens.

Many children will outgrow some or all of their food allergies; a significant number will outgrow them before kindergarten. Studies suggest that 85 percent of children who are allergic to milk and eggs will outgrow these allergies by their fifth birthday (Sicherer, 2006); therefore, parents and other caretakers will be responsible for managing their food allergies for the duration of the condition. Children who do not outgrow their allergies will learn to manage them over time. Children with multiple allergies and allergies to tree nuts, peanuts, fish, and shellfish are less likely to outgrow their allergies; however, it is possible to outgrow an allergy at any age. Children with food allergies are retested for their allergies yearly. An allergist reviews their medical history, reports of recent reactions, and compares the blood levels of allergens from year to year. When the allergist believes there is a good chance the child will tolerate the food, a food challenge may be suggested. Food challenges must be carefully considered because they may cause fear and anxiety for the child and the parents. Also, there is still a considerable chance that the food challenge will not be successful, as was the case of Ana, a six-year-old girl with multiple food allergies who was scheduled for a food challenge for peanuts. Once her mother began preparing for the food challenge, Ana became fearful of the allergist. Ana confided in her mother that she was afraid of what might happen if she ate peanuts. Ana has avoided peanuts her whole life. She is able to remember a significant reaction to milk when she was four that caused her to go to the emergency room. Ana said, *"I'm fine without peanuts. I like not eating peanuts."* Ana's parents found that the other children Ana was friendly with that had allergies were all allergic to peanuts. When Ana was asked about this, she said, *"I finally have friends like me with allergies. I want to be like them."* After Ana's parents tried to explain how adding peanuts to her diet would add more foods to her diet, Ana appeared mistrustful of her parents and became reticent. She also became anxious about medical appointments, which had never happened before. Her mother cancelled the food challenge appointment, reasoning that it would be more important in the long term for Ana to continue to trust her parents and her allergist than to try to struggle through a peanut challenge that might fail anyway. Now Ana continues to see the doctor without visible anxiety.

Children who grew up without certain foods may not understand the purpose of continued allergy testing and undergoing a food challenge. Some children do not want to have a food challenge because they are happy without the food. This presents a problem for the rest of the family, particularly if siblings want to bring the offending food back into the house. Without the food challenge, the parent has no reliable way of knowing whether it is safe to do this. The mother of eight-year-old Charlie wanted him to have a food challenge for peanuts so that she could bring peanut butter back into the home, but he was afraid to. It is difficult to have a food challenge with an uncooperative child. Many parents just try to wait for their child to get over his or her fear or be motivated by another child having a successful food challenge. Many food challenges are unsuccessful but can be helpful because they confirm that the family is avoiding a food for good reason. It also allows the parent to see the child having a reaction in a controlled setting, which, if the child was diagnosed through allergy testing only and not through a reaction from exposure, could demystify what a reaction looks like.

Children with food allergies are more likely than children without food allergies to have conditions such as asthma and eczema. These conditions are also related to immune responses. Children with food allergies who also have asthma are more likely to suffer fatal reactions to a food allergen than children with food allergies who do not have asthma. The combination of illnesses adds stress and complicates the ways families manage the illnesses. Sometimes an anaphylactic reaction is mistaken for an asthma attack, and asthma medication is administered instead of epinephrine. This has resulted in fatalities (Sicherer 2006, p.134). Children with asthma usually take daily medication, and parents of children with asthma learn to prevent asthma attacks by recognizing asthma triggers and the signs of increasing symptoms. Triggers for some children could include a cold, respiratory viruses, or exercise. Children with eczema might require special care of their skin and may be required to wear certain fabrics. Parents have to recognize what triggers their child's eczema and try to prevent outbreaks. Triggers might include ingesting certain foods, sweating, or being around certain animals. Parents who are watching for signs of allergic reactions, such as hives, need to be aware of the condition of their child's skin each day. Monitoring a child's allergies, asthma, and eczema triggers is time-consuming and stressful, and siblings of a child who receives attention because of medical issues might also want to compete for parents' attention. Also, the child with allergies might crave attention that has nothing to do with the allergies or asthma, and in turn resent how parents spend time acting like nurses and not mommies or daddies.

Protecting the Child Away from Home

Many initial allergic reactions happen while children are very young. After the diagnosis, all areas of normal life are affected. Safety at school and day care is an issue; participation in extracurricular activities can be a challenge; air travel can be particularly stressful. Stories have circulated about fatalities on airplanes from allergic reactions, and most of the stories involve peanuts. Studies show that most allergic reactions on airplanes are mild; however, because flying involves being unable to get to a hospital, the risk of anaphylactic reaction is serious. The concern about peanut exposure is related to the large number of people opening vacuum-packed peanut snacks at once in an air-tight plane. Also, peanut residue can be found on all plane surfaces. Small children who like to touch everything and put their fingers in their mouths can react from this type of incidental exposure.

Recently, schools have improved the experiences of students with food allergies. Many schools have developed peanut-free table policies in the cafeteria. Some have peanut-free classrooms. School nurses and other school personnel have been trained to use epinephrine. States have passed laws allowing children to carry their own epinephrine, when they are capable. Organizations such as the Food Allergy and Anaphylaxis Network (FAAN) have set up allergy awareness weeks every spring and distribute educational materials to school districts. There is a book and video series for young children about an elephant that is allergic to peanuts, a lion that is allergic to milk, and other characters with different allergies. The series was created by two sisters, one of whom had food allergies when she was young. The series, available through FAAN, teaches children about doing things like going to school, trick or treating, and going to the supermarket safely.

Linda, a five-year-old with peanut and tree-nut allergies watched Alexander the Elephant goes to School *with her kindergarten class during Food Allergy Awareness Week. Her classmates recognized that Linda had a peanut allergy, just like Alexander. Linda was happy to talk about her allergy to her friends. Linda asked to take the video home so she could show her family. Linda's dad said the entire family watched it all weekend.*

According to the C.S. Mott Children's Hospital National Poll on Children's Health (2009), one-half of parents who have children with food allergies believe that people at school accommodate their child's allergy *very well*, and another 44 percent believe the child is *somewhat* accommodated. Overall, 22 percent of families that had a child in day care or preschool, and 25 percent of families who had a child in elementary school, knew of a child with a life-threatening food allergy in their child's school. Almost one-half of parents who did not have children with food allergies reported that it was *not at all inconvenient* to accommodate for another child's food allergy in school. The most commonly cited accommodation identified by parents were bans treats from home, followed by food allergy plans, special classroom assignments, and separate eating areas. Although it is impressive that so many parents of nonallergic children are not inconvenienced by food restrictions, one-third of parents of nonallergic children feel that it is inconvenient. The authors of the study express concern that the one-third of parents that are inconvenienced may be obstacles to expanding accommodations and point out that the parents of children without food allergies may influence how food allergy policies are developed in schools.

The most common food that causes allergic reactions in school is milk. More school-age children have a peanut allergy than a milk allergy, however, it is more common for milk to be accidentally ingested. Approximately 15 percent of food allergic reactions in school are treated with epinephrine. Sixty percent of reactions involve the skin (hives), and 30 percent involve wheezing. It is extremely rare that blood circulation is also involved in food allergic reactions in schools (Sicherer, 2006, p. 188). Most food allergy reactions in school happen in day care and preschool settings. A significant number of peanut reactions have occurred from peanuts being used in craft projects, such as peanut butter bird feeders.

Lunchrooms that have peanut-free tables often rely on small children knowing what is in their lunch box when they sit down. Children without allergies often are able to move between the tables; for example, one day they might sit at the no-peanut table but the next they might sit at the general class table because they have peanut butter and jelly for lunch. Children with allergies are often at the peanut-free table every day. For some this is a normal experience, and they sit with friends. Others may feel isolated if only children with allergies are allowed to sit at the table. The table would have a variety of grades sitting together and would be an unnatural grouping, and for children with food allergies other than peanuts, this can be confusing.

Anita, the mother of Arun, who is five, put it this way: *"I was so mad at the school when they told me Arun would have to sit at the peanut-free table. He is allergic to eggs only, not peanuts. He could still be sitting next to someone eating egg salad. I feel like he is being punished for his allergy. There is no convincing the school of changing this."*

Ana's mom said, *"I find it a little funny that they make her sit at the peanut table since she has a multitude of allergies, most significantly to milk. She sits with kids drinking milk. She has in the past had reactions from other children's milk-containing food, some of them very serious reactions. Those reactions happened in preschool, though, when the kids were so much messier when they ate. If she were to sit with kids who only had the same allergies as she does, she would be sitting alone. I would complain about her being required to sit at the peanut-free table, but she loves it. She has friends with peanut allergies, and she doesn't mind that they have less allergies than she does."*

> *Morgan is a fourth-grader who discovered she was allergic to peanuts and tree nuts in second grade after eating a cookie with almonds in it and had an anaphylactic reaction that was treated with two EpiPen juniors on the way to the hospital. Morgan's parents reported that Morgan was initially afraid to eat anything unless her mom checked it first. She was reluctant to attend parties and withdrew from her friends and activities. Her parents were surprised when she asked them to let her sit at the regular classroom lunch table at the beginning of the school year. Morgan said, "I felt isolated at the peanut-free table because most of the other kids were much younger. There was no one from my grade at the table." Her mother said, "My husband and I met with the nurse and the principal and we were able to convince them that Morgan was aware enough of her allergies to sit at the general table. It has been a good thing for her. It helped her feel more independent. She learned to use her EpiPen herself this year as well and carries it now in her backpack."*

Parents of children who do not have food allergies but are in class with children who do express different feelings about allergy-safe classroom parties. At one kindergarten party, a group of parents were discussing the food issue. One mother said, *"I don't know why those kids with allergies just don't bring in their own snacks all the time. Why do the other parents have to try to be bothered with this? I don't want my child eating the allergy food. I want him only eating regular food."* But another mother said, *"I want my son to understand that we go out of our way to make sure all the kids can be safe at the party. I don't want him growing up thinking that it is okay to ignore another person's needs."*

Some parents want to follow the allergy rules but find it extremely difficult. As parents of children with food allergies know, it can be a painstaking process to find ingredients that are safe for their children. This also makes it difficult to trust another parent to make foods for a school party that are safe for children with allergies. Many parents who have children with food allergies are happy to send their own treat or even to send treats for the whole class.

Teachers are on the front lines of protecting children with food allergies. One teacher explained that her school has a policy stating that no foods containing peanuts or tree nuts are allowed in the school. This includes the school lunch program, lunches brought from home for children and staff, and all food brought in for parties in school. Teachers who have children in their classrooms with food allergies carry auto-injectors in the classroom, throughout the school building, and outside the building on field trips or the playground. At lunch, a staff member carries an auto-injector in the cafeteria at all times. The school does not have a full-time nurse, so responsibility for carrying the auto-injector has been delegated to the staff that is with the children throughout the day. She reported, *"It is everyone's responsibility to make sure the children with food allergies are safe, not just the nurses. The administration fosters a culture of working together. Honestly, I don't hear grumbling about EpiPens and checking the ingredients on cupcakes that come into school for birthday parties. It's just part of our job. I don't think about it anymore as an additional thing to do; it is just part of my day now."*

Another teacher reported that there were no peanuts or tree nuts allowed in her school or in the schools in which she did her student teaching. The idea of checking lunches and party foods and carrying an EpiPen were described as a natural part of an elementary school teacher's day. This was repeated by other elementary teachers, including teachers of special education. Some schools also have begun to discourage food at parties and instead encourage games or activities to celebrate a birthday or holiday. Many teachers send out letters in the welcome-back-to-school packets explaining the no-peanut and no-tree-nut policies of the classroom or the school. Some teachers also dictate the foods that are to be brought into a party (e.g,. fruit salad, bagels) to prevent tree nuts and peanuts entering the classroom.

One teacher described a classroom holiday party where a child who was allergic to peanuts ate a cookie that contained trace amounts of peanut and became quite ill. The parent was in the room at the time and had allowed the child to eat the cookie. The parent was upset at the teacher for not checking the ingredients better. As a result, the teacher disallowed any food at parties to prevent another accidental exposure. This upset other parents because birthdays could no longer be celebrated with cupcakes. Unfortunately for this class it was known who the child involved was, and there were negative feelings between the families of those with allergies and those without.

Families that have a child with only one or two allergies, especially if they are peanut and tree-nut allergies, and the school or classroom is peanut and tree-nut free, may be more relaxed about the participation in parties.

Charlie's mom said, "My son is good about saying, I can't eat nuts. Does this have nuts? I'm allergic. The teacher is great about checking ingredients. I don't send special treats on party days. Most of the other parents are responsible about what they send in. Once someone sent in a treat with nuts, but the nuts were obvious. The teacher realized right away and found another

treat for my son. When my son was younger I was more cautious, but now
he reads and is able to speak up for himself."

The different levels of severity of allergies may contribute to the confusion of families that don't have a child with food allergies. For instance,
why does one child need to bring a special snack while another child with
a food allergy can get by with just the teacher double checking the ingredients? Also, sometimes people misuse the word *allergy* when they really
mean aversion. For example, families with children who are picky eat-
ers may want their child to have peanut butter in school because it is the
only thing the child will eat, but families with children who eat a variety
of foods will not be greatly affected by restrictions placed on outside food.
Children who have special diets for reasons other than allergies, such as
diabetes, and who are already on restricted diets that need to be carefully
monitored, may also be burdened by classroom food restrictions. For children who are very young or require assistance eating because of physical
disabilities, problems may occur if the family and school don't regularly
communicate about the changing status of allergies. A teacher, for example, may find a food in the child's lunch box that has an ingredient the
teacher believes the child is allergic to. However, the doctor may have told
the parent at a recent appointment that the child is outgrowing the allergy
and could eat foods that were previously forbidden. Since the teacher is
not aware of this, he or she may take the food away from the child and
substitute it with something else. This may cause a conflict between the
family and the school. It is also possible that the teacher may receive training about food allergy awareness that is more comprehensive than the information the family has. If the child has a relatively mild food allergy, the
family may not perceive that the child's eczema or asthma symptoms are
attributable to trace amounts of an allergen in their food and continue to
allow the child to eat foods that are exacerbating their symptoms. A variety of school personnel, including the teacher, school nurse, social worker,
or psychologist might interpret the parent's behavior as neglectful when,
in truth, no clear connection has been made between eating the food and
the symptoms. Perhaps the family needs more information about food allergies, or perhaps the school is making a mistake in not believing that
the parents are doing the right thing with the foods. Maybe the eczema or
asthma is related to another allergy, such as an environmental allergy.

Another area of concern for mealtimes is the washing of tables and
hands. Especially when children are very young and put things in their
mouths, including other children's hands, the possibility of a reaction
to food residue is real. In school children don't have much control over
whether the other children wash their hands after they eat. The growing
use of hand sanitizer in place of soap and water is cause for concern, because hand sanitizer is not proven to remove food proteins that contain
the allergen. In Perry, Conover-Walker, Pomes, Chapman and Wood's 2009
study published by the Food Allergy and Anaphylaxis Network, scientists

recreated a cafeteria in which people ate peanut butter. Their hands and tables were then cleaned and checked for Ara h 1, which is a major peanut allergen. Scientists discovered that common household cleaners removed peanut allergens from tabletops; however, dishwashing liquid left traces of peanut allergen on one-third of the tables studied. The use of hand sanitizer left peanut allergen on the hands of half of the group studied. Liquid and bar soaps used with water were found to be very effective in removing peanut residue. Wipes were also found to be effective.

Parents of children without food allergies may be unaware that it is not just the staff and the other families that are making accommodations for the food allergy. The parents of the child with food allergies are responsible for several things, including medical paperwork from the doctor that is usually updated annually or whenever there is a change in medication. They also must provide the medication to the school and keep the medications current. For many children this will include several medications such as epinephrine, liquid antihistamine, topical steroid for eczema, asthma medication, and a spacer or nebulizer attachments. The family must also provide safe treats to be kept in the classroom, and the parents must play a large role in educating their child about his or her allergy. Children with allergies have a lot of responsibilities in keeping themselves safe. For instance, even very young children are given the responsibility of never sharing food with another child and never taking food from any adult other than the adult designated to ensure that the food is safe. They are responsible for reporting when they think they might be having a reaction. They may be responsible for wearing a medical alert bracelet. As they enter the upper elementary and middle school grades, they become responsible for carrying their own epinephrine and liquid antihistamine. At extracurricular activities, they are responsible for not eating what other kids are eating. They must recognize art materials they cannot handle. They must not touch foods containing allergens at social events and may have to skip events. For example, a girl with a severe milk allergy may not be able to attend a party that serves buttered popcorn because the butter will be all over the hands of the other guests. The children must take responsibility for keeping themselves safe, which also means they have to become aware that their allergy is potentially fatal. This is a lot of responsibility for a growing child and can lead to emotional difficulties including jealousy of other children without such issues, acting out behaviors, and withdrawing from others to avoid possible dangerous situations.

Bullying is a growing problem in school. The National School Safety Center reports an increase in bullying in grades 6–12 between 1999 and 2003. In April 2008, ABC News aired a report, *Peanut Butter and Deadly Taunts*. The report highlighted a horrific example of bullying by a group of students toward a 14-year-old girl, Sarah VanEssendelft, with a severe peanut allergy. A group of five girls brought peanut butter sandwiches to school so that she would stop sitting at their lunch table. Two weeks following that incident, a boy in Sarah's class opened a peanut butter cup in the classroom and she had a reaction that landed her in the emergency room. Dr. Scott Sicherer, professor of pediatrics at the Jaffe Food Allergy Institute at Mount Sinai School of Medicine, reports that in the workshops he has conducted with teenagers who have food allergies, most report being bullied because of their allergy (Cox, 2008). In Sarah's case, the bullying increased after she went to the emergency room and included a plot to have a "peanut party" in the cafeteria and watch her face "blow up." The school administration failed to discipline the students involved, so the VanEssendelfts applied for a section 504 plan. Now if Sarah is bullied in school, the bullying is considered discrimination against her disability. Online message boards for parents of children with food allergies include many comments about this type of bullying as a parent's worst nightmare scenario. While it is an extreme example, it is not alone. *Allergic Living Magazine* reported in the summer of 2008 that an eighth-grade girl was arrested in Kentucky on felony charges for putting peanut butter cookie crumbs in a classmate's lunchbox that she knew was allergic to peanuts. The child did not eat the peanuts and did not have a reaction, but the potential for a serious reaction was determined to be enough for charges to be brought. In the VanEssendelft case, Sarah's parents report that after Sarah had a reaction that led to a four-day hospitalization, the school became much more responsive to Sarah's needs. On the Web site nopeanutsplease.com, it was announced that wordspy.com, which tracks new phrases, added *food allergy bullying* to its list in April 2009. In the teen workshops that Dr. Sicherer leads, most teenagers report that they want their peers, not adults, to be educated about food allergies. Anne Munoz-Furlong, founder of the Food Allergy and Anaphylactic Network, reported that teenagers call their friends their "body guards." FAAN has a program for schools called PAL: Protect A Life. The program provides educational materials to teach children how to protect their friends with food allergies from accidentally eating something they are allergic to. It also teaches how to recognize the signs of, how to treat, and how to get help for the reaction. PAL heroes are children who acted to prevent a reaction, treated, or got help to treat a reaction. This is a proactive program to educate peers and prevent bullying behavior that might be created because of curiosity about what might happen in the event of an allergic reaction.

More typical cases of food bullying are children being taunted by their peers about their food allergies, but some parents report that their children are actually exposed to the food.

Carol, mother of Lydia, now in sixth grade said, "When she was in second grade she had a peanut butter cookie shoved in her face in the cafeteria. She broke out in hives and vomited. The principal wasn't going to discipline the kids because he felt she needed to learn to manage her allergies. We went over to the school and did not let the issue drop until something was done.

We have not had another problem that severe, but the teasing still goes on. Fortunately, as she gets older, she has more friends that really look out for her and are aware of her allergies."

Children with food allergies that always bring their own treat to birthday parties may not feel special about this. As children grow up and focus increasingly on peer acceptance, they may want to try their friend's food or believe they can decide for themselves what is safe to eat. The development of a peer group that understands food allergies is vital to keeping growing children safe as they do more and more activities out of sight of their parents.

Psychological Consequences

Living with the stress of a food allergy can take an emotional toll on the individual and on the family system. Individuals and families might feel isolated in different settings, such as school, work, birthday parties, or family parties. A lack of a strong support network can isolate a person and a family further. Without the help of extended family members participating, family gatherings can be nearly impossible. Feeling judged by family members or friends can be painfully isolating. Friends who are not sympathetic, or fail to get it, can jeopardize a child's safety, and parents may have to decide that such friends need to be dropped from further contact. The impact on the family's quality of life has been determined to be similar to the effect on families with children with chronic diseases such as diabetes, according to FAAN.

At this time there is no cure for a food allergy. Once a child is diagnosed, the parents become the protector from the allergens. Parents read food labels at the grocery store, they search the Web for allergy-friendly products, and they cook from scratch items that can't be purchased. This often includes foods for special occasions, such as birthday cakes. Often, there are few restaurants from which a family can safely eat. The food court at a mall is usually not safe. Spontaneous outings are difficult or impossible, depending on the severity and number of allergies. The constant planning ahead for going anywhere, coupled with the stress of knowing that if you were to let your guard down your child could have an accidental exposure, which could be fatal, is very stressful to most families. Stress, especially chronic stress, is known to have physical and psychological consequences in people. Families who experience other types of chronic stress on top of the stress of caring for a child with food allergies, such as financial stress, may suffer further. Also, parents who have an underlying mental illness or who have limited cognitive abilities may experience exacerbated stress. The stress of managing the food allergies comes from many places other than planning to go out or the lengthy process of reading every label in a grocery store. There are expectations from the school, doctors, neighbors, and extended family. There are many opportunities for parents to feel judged by others in their care of their child, such as whether they are over-zealous or too passive. Parents of children with food allergies may have more contact with school personnel about food safety issues. Many parents are not comfortable communicating with the school and may find this to be an enormous stress, especially if they do not perceive the school to be sympathetic to their child's needs. Relationships in the extended family can suffer. If the grandparents and aunts and uncles don't recognize the severity of the allergy, they can work to pit spouse against spouse, especially if one parent of a child with a food allergy is much more concerned about the allergy than the other parent.

To develop support networks, though, parents must be willing to reach out to other families. This is where a diagnosis of depression may really stand in the way of a family moving forward, because people with depression often don't have the energy to get out of the house or to recognize they are depressed and thus fail to seek help. This may take a toll on the family and jeopardize their child's safety.

Children with food allergies also experience stress and anxiety about accidental exposure allergens. If they have experienced a severe allergic reaction and were old enough at the time to remember it, their fear may be very high. Also, children who have repeated anaphylactic reactions may be more likely to suffer from anxiety about eating. As children grow up they may become more aware of the possibility of a fatal reaction. They also take on more responsibility for managing their own allergies and may be overwhelmed with how complicated it is to check every food label, ask every server in a restaurant about ingredients, and constantly keep track of their medicine. It is possible for some people with food allergies to become so fearful of eating that they become malnourished or develop eating disorders (Melina, Stepaniak, & Aronson, 2004). Taking steps to feel less helpless and more in control of what is eaten can help reduce the impact of fear. Having some fear of food has been known to aid people with food allergies in the prevention of accidental ingestion, because it decreases the chance that they will eat a food that seems doubtful at a party or restaurant. If fear is known to be a protector, people with food allergies, or parents protecting a child from food allergies, can use fear as a motivator to act with competence. Becoming educated about their food allergies, developing confidence in how to use their auto-injector, and taking the time to always carry their medicine pack and wear a medic-alert bracelet can help reduce the stress on persons with food allergies because it increases the amount of control they have over their safety.

Guilt is another common feeling experienced by parents of children with food allergies. Many parents feel guilt for possibly having caused the allergy. Mothers may worry that what they ate while nursing or pregnant caused the allergy. Parents may feel guilty for giving the child the food that caused the anaphylaxis, especially if more than one incident of anaphylaxis occurred. Children with food allergies may also feel guilty because of the perceived burden they are putting on their family (Melina et al., 2004). Siblings of children with food allergies may feel guilty for not having allergies and for having an easier time managing social outings. Other family members may also feel guilty if they doubted the seriousness of the allergy and did not provide support to family members due to a lack of information about allergies.

Some children develop responses to the anxiety surrounding their food allergies. Patterns of behavior include food refusal, generalization of reactions, and a panic response. Children who feel stress from worrying about their safety when they eat may want to stop eating because there is no pleasure in it. Some children will have mild allergic reactions to a variety of foods, making it difficult to know if the food is safe to eat. Children might have a reaction to an environmental allergen but believe it is from food they are eating. If they then stop eating that food, they restrict their diet. If they have multiple food allergies, restricting the diet further can impact their nutritional status. Some children who have had anaphylactic reactions to foods may develop posttraumatic stress disorder (Sicherer, 2006). A child may have the physical symptoms of a severe allergic reaction that is caused by emotional rather than an actual physical response to an allergen.

Linda began in second grade to be fearful of food in the classroom that was sent in by families for parties. Prior to second grade, Linda was fine about eating food at parties that the teacher had checked the ingredients on. After she felt sick during a birthday party in the classroom and the teacher rushed her to the nurse fearing an allergic reaction, Linda began to refuse other children's party food. During a school party, Linda would say she felt sick and needed to go to the nurse. Linda's father said, "The school's hyper vigilance about food coming into the classroom made Linda much more fearful of her allergies. It got to the point where the school nurse thought she had school phobia. I asked the school not to draw so much attention to her allergies. I assured the school that she had been safe before in kindergarten and first grade, and her allergies had not changed. Once the school relaxed, Linda started to get back to normal."

Family members may experience sadness and depression from living with the food allergy. However, the depression could have preexisted and been exacerbated by the stress of living with the food allergy. Many families with children with food allergies are coping well, even thriving. Most families go through a period of grief when the diagnosis first happens. Many parents worry about accidentally harming their child. Some also feel guilty and consider the possibility that they may have been able to prevent the allergy itself or prevent the allergic reaction even before knowing the child had an allergy. Learning the diagnosis and hearing the words *possibility of a fatal reaction* can be traumatizing. Families who lack positive coping skills and or lack supportive family and friends may become isolated and experience difficulties in their family dynamics.

Marshak and Prezant (2007) explained that depression and grief can manifest themselves in similar ways but are not the same thing. Depression is an illness that affects the entire body. One of the classic symptoms of depression is the inability to find pleasure in anything that would have normally brought a person pleasure. People who are depressed often have a sense of hopelessness and lack resiliency in the face of a crisis. The stress of caring for a child with severe food allergies will become more manageable for a person who is able to find a supportive network and can develop confidence in their abilities to keep their child safe. Depression could compromise parents' abilities to care for their children, contribute to their inability to develop confidence in handling food allergies, and limit their ability to form a supportive network. Often, people who are depressed can miss seeing themselves as depressed, preventing them from getting the treatment that they need. People who have children with special needs may believe that every parent who has a child with special needs feels sad all the time or feels unable to get out of bed in the morning every day. Treatments for depression are advertised on television and talked about on the news and joked about in comedies, but many people still do not know the symptoms of depression or the myriad treatments. While medication for depression is widely advertised and is helpful to many, other treatments also work. Psychotherapy has been shown to be effective in treating depression. Psychiatrist, psychologists, clinical social workers, marriage and family therapists, and mental health counselors are qualified to treat emotional concerns and conditions. Mental health professionals use a variety of methods to treat psychological symptoms that include both short- and long-term treatment models. Many mental health professionals will advertise themselves as psychotherapists or counselors. Psychotherapy is usually thought of as talk therapy. Depending on the setting where the therapy takes place, the person receiving the service is referred to as a patient, client, or consumer. When choosing a mental health provider, it is helpful to consider what services and which providers are covered under the client's health insurance plan. Since persons seeking the service may not know what type of treatment they need, they may interview a few different therapists to try to find the best treatment option, or they may obtain referrals from friends, family, and their doctor. Some people are reluctant to begin psychotherapy because of misperceptions about what will be expected in the therapist's office. The client should feel listened to and understood by their therapist. Many people suffering from severe depression benefit from a combination of psychotropic medication and psychotherapy.

Young children who experience fear or anxiety about their food allergies to such a degree that they avoid food may benefit from professional help. Children with emotional difficulties are often successfully treated with play therapy. Play therapy allows children to play in a controlled environment so that they may express their feelings through play. Children may be treated very quickly through play. Generally, the therapist meets with the parents first, then with the child, and then again with the parents. The therapist will alert the parents to what the play reveals so that the family can address the child's fear directly. This is very different from psychotherapy with adolescents, where confidentiality would be kept between child and therapist and the parents would likely receive much less information from the therapist in consultation sessions. Even adolescents may use elements of play or creative expression in therapy to increase the amount of feelings they express. Older children may use board games with the therapist or art projects. A child with an interest in music or writing may use journal writing or song writing to express feelings. The treatment of psychiatric symptoms in children with food allergies would be the same as for children with other ailments. The only difference may be that the therapist would likely need to know something about the child's physical issues in order to be sensitive in the therapeutic process and to understand the way the food allergies impact the child's daily life.

Some children develop resiliency in managing their food allergy.

Kim, a fifteen year-old daughter of immigrants and allergic to egg, manages her allergies very independently. She reads food labels herself, knows how to call food manufacturers, translates for her mother at medical appointments and asks questions about ingredients to the lunch room staff when her lunch, which she receives through the free lunch program, looks "iffy." "I just ask what I need to ask. People help me. It's not a big deal."

Families engaged in conflict related to the food allergy may be helped through family therapy. Treating only the depressed parent or the teenager who is acting out may miss that the whole family is suffering. Often, one person in a family exhibits the symptoms that the family system is experiencing. That person may be referred to as the identified patient. If the identified patient is the child with food allergies and is sent to individual therapy, the child may feel further like the patient, or the problem in the family. In family therapy, the underlying tensions in the family may be more quickly brought to the surface and dealt with. Also, it may be a way to address the emotional needs of other family members, such as siblings and spouses, who feel neglected because of the attention the child with food allergies is receiving. Family therapy sessions tend to be longer than individual therapy sessions to allow all family members to have a chance to express themselves.

Psychotherapeutic groups are another treatment option. Sometimes this can be a more affordable option if the family is paying out of pocket. This is different from a support group but is also a way to find support from other people. The main difference will be that the therapy group will be lead by a mental health professional and it is less likely that the members of the group will all have a child with a food allergy. The therapist will prescreen group members to make sure that the group will be cohesive and that each member is appropriate for the group. Group psychotherapy is a way for an isolated parent to reduce some of their isolation and learn through group process to see how others experience them. This can provide insight into more effective communication styles and provide an opportunity to see oneself in a more realistic manner. Many people underestimate their worth and through group process come to see that they have much to offer.

Support groups for parents of children with food allergies are an excellent way for parents to meet other parents going through similar experiences. This may decrease feelings of isolation and provide an opportunity to learn from others who are at different stages of adjusting to their child's diagnosis. Online support groups and chat rooms are increasingly popular. They provide an excellent source of information and provide a way to connect with other parents. They also allow parents to participate at all hours of the day and do not require travel.

Food allergies are a manageable condition. More than three million children and their families are living with food allergies every day. While there is currently no cure for food allergies, new legislation has made it easier through food labeling laws and school safety laws to manage them. Children with food allergies every day participate in day care, school, extracurricular activities, sports, music, scouting, and myriad other activities. For families who have difficulty managing the emotions surrounding food allergies, there are multiple treatment options available.

References

Coss, L. M. (2004). *How to manage your child's life-threatening food allergies: Practical tips for everyday life.* Lake Forest, CA: Plumtree Press.

Cox, L. (2008, April 17). *Peanut butter and deadly taunts: A combination of bullying and peanut allergies may put some kids in the ER* [Television broadcast]. New York: American Broadcasting Company. Retrieved from http://abcnews.go.com.

Davis, M. M., Leo H., Singer, D. C., Butchart, A., Clark, S. J. (2009, May). Are schools doing enough for food allergic kids? C. S. Mott Children's Hospital National Poll on Children's Health, University of Michigan 6(3), May 2009. Retrieved from http://health.med.umich.edu/homenpch.cfm?id=325.

Food Allergy & Anaphylaxis Network. (2009). *Cleaning methods: The distribution of peanut allergen in the environment.* Retrieved from http://www.foodallergy. org/page/cleaning-methods.

Food Allergy Initiative. *Section 504 plans.* Retrieved from http://www.faiusa. org/?page=section_504_plans.

Gagne, C. (2008). Bullying case grabs attention. *Allergic Living Magazine,* Retrieved from http://allergicliving.com/index.php/2010/07/02/food-allergy-bul lying-case/print.

Marshak, L. E., & Prezant, F. P. (2007). *Married with special-needs children: A couples' guide to keeping connected.* Bethesda, MD: Woodbine House.

Melina, V., Stepaniak, J., & Aronson, D. (2004). *Food allergy survival guide.* Summertown, TN: Healthy Living Publications.

Sicherer, S. H. (2006). *Understanding and managing your child's food allergies.* Baltimore: The Johns Hopkins University Press.

Resources

Allergy and Asthma Network/Mothers of Asthmatics, Inc. (AANMA). www.
    aanma.org
American Academy of Allergy, Asthma and Immunology; www.aaaai.org
Asthma and Allergy Foundation of America; www.aafa.org
The Food Allergy & Anaphylaxis Network (FAAN); www.foodallergy.org; (800)
    929-4040
Offers books, videos educational materials for families with children with food
allergies as well as training materials for schools and restaurants. Raises money for
research. Web site provides easily accessible and life-saving information for fami-
lies on things likes how to read a label for allergens.
The Food Allergy Initiative; www.foodallergyinitiative.org
Medic Alert; www.medicalert.org
Nonprofit group that makes jewelry with identifying medical information on it.
Maintains medical information for members so that emergency responders can get
the information they need about the wearer's condition immediately.
www.nopeanutsplease.com

CHAPTER 10

Debates Surrounding Childhood Gender Identity Disorder

Eliza A. Dragowski,
María R. Scharrón-del Río, and
Amy L. Sandigorsky

Mark is a 6-year-old boy, who lives with his mother and two siblings. He was referred for a psychological evaluation by his pediatrician, after his mother approached the doctor about Mark's school-related anxiety. As relayed by the pediatrician, although a good student, Mark was having difficulties making friends and participating academically in school. Mark was most upset about the fact that nobody in school liked him and that children made fun of him and called him names. Additionally, he liked to play with typically girl toys, favored colors like pink and purple, and wanted his school materials to picture Disney princesses instead of trucks and cars. Although he got along with his older brother, he never played with him, as the two boys appeared to have nothing in common. Mark was also disinterested in playing with other boys, as he disliked the sports and war games. The pediatrician's diagnostic impression included Childhood Gender Identity disorder and Social Anxiety Disorder.

Charlotte is a 7-year-old girl who was born biological male and named Charlie. At 25 months of age, Charlotte stood by her mother every morning, observing her make-up routine and insisting that she, too, needed to put on lipstick. When denied, Charlotte would go into her older brother's room, pick up a red magic marker, and paint her lips. She cried and protested during haircuts and eventually negotiated with her parents to let her hair grow long. At the age of three, she wrapped scarves around her waist, pretending to be wearing skirts. She also insisted that she was a girl. When these activities were forbidden by her parents, Charlotte became anxious and depressed. She cried every day and kept saying that she hated herself. She also refused to look at her genitalia and often inquired when she would grow a vagina.

After numerous consultations with a myriad of mental health professionals, Charlotte's parents decided to let her live as a girl.

****

In recent years, transgender children seem to be featured on almost every popular talk and news show, including *20/20* (April 27, 2007), *Oprah* (Sept. 28, 2007), and *Dr. Oz* (Feb. 18, 2010). With the bright spotlight currently shining on children who do not conform to traditional gender norms, we are beginning to understand their lives, experiences, and needs. However, we are truly just beginning: Pediatricians and mental health clinicians, although schooled in diagnostic issued surrounding childhood gender nonconformity, often feel inexperienced or unprepared to work with these children and their families, who, as a result, struggle as they try to find appropriate support.

In this chapter, we review developmental, cultural, diagnostic, and treatment issues surrounding children whose gender identity and expression do not correspond to our society's expectations. We begin by clarifying terminology and continue with a brief overview of what is currently known about development of typical and atypical gender identity in childhood. We follow with a critical consideration of the diagnosis of Gender Identity Disorder in Children (GIDC) and the available treatment options. We conclude this chapter by answering questions often asked by families of children who do not fit with our society's gender templates.

Part One: What Is Gender?

In our daily lives, we rarely think about gender. We rarely question what makes a boy a boy, a girl a girl, or how we know our own gender. Most of us assume that an infant born with a penis will grow up to be a boy, who will like to play with trucks and who will eventually develop attraction to girls. Likewise, most of us believe that a baby born with vagina will grow to be a girl, who will love dolls and who will be attracted to boys. These assumptions, while congruent with the experience of a majority of individuals, are just assumptions: They do not reflect the diversity of human experience. Let's begin by clarifying terminology used when speaking about gender-variant children.

Understanding Terminology *Biological sex* refers to a person's anatomical and reproductive structures. Typically, a binary determination is made at birth based on external genitalia.

Gender is a culturally defined construct referring to one's personal sense of being a man or a woman. As the saying goes, no one is born a boy/man or a girl/woman but becomes one through a complex process of socialization.

Gender identity relates to one's subjective and internal identification with a particular gender category. Typically, a biological male perceives himself to be a boy/man, and a biological female sees herself as a girl/woman.

Gender expression is a public display of gender identity through behavior, clothing, or body shape and mannerisms.

Transgender is an umbrella term used to describe people who, to a larger or smaller degree, violate conventional conceptualizations of what it means to be a man or a woman or who mix various aspects of gender roles and identity commonly associated with being a man or a woman (Diamond & Butterworth, 2008). Included in this umbrella term are *transsexuals, cross dressers, androgynous,* and other gender nonconforming people. Recent media attention has focused on transsexuals, people whose gender identity does not correspond to their physical bodies and who sometimes choose to transform their bodies into congruence with their identity. This process, called "transition," may involve hormone therapy, surgery, and other medical and cosmetic interventions. According to some scholars, the term *transsexual* best describes adults, not children (Diamond, 2002). People that *transgress* conventional gender roles are also described as *gender-nonconforming* or *gender-variant*. Throughout this chapter, we will use the terms *gender-variant* and *gender-nonconforming* interchangeably to describe children whose gender expression, gender role behavior, and/or gender identity does not conform to the traditional gender norms.

Sexuality/sexual orientation refers to people's romantic and/or sexual attraction to people of a particular gender. Most commonly, we use the term *heterosexual/straight* to refer to a person who is attracted to a member of another gender, *homosexual/gay/lesbian* to describe an individual attracted to the member of the same gender, and *bisexual* to refer to a person attracted to a member of any gender. A person's gender identity is independent from his or her sexual orientation.

The most common combination (the norm) is that of a biological male, who has a gender identity/expression of a boy/man and is attracted to girls/women, or a biological female, who has a gender identity/expression of a girl/woman and attraction to boys/men. However, it is entirely possible for a person whose biological sex is that of a traditional female to have a gender identity and expression of a boy/man, to self-identify as transgender or transsexual and live as a man of any sexual orientation. To give another example, a biological female can have a gender identity of a girl/woman, who is attracted to other women and identifies herself as a lesbian. It is also possible, however, for a biological male to have a gender identity of a man, to have gender expression conveying the social scheme of a woman, and to be affectionately, romantically, and erotically attracted to other men.

The number of potential combinations of biological sex, gender, and sexual orientation is extensive, especially when considered against the background of world cultures. Numerous societies recognize more than two genders, including Samoa, Hawaii, Siberia, and various American Indian/First Nation groups. In the American Indian groups, for example, persons who take on the role and status traditionally associated with the opposite sex are known as the highly regarded *Two-Spirit* people, who are considered as a third gender (Jacobs, Thomas, & Lang, 1997).

Part Two: Gender Identity Development

While our understanding of prenatal sexual differentiation has increased greatly during the last several decades, we have gained less insight into what determines gender identity. In this section, we provide an overview of what is currently known about typical and atypical gender identity development. We review developmental biology of prenatal sexual differentiation as well as environmental forces known to shape our gender identifications. At the end of this section, we offer an integrative paradigm of gender identity development.

The Nature Path

Typical Development

Our chromosomal makeup is set at the time of conception, with most humans having 46 chromosomes arranged in pairs. In typical males, one pair is composed of one X and one Y sex chromosomes (46,XY karyotype), whereas females generally have one pair made up of two X sex chromosomes (46,XX karyotype). All fetuses begin existence with the same set of gonads that have a potential to differentiate into male or female reproductive organs. Between 6 and 12 weeks of gestation, most fetuses will differentiate into typical male and female bodies. Usual male development will be prompted by the SRY gene beginning production of testosterone and development of Wolffian ducts, which will differentiate into a male genital system. This process will be followed by dihydrotestosterone (DHT), prompting development of male typical genitalia. Typical female development proceeds when undifferentiated gonads develop into ovaries and Mullerian structures develop into the uterus, fallopian tubes, and upper segment of the vagina.

Atypical Development

Although under the current guidelines of the *Diagnostic and Statistical Manual of Mental Disorders, Fourth Edition, Text Revision* (DSM-IV-TR, 2000), children with Disorders of Sex Development (DSD) cannot be diagnosed with GIDC, knowledge of these conditions deepens our understanding of the relationship between person's biological sex and gender identification. Moreover, the proposed revisions to the upcoming (fifth) edition of the DSM request that children with DSD be eligible for the GIDC diagnosis. Consequently, we begin this section with a brief review of DSDs and follow with an overview of development of atypical gender identity development without concurrent intersex conditions.

Disorders of Sex Development

Present classification of DSDs is based on their objective descriptions and, where available, includes genetic etiology. This system recognizes three general categories: Sex Chromosome DSDs; 46, XX DSDs; and 46, XY DSDs (Hughes, Houk, Ahmed, & Lee, 2006). The following is a general and non-exhaustive list of these conditions.

Sex Chromosome DSDs are caused by erroneous cell division, resulting in the zygote cells that are either missing one sex chromosome or containing additional ones. Included in this category are *Turner Syndrome* and *Klinefelter Syndrome*. Most individuals affected by these syndromes tend to acquire typical gender identity and roles (Blakemore, Berenbaum, & Liben, 2009; Pasterski, 2008).

46, XX DSDs affect individuals who are born with a typical female karyotype (46, XX) and masculinized appearance, due to a genetic disorder or exposure to masculinizing hormones in utero. The most frequently occurring type of 46,XX DSD is Congenital Adrenal Hyperplasia (CAH), which is characterized by ambiguous genitalia and female internal structures (Blakemore et al., 2009). Infants affected by CAH are typically raised as girls, who often show some gender nonconforming behaviors including preference for play with boys and typically boyhood toys, increased physical activity, and greater likelihood of being attracted to women in adulthood (Paterski, 2008).

46, XY DSDs occur in individuals born with a typical male karyotype (46,XY) and undermasculinized appearance. Included in this category is the Androgen Insensitivity Syndrome (AIS), caused by hormonal irregularities interrupting typical development of the penis and scrotum. Persons with Complete Androgen Insensitivity Syndrome (CAIS) are born with completely feminine external genitalia and raised as girls, who typically adopt female gender identity and roles. Partial Androgen Insensitivity (PAIS) is characterized by ambiguous genitalia and variable satisfaction with assigned gender roles among those affected (Paterski, 2008).

Girls with CAIS are typically diagnosed after failure to menstruate and ultrasound examination , which reveals testes and no uterus (Paterski, 2008). Caster Semenya, the South African female runner, was required to undergo genetic and sex-determination testing after winning the gold medal at the 2009 track and field world championships in Berlin. In spite of activists and family members' requests to keep results private, various media sources reported that she had no womb or ovaries and that her levels of testosterone were much higher than would be expected for a woman. These results are consistent with CAIS.

Atypical Gender Identity in Absence of Disorders of Sex Development

Another type of gender atypical identification occurs in persons who, in absence of biological anomalies, experience their gender identity as incompatible with gender assigned at birth. According to the Gender Identity Research and Education Society (GIRES, 2006), atypical gender development can be influenced by (1) atypical androgen levels during fetal development, (2) anomalous brain development in the course of prenatal sexual differentiation, and (3) genetic and prenatal chemical influences during periods critical to gender identity formation.

The Nurture Path

Typical Development

According to selected social science theories, children learn gender norms through identifications with parents during early childhood, being reinforced for following normative behaviors and punished for atypical gender behaviors, and cognitive understanding and learning about gender and gender behaviors (Blakemore et al., 2009). It is clear that children in our society are continually encouraged to act according to the accepted gender norms. Even during early infancy, most parents see their little girls as beautiful and delicate and boys as strong and handsome. They encourage gender stereotyped behaviors and disapprove of behaviors that do not reflect society's gender expression expectations. Supporting parental efforts is the American culture, abounding with examples of gender differentiation in television commercials, store layouts, and books designed and marketed separately to boys and girls. By preschool age, children will understand that boys and girls are different and that they express themselves differently in terms of dress and behavior.

Atypical Development

Early theories of atypical gender identification explained it in the context of an intra-psychic conflict, stemming from environmental/familial instability. Some of the current theories name the child's temperament coupled with familial upbringing as contributors to the development of an atypical gender development in children. Zucker and Bradley (1995) as well as Meyer-Bahlburg (2002) see gender-nonconforming children as temperamentally inhibited and sensitive to dysfunctional family dynamics, which contribute to their gender-nonconforming identity and expression.

Nature and Nurture Path

> *I'd like to stop dividing us up as 'nature vs. nurture' and look at our bodies as an intricate system.*
>
> —*(Dr. Anne Fausto-Sterling, speaking at*
> *a public lecture at Wabash College)*

Many scholars and clinicians consider environmental theories of etiology of nonconforming gender identity as dated and sexist. At the same time, while some studies offer support for the neurodevelopmental origin of gender identity and expression, no available evidence is conclusive at this time. While debate about biological versus environmental determinant of gender identity continues, proposals for a more integrative paradigm have been offered. Such thinking conceptualizes gender identity formation as a complex developmental process involving both nature and nature and taking place within a specific sociopolitical context.

According to Diamond's (2006) biased-interaction theory, a child is born with a set of genetic and gestational influences that bias him or her toward a certain pattern of gender expression, which, at the same time, depends on the child's upbringing and the degree of societal tolerance. As children learn about the ethos of the world around them, they start comparing themselves with others. In the process, they analyze their feelings and behavior preferences, wondering who they are like and who they are unlike. For the majority of human population, possession of XX chromosomes corresponds with phenotypically female bodies, which develop into girls/women with characteristics seen as appropriate by their society. Similarly, chromosomal makeup XY typically produces phenotypic males who mature into boys/men with masculine characteristics that are seen as appropriate by their culture. Some individuals, however, take a different developmental path, bringing about atypical gender identifications.

The gender-variant biological male, for example, does not perceive himself to be the same as others of his assigned gender, but sees himself as different in behaviors, preferences, and attitudes. Such a child, after an initial period of confusion, may eventually conclude that, since the only other category he knows is *girl,* maybe he is a girl, too. Within cognitive constrains of childhood, he may even believe that he will grow up to be a woman. As noted by Diamond (2006), the child's ability and willingness to express his or her core feelings about gender will depend on how restrictive or permissive the culture is with respect to accepted gender behaviors and attitudes.

Part Three: Diagnosis, Critique, and Treatment
of Childhood Gender Identity Disorder

It was during a regular well-baby exam. The pediatrician was looking at her. He got really quiet and just sort of watched her for a while, and he brought up a term Gender Identity Disorder. *Excuse me? What's that? He said, you know, like, transgender. I was like, could you spell that for me? I had no idea what he was saying.*

—*(Mother of a transgender child, Dr. Oz Show, February 18, 2010)*

Diagnosis

According to the *DSM-IV-TR* (2000), GIDC has two main features: "a strong and persistent cross-gender identification" signifying a desire to be or assertion of being of the other sex (Criterion A); and the "persistent discomfort with his or her sex or sense of inappropriateness in the gender role of that sex" (Criterion B).

Boys diagnosed with GIDC tend to be preoccupied with activities traditionally associated with stereotypically feminine activities, toys, and clothes (they especially like to play with princesses, Barbie dolls, and enacting the mother role and female fantasy figures). This is matched by lack of interest in typical boyhood toys, avoidance of rough-and-tumble, or sport games. These boys can but don't have to have an expressed wish to be a girl or belief that they will become a woman. They may prefer to sit for urination and pretend that they do not have a penis. Occasionally, these children are disgusted by their genitalia or desire to have a vagina (*DSM-IV-TR*, 2000).

In girls, this condition is associated with rejection of traditionally feminine attire in favor of more masculine clothing. In play, they gravitate to boys, masculine fantasy heroes, rough-and-tumble play, and other stereotypical boyhood games and have little to no interest in dolls and other feminine play activities. These girls may insist on urinating standing up, and believe that they will grow up to be a man with a penis (*DSM-IV-TR*, 2000).

GIDC diagnosis can only be made if the preceding behaviors are accompanied by "clinically significant distress or impairment in social, occupational, or other important areas of functioning" (Criterion C). In young children, such distress is manifested by expressed unhappiness with their biological sex assignment. Older children, in turn, do not develop age-appropriate same-sex friendships and may refuse to attend school in order to avoid teasing and the necessity to dress in traditional gender clothing. The last diagnostic criterion (D) specifies that GID cannot be given to individuals who have concurrent Disorder of Sex Development.

Critique

Ever since its introduction to the *DSM*, GIDC has been a source of intense debate. Those opposed to the diagnosis do not see atypical gender identity as maladaptive and postulate that treatment of GIDC further feeds into gender stereotypes. In their review and evaluation of the diagnosis,

Dragowski, Scharrón-del Río, and Sandigorsky (in press), question the status of GIDC as a mental disorder, due to its flawed diagnostic criteria and strong link to adult homosexuality.

One of the most prominent issues with the diagnosis of GIDC is the fact that it can be made in the absence of the child's discomfort with her or his own sex or desire to be of the other gender. The *DSM-IV-TR* diagnosis is made when children exhibit behaviors or identifications congruent with a set number of indicators included in the four criteria. For example, Criterion A, which examines cross-gender identifications, has five indicators, but manifestation of four of them is enough for diagnosis; any one of the behaviors listed in Criterion B (examining discomfort with sex or gender role), however, needs to be manifested for diagnosis. Therefore, a boy who strongly prefers to wear more stereotypically feminine clothes (indicator A2), to play out princesses (indicator A3) and other stereotypically feminine games (indicator A4) with girls (indicator A5), and who rejects rough play with other boys (Criterion B) can be diagnosed along with children who are unhappy with their sexual anatomy and gender assigned to them at birth. The two children introduced at the beginning of this chapter illustrate the disparity in a range of behavior that is grouped together and seen as the same disorder.

This issue brings about another concern: In spite of media portrayals of all transgender children growing up to be transsexual adults, research shows that a majority of gender nonconforming children grow up to acquire homosexual identity, with a small minority identifying as transsexual (Zucker & Spitzer, 2005).

Diagnosing children with GID when homosexuality is their most likely psychosexual outcome is problematic to many mental health professionals and scholars. Although homosexuality is not recognized as a disorder in the *DSM-IV-TR* (2000), GIDC diagnosis and treatment are seen as a back door to preventing homosexuality. In fact, some scholars claim that GIDC should not be a diagnosis at all , as it fails to cause significant distress or impairment in the children's functioning. As stated in the *DSM-IV-TR,* to be considered a mental disorder, the dysfunction cannot be based in conflict between the affected person and society. Thus, a child's gender nonconformity, not the societal condemnation and rejection of that child, has to be causing distress. However, available literature indicates that societal ostracism is the main course of disturbance among gender-nonconforming children (Bartlett, Vasey, & Bukowski, 2000; Zucker & Cohen-Kettenis, 2008).

Work is currently underway to revise and publish the new edition of the *DSM*. The *DSM-5* Development Sexual and Gender Identity Disorders Work Group (American Psychiatric Association [APA], 2010) has proposed several revisions to GIDC. some of these changes include (1) change of name to Gender Incongruence in Children; (2) removal of the distress/impairment criterion in acknowledgement of psychiatric problems among gender-variant children being a result of societal stigma; (3) manifestation of "a strong desire to be of the other gender or an insistence that he or she is the other gender" as necessary for diagnosis; and (4) inclusion of persons with Disorders of Sex Development as eligible for diagnosis. The proposed revisions continue to draw heated conversations , and it is certain that the discussion about this diagnosis will continue.

Available Treatment Options

Once she was allowed to express herself authentically, once we allowed her to live in her normal role, without trying to force her into a mold that didn't fit her, then she just blossomed. You know, she was on, she took 17 doses of medications a day, 14 different medications to try to get her to fit into this mold, for depression, anxiety, ADHD, she was, you know, Tourette's went in there at the end, just all kinds of things . . . and you know all of those medications went away. Every single one. She is on no medications now. You see her. She can't stop smiling and giggling and, you know, she's just a happy little girl. That wasn't her.

—(Mother of a transgender child, Dr. Oz Show, February 18, 2010)

Rationales for treatment of children diagnosed with GIDC include attempts to reduce ostracism, treatment of underlying psychopathology and stress, as well as prevention of adult transsexuality and homosexuality (Zucker & Cohen-Kettenis, 2008). In general, treatment of GIDC can be divided into corrective interventions designed to eradicate gender nonconforming behavior and supportive treatments aimed at promoting family resilience in the face of societal ostracism and acceptance of gender-variant children.

Corrective treatments are designed to promote normative gender behaviors by working with children and their families. In their work with gender-variant children, therapists reward gender-typical behaviors while ignoring and possibly punishing gender-nonconforming ones. Therapeutic work with parents involves exploration of their contributions to the cross-gender identifications and behavior and understanding and learning how to limit gender-variant behaviors (Zucker & Cohen-Kettenis, 2008).

Supportive treatments, developed by clinicians who do not perceive gender nonconformity as a disorder, concentrate on facilitating the family's acceptance of the child, supporting the child's gender-role expression, helping the family weather societal ostracism, and promoting adjustment (Zucker & Cohen-Kettenis, 2008). A supportive medical treatment involves delaying puberty of the gender-variant children who wish to postpone sexual differentiation associated with puberty in order to (1) provide the child and family with more time before making a more permanent decisions (such as beginning the process of transition), (2) prevent results of puberty from altering the child's body, and (3) help children avoid discrimination based on appearance. The medical term for drugs that postpone puberty is *GnRH inhibitors,* or *GnRH analogues.* Commonly called *"blockers,* these medications stop pubertal development. If the child discontinues intake of these drugs, the body resumes its natural developmental path within six months, making effects of these drugs entirely reversible (Brill & Pepper, 2008).

Part Four: Common Questions and Concerns

Upon hearing for the first time about the diagnosis of GIDC, a parent of a gender-variant child is likely to go to use Google and type in "GID children." Such a search conducted on August 30, 2010 yielded over 5,000,000 results. The first result, titled "How Should Clinicians Deal with GID in Children?" leads to the Web page of the National Association for Research and Therapy of Homosexuality (NARTH), described as a professional and scientific organization that ". . . upholds the rights of individuals with unwanted homosexual attraction to receive effective psychological care and the right of professionals to offer that care." Exploration of the site leads to intervention models based on theories that conceptualize families of children with GIDC as pathological: frequently absent fathers and mothers who are emotionally unavailable, disturbed, and/or intrusive. Ineffective parenting and lax moral views about gender roles are also named as contributors to the development of the disorder. Finally, the relationship between GID and homosexuality is highlighted. This unwanted long-term psychosexual outcome of GID is seen as demanding prevention and intervention.

If the parent is able to go back to the search results and click on the following link, another very different perspective appears. This next link, from the *GID Reform Advocates* includes information questioning the validity of the GID diagnosis and its misuse in a moralistic agenda intended to prevent homosexuality. This organization offers papers, a list of advocates, and links to affirmative organizations. There are many other links, some affirmative, some condemning, and some written in language that is difficult to understand. Likely flooded with guilt, shame, and confusion, parents may ask themselves: Who to believe? Where to start? Who is right? And more importantly, how can I help my child?

This section was written with such parents in mind and is based on our belief that the rejection of traditional gender roles does not constitute psychiatric illness, but that it does increase vulnerability to societal ostracism and need for social support. We will address various common questions and some of the practical dilemmas faced by parents of gender-variant children. We aim to help synthesize the information introduced thus far. We also provide a list of resources for parents, educators, and mental health practitioners who want to support gender-variant children. We have arranged this section according to answers commonly asked by those who love and are concerned about the well-being of these children.

What Is Wrong with My Child?

> *He is so lonely. His brothers are embarrassed by him. We are embarrassed*
> *by him. Why won't he just change? Why can't he be normal? . . .*
> > —*Parent of a six-year-old gender-variant boy*
> > *(Brill & Pepper, 2008, p. 81)*

We tend to see gender as a concept with two opposing and mutually exclusive options—men and women. What would happen if we saw men
and women residing on a continuum containing traditional gender identifications and behaviors as well as the less traditional ones? From this perspective, a child who feels and behaves in ways that do not correspond
to our traditional gender roles would be considered different but not abnormal. And, while we are on the topic of normalcy, let's consider the concept in more detail.

The information coming from the media, Internet, family members,
friends, and medical and mental health practitioners about what is or is
not normal about a child can be overwhelming and confusing because of
the relativity of the term. We can determine normalcy by what is familiar
to our experiences, what is most frequently observed, what is perceived as
ideal or what is culturally appropriate (Tiefer, 1995). Clinical standards for
normalcy, which purport to utilize objective scientific data to make judgments about health and illness, are not disconnected from the sociopolitical contexts in which they are made. History shows that psychiatry has
been used to pathologize race, gender, ethnicity, and sexual orientation.
One need only look at the history of the eugenics movement to quickly
identify current eugenic trends in some of today's scientific debates regarding intelligence. Clinical standards have also been used to perpetuate
oppressions in the lesbian, gay, bisexual, and transgender (LGBT) community. Until 1973, homosexuality was classified as a psychiatric diagnosis,
in spite of research demonstrating that LGBT persons were living productive and self-fulfilling lives.

Our accepted definition of normal "maintains sets of hierarchical political structures, economic systems, and social conventions that benefit those
at the top" (Girshick, 2008, p. 5). Furthermore, it shames, stigmatizes, and
discriminates against those who deviate from the accepted canon of nor-
mality. Thus, when faced with children who violate accepted definitions
of gender, we tend to label them as abnormal, difficult, or sick. Rarely do
we stop and think that we can choose to question the system that op-
presses those who are not the norm. It is our choice, however, to question
our assumptions and to become accepting and affirming of difference and
diversity.

Is this My Fault?

It is a common response for parents of gender-nonconforming children
to think about how they could be responsible for their child's gender

variance. While there is no clear consensus about etiology of atypical gender identity, available research suggests that gender identity is a result of
complex interplay of biology and environment.

Mental health theorists and practitioners, dating back to Freud, have
argued that both gender identity and sexual orientation are both heavily influenced by rearing practices. This is an often recurrent myth stemming from the belief that deviation from traditional gender roles is an
illness (Brill & Pepper, 2008; Goldman, 2008). The families of gender-
nonconforming children and adults are no different than the families of
gender-conforming children and adults. Furthermore, there are many
gender-nonconforming children who come from families steeped in stereotypical gender roles.

It is possible for parents to be gender conforming and also be affirming
of their children's identity and behaviors. Stephen Orr narrates an episode
of his childhood that took place in 1971 in Abilene, Texas:

> My father was tossing a football with my brothers in the front yard.
> Seeing me sitting alone on the steps, my mother took my dad aside.
> "Dub," she said, calling my dad by his nickname, "I think Steve is feel-
> ing a little left out. Why don't you ask him if he'd like to play too?"
>
> So my dad walked over. "Wanna throw the football some?" he
> asked.
>
> "I'd really rather go pick flowers," I replied.
>
> *And we did.*
>
> My father, a former football coach, spent the rest of the afternoon
> picking flowers with me in a nearby field. (Orr, in Trachtenberg,
> 2005, p.4).

Is GID a Mental Disorder? Is It a Disability?

Inclusion of GID in the *DSM* signifies that the mainstream psychiatry and
psychology consider gender nonconformity a psychiatric condition. As
described in this chapter, however, many scientists, mental health professionals, and advocates question the validity of pathologizing gender variance, adding that it perpetuates the social stigma already associated with
gender nonconformity and that it enables practitioners to diagnose young
boys and girls who display stereotyped sissy or tomboy behavior. It is our
position that childhood rejection of traditional gender roles does not constitute disability. While examples of children distressed with their biological sex exist in the literature, such cases are not very common.

Mark, introduced at the beginning of this chapter, was a patient of one
of the authors (MSR). Along with Mark's mother, teacher, and school counselor, the clinician designed a multimodal intervention, which included
play therapy, progressive desensitization and positive reinforcement
around social interactions with peers, and participation in a social skills
counseling group at school. Mark's anxiety eventually lessened, and he

became more socially involved with his peers. His academic performance improved, and he began to attend play dates and peer birthdays. Mark's gender variance was discussed with his mother, who had many questions, similar to the ones discussed in this chapter. She was accepting of the possibility that Mark's gender-variant behaviors would continue and was adamant about expressing unconditional positive regard to him at all times. This clinician's decision to listen to the family's chief complaint of distress (social anxiety) instead of focusing on his gender-variant behaviors represented an approach to treatment that was different from that initially promoted by the pediatrician.

Is this Just a Phase?

Each child's development is both unique and shared. As such, it has to be considered within its particular context, culture, and time. Not everyone fits neatly into the many available theories of human development: Healthy development can happen in many ways and have different end results (Savin-Williams, 2005, as noted by Brill and Pepper, 2008):

> For some children, expressing gender variance may be a phase; for others, it is not. The longer a child has identified as cross-gender, the easier it becomes for a parent to answer this question. Regardless of the eventual outcome, the self-esteem, mental well-being, and overall health of a gender-variant child relies heavily on receiving love, support, and compassion from their parents. (p. 32)

When parents ask about whether their children will outgrow their nonconforming behaviors, they are worrying about many different matters, which include (1) their own preconceptions about gender roles (sexism) and sexual orientation (heterosexism/homophobia); (2) desire for crossgender behaviors to stop, as they bring about uncomfortable feelings; and/or (3) anxiety over the challenges to be faced in the future. Let's address each one of these separately.

Sexism and Heterosexism

Most of us have been raised in a culture that not only lauds heterosexuality but also equates an ideal male with heterosexuality. Children (especially boys) who do not conform to gender norms face daily ostracism from society at large. It is our contention that such ostracism is a result of sexism and heterosexism deeply ingrained in our society. Let's define both concepts.

Sexism, as defined by Girshick (2008) is "the belief system that men are better or superior to women, combined with the institutional advantages men have over women to entitle them in law, employment, power, and so forth" (p. 205). While not many people would openly say that men are better than women, many value masculine over feminine qualities. For example, aggressiveness is often valued over passivity in both men and women. When applied to gender-nonconforming children, sexism plays into the double standard regarding treatment of gender-variant boys as opposed to gender-variant girls. Since feminine behavior is considered less desirable than masculine behavior within our society, feminine boys are less tolerated than masculine girls.

Heterosexism is the marginalizing belief system and dominant discourse that values a heterosexual sexual orientation as the norm and devalues all departures (Croteau, Lark, & Lance, 2005). Sometimes labeled as *heteronormativity*, this system considers "heterosexuality as the standard with which to compare any other sexual orientation, where heterosexuality is normal, natural, and right" (Girshick, 2008, p. 203) as contrasted with the abnormal, unnatural, and wrong people of a sexual orientation different from heterosexuality.

Although gender identity and sexual orientation are two different concepts, in the case of gender-variant children, sexism and heterosexism are intricately related. One often hears people who claim to be okay with gay people as long as they don't flaunt it. Gender transgressions are heavily policed, particularly in boys, because they are thought to be related to homosexuality. Oftentimes, when parents hope that the gender-variant behavior is just a phase, they are hoping that their child will not be gay. Not all children who exhibit gender-nonconforming behavior will later identify as gay/lesbian/bisexual/transgender/transsexual/queer (LGBTQ). However, as described in earlier parts of this chapter, the majority of children diagnosed with GIDC grow up to acquire a homosexual identity. Therefore, parents of gender-variant children should face the possibility that their child might grow up to be gay.

Uncomfortable Feelings

While Jazz's parents now fully accept their son as their daughter, the transition has not been without considerable doubt and stress. Many parents grieve for the child that never was. "I mourn the loss of the idea of my son," Renee said. "I see pictures and the video, and that child's gone. But there's a wonderful person now that's with us."

—(Goldberg & Adriano, 2007)

Parental dreams and expectations exist even before the child's birth. Many of these dreams materialize in milestones and achievements, like graduations, weddings, or championships. Some of these dreams are modeled after the parents' own interests and childhoods or in response to them: a blue-collar family may dream of their child becoming a famous doctor; a father who excelled in sports may dream about driving his son to practice; a mother who loves pageants may fantasize about her daughter entering beauty competitions. When children grow up and express their own desires and ambitions, parents may need to let go of some of those dreams and embrace those of the children. While this is true for most families, parents are often not prepared to let go of the gendered dimension of these dreams. Having birthed a baby boy, parents may find it hard to picture their child in a flowery dress and stockings. When parents express a desire for the gender-variant behavior to be just a phase, their wish may stem from not wanting to let go of, or adjusting, many of these dreams.

The Outreach Program for Children with Gender-Variant Behaviors and their Families from the Children's National Medical Center in Washington, DC, urges parents to take a look at their own feelings and examine them:

> You may have to adjust your dreams of how you expected parenting and your family to be. If these changes must occur, you may experience some of the emotions associated with loss, such as shock, denial, anger, and despair. These feelings are all part of the process towards acceptance. You must reach acceptance in order to affirm your child's uniqueness. (p.13)

Having a support network of other families with gender-variant children can be an invaluable resource to deal with this process. Consulting a mental health professional can also be a beneficial source of support during the mourning process that can result as we let go of our dreams.

Can My Child Be Cured?

As described in the earlier part of this chapter, there are a number of treatment options available to parents of gender-nonconforming children. However, while some treatment effectiveness studies have been conducted, it is impossible to truly evaluate their efficacy. In other words, no treatment method has been unequivocally shown to be successful. As previously stated, we, along with a number of national mental health associations, support treatments concentrating on helping the family accept their children, supporting their children's gender expression, withstanding ostracism, and promoting adaptive functioning and adjustment.

Won't My Child Have a Harder Life?

Studies demonstrate that the cross-gendered behavior of children (especially boys) is likely to elicit negative reactions from peers and adults. In fact, the amount of stigmatization seems to be directly related to the degree of gender nonconformity exhibited. Available literature on the topic demonstrates negative peer relations, rejection, and even victimization (Bartlett et al., 2000; D'Augelli, Pilkington, & Hershberger, 2002).

As aforementioned, these negative societal reactions are likely to stem from sexism, heterosexism, and the inflexible attitudes about gender in our society. Practitioners who support treatments designed to eradicate gender nonconformity in children claim that their interventions are designed to help children avoid the future distress of experiencing sexism and heterosexism. However, in our opinion, making the child the focus of intervention is likely to convey the message that there is something inherently wrong with the child.

Many national mental health professional associations (such as the American Psychological Association, the American Counseling Association, and the National Association of Social Workers) oppose the use of reparative and conversion therapies that aim to change sexual orientation, insisting that "scientific evidence does not support the efficacy of reparative therapy" (Carroll, 2010, p. 37). While there is no clear consensus on the approaches to the treatment of GIDC, the mental health professions have consistently moved to more affirmative approaches towards gendernonconforming clients. We, too, believe in affirmation of diversity and variance in gender and sexual orientation. Along the same lines, we believe in questioning and eradicating social and institutional sexism and heterosexism. Teaching children to suppress and deny their self-identification puts them at increased risk for engaging in substance and alcohol use, risky sexual behaviors, school problems, and suicide (Chesir-Teran & Hughes, 2009; Grossman & D'Augelli, 2007).

How Can I Help Protect My Child from Suffering and Harm?

There are many things that parents can do to be affirming and contribute to their gender-variant child's well-being. The Outreach Program for Children with Gender-Variant Behaviors and their Families, part of the Children's National Medical Center, in Washington, DC, suggests the following (n.d., 6–9):

- Love your child for who he or she is.
- Question traditional assumptions regarding gender roles and sexual orientation.
- Create a safe space for your child.
- Seek out socially acceptable activities.
- Validate your child.
- Seek out supportive sources.
- Talk to other significant people, including siblings, extended family, friends, and caretakers.
- Prepare your child to deal with bullies.
- Be your child's advocate.

The brochure also includes a list of pitfalls, which include finding fault, pressuring the gender-variant child to change, and blaming the child (p.11).

Parents may choose to educate themselves and others to be accepting, affirmative, and nonjudgmental of their children and themselves and to activate a support network, which may include family, friends, support groups, and/or mental health professionals. It is also important for parents to be proactive in their children's schools by meeting with teachers and administrators, advocating for professional development, and help-ing to create antibullying policies, which are just some of the advocacy activities.

Where Can I Seek More Information?
Where Can I Reach Out for Help?

In today's world, whenever we need to learn about anything, we tend to turn to the Internet first. As illustrated at the beginning of this part of the chapter, the Internet, while immensely useful, can be the source of con-tradictory information and devoid of the human contact needed to make sense of perplexing facts. We urge interested readers to contact local LGBT centers and outreach organizations. Parents may also consider seeking support from mental health professionals, including psychologists, psy-chiatrists, counselors, social workers, and other therapists who may pro-vide crucial support in difficult times. It is important to keep in mind that not everyone will have the expertise to deal with issues regarding gender variance. Thus, it is important to ask service providers about how experi-enced they are with gender-identity and gender-variance issues as well as ask about their approach. You want to seek services from someone knowl-edgeable, affirming, and supportive of diversity.

We are including a short list of resources. Following these links and searching for these organizations on the Web will offer more information as well as local and national resources.

Organizations

- Local LGBT Centers
- GLSEN—Gay, Lesbian, and Straight Education Network—http://www.glsen.org/cgi-bin/iowa/all/home/index.html
- PFLAG—Parents, Families, and Friends of Lesbians and Gays—http://community.pflag.org/Page.aspx?pid=194&srcid=-2
- Mermaid Support Groups
- Outreach Program for Children with Gender-Variant Behaviors and Their Families
- Children's National Medical Center

Books

Brill, S., & Pepper, R. (2008). *The transgender child: A handbook for families and professionals.* San Francisco: Cleis Press.
Girshick, L. B. (2008). *Transgender voices: Beyond women and men.* Lebanon, NH: University Press of New England.
Rottnek, M. (1999). *Sissies and tomboys: Gender nonconformity and homo-sexual childhood.* New York: New York University Press.

Other Organizations and Web Sources

- www.transfamily.org
- http://www.transkidspurplerainbow.com/
- http://genderspectrum.org/

References

American Psychiatric Association. (2000). *Diagnostic and statistical manual of mental disorders* (4th ed., text rev.). Washington, DC: Author.

American Psychiatric Association. (2010). *302.6 Gender identity disorder in children: Proposed revision.* Retrieved July 8, 2010, from http://www.dsm5.org/ProposedRevisions/Pages/proposedrevision.aspx?rid=192.

Bartlett, N., Vasey, P., & Bukowski, W. (2000). Is gender identity disorder in children a mental disorder? *Sex Roles, 43*(11), 753–785.

Blakemore, J.E.O., Berenbaum, S.A., & Liben, L.S. (2009). *Gender development.* New York: Psychology Press.

Brill, S., & Pepper, R. (2008). *The transgender child: A handbook for families and professionals.* San Francisco: Cleis Press.

Carroll, L. (2010). *Counseling sexual and gender minorities.* Upper Saddle River, NJ: Prentice Hall/Merrill.

Chesir-Teran, D., & Hughes, D. (2009). Heterosexism in high school and victimization among lesbian, gay, bisexual, and questioning students. *Journal of Youth and Adolescence, 38*(7), 963–975. doi:10.1007/s10964-008-9364-x.

Croteau, J.M., Lark, J.S., & Lance, T.S. (2005). Our stories be told: Deconstructing the heterosexist discourse in the counseling professions. In J.M. Croteau, J.S. Lark, M.A. Lidderdale & Y.B. Chung (Eds.), *Deconstructing heterosexism in the counseling professions: A narrative approach* (pp. 1–15). London: Thousand Oaks, CA: Sage.

D'Augelli, A., Pilkington, N., & Hershberger, S. (2002). Incidence and mental health impact of sexual orientation victimization of lesbian, gay, and bisexual youths in high school. *School Psychology Quarterly, 17*(2), 148–167. doi:10.1521/scpq.17.2.148.20854.

Diamond, L.M., & Butterworth, M. (2008). Questioning gender and sexual identity: Dynamic links over time. *Sex Roles, 59,* 365–376.

Diamond, M. (2002). Sex and gender are different: Sexual identity and gender identity are different. *Clinical Child Psychology and Psychiatry, 7*(3), 320–334. doi:10.1177/1359104502007003002.

Diamond, M. (2006). Biased-interaction theory of psychosexual development: "How does one know if one is male or female?" *Sex Roles, 55,* 589–600.

Dragowski, A.E., Scharrón-del Río, M.R. & Sandigorsky, A.A. (In press). "Childhood Gender Identity. . . Disorder?" *Childhood psychological disabilities: Current controversies.* Ed. A. Bursztyn. New York: ABC CLIO.

Gender Identity Research and Education Society. (2006). Atypical gender development: A review. *International Journal of Transgenderism, 9*(1), 22–44.

Girshick, L.B. (2008). *Transgender voices: Beyond women and men.* Lebanon, NH: University Press of New England.

Goldman, L. (2008). *Coming out, coming in: Nurturing the well-being and inclusion gay youth in mainstream society.* New York: Routledge.

Goldberg, A. B., & Adriano, J. (2007, April 27). "I'm a girl": Understanding trans-gender children. *ABC News*. Retrieved from http://abcnews.go.com/2020/story?id=3088298&page=1.

Grossman, A., & D'Augelli, A. (2007). Transgender youth and life-threatening be-haviors. *Suicide and Life-Threatening Behavior, 37*(5), 527–537.

Hughes, I., Houk, C., Ahmed, S., & Lee, P. (2006). Consensus statement on man-agement of intersex disorders. *Archives of Disease in Childhood, 91*(7), 554–563.

Jacobs, S. E., Thomas, W., & Lang, S. (1997). *Two-spirit people: Native American gender identity, sexuality, and spirituality.* Urbana and Chicago: University of Illinois Press.

Meyer-Bahlburg, H.F.L. (2002). Gender identity in young boys: A parent- and peer-based treatment protocol. *Clinical Child Psychology and Psychiatry, 7*(3), 360–375.

Newman, L. K. (2002). Sex, gender and culture: Issues in the definition, assessment and treatment of gender identity disorder. *Clinical Child Psychology and Psy-chiatry, 7*(3), 352–359. doi:10.1177/1359104502007003004.

Pasterski, V. (2008). Disorders of sex development and atypical sex differentiation. In D. L. Rowland & L. Incrocci (Eds.), *Handbook of sexual and gender identity dis-orders* (pp. 354–375). Hoboken, NJ: Wiley.

Tiefer, L. (1995). *Sex is not a natural act and other essays.* Boulder, CO: Westview Press.

Trachtenberg, R., & Bachtell, T. (2005). *When I knew.* New York: Regan Books.

Wabash College. (2007). *Fausto-Sterling: "Our bodies are intricate systems."* Retrieved January 23, 2010, from http://www.wabash.edu/news/displayStory_print.cfm?news_ID=4313.

Zucker, K. J., & Bradley, S. J. (1995). *Gender Identity disorder and psychosexual prob-lems in children and adolescents.* New York: Guilford Press.

Zucker, K., & Cohen-Kettenis, P. (2008). Gender identity disorder in children and adolescents. *Handbook of sexual and* gender identity disorders (pp. 376–422). Hoboken, NJ: Wiley.

Zucker, K., & Spitzer, R. (2005). Was the gender identity disorder of childhood diagnosis introduced into DSM-III as a backdoor maneuver to replace ho-mosexuality? A historical note. *Journal of Sex & Marital Therapy, 31*(1), 31–42. doi:10.1080/00926230590475251.

CHAPTER 11

Disabilities, Families, and Schools

Alberto M. Bursztyn

In American culture, childhood is lived primarily in the contexts of home and school. As noted in preceding chapters, the experience of residential placement has remained an option only for children with the most severe disabilities. Children with disabilities are now more likely that ever to be integral participants in the life of home and the neighborhood school. Throughout the United States, schools are increasingly accommodating children with special needs in the same classrooms as those attended by typically developing children, following legal mandates and parental pressure. Schools attended exclusively by children with special needs are shrinking in number and struggling to justify their existence. Still, advocates and parents point out that these changes have been hard won and that quality education for children with special needs is still an aspiration, not a reality.

Families have played a central role in the development of contemporary special education in public schools. In fact, parental advocacy for access to free and appropriate education for their children with disabilities in the 1960s culminated in the landmark legislation that established special education services as a right in the mid 1970s. Shaped in the contentious climate of the struggle for access, the relationship between schools and parents of children with disabilities is now regulated by federal law and court mandates, giving parents rights and degrees of control over their children's education that extend beyond those available to other parents. Despite the legal scripts and protections, however, parents of children with disabilities and schools are often at odds over expectations, educational placements, and the nature, quality, and frequency of services.

Conflicts between parents and schools are multilayered, but we may distinguish between disputes about classification, parental demands for a child's integration within the school's general education program, and conflicts that arise from parental demands for specific services and therapies. There might not be a concern about classification if the child has a severe condition that was identified at birth or soon thereafter; conflict is more common when the child's needs are identified by others in the context of child care or schooling.

In the current educational policy context, where only the most disabled students are precluded from high-stakes testing, and when federal oversight frowns upon special education self-contained classes, there is little incentive to classify students. More often, these days, administrators will recommend that children with low scores repeat grades—despite evidence that this approach does not improve learning outcomes. Initial referrals from teachers are generally discouraged but are more likely to be approved by administrators and testers if the identified child has severe learning problems or is behaviorally disordered or unmanageable in the classroom.

When there are differences of perception regarding the nature of the child's difficulties, parents may opt to deny consent for a formal assessment, seek a private evaluation, and/or contest the classification recommended by the school district. Although multidisciplinary teams in schools seek to identify the disability and degree of impairment with a degree of objectivity, their internal deliberations might take into account the parents' willingness to agree to the designation or label suggested by the assessment. This is of particular concern when the child is recommended for a classification that carries a negative connotation, such as Emotionally Disturbed. The stigma associated with the label makes some parents recoil and withdraw their cooperation with the assessment process. There are similar concerns regarding autism and cognitive disabilities.

Although not a sanctioned practice, I have witnessed school-based assessment teams compromise on a label that the parents are willing to accept. School assessment professionals justify the practice, pointing out that once children have Individualized Education Programs (IEPs) they are eligible for most services available through special education, regardless of classification. This arrangement presents its own set of drawbacks; the parents may continue to deny the nature of the child's difficulties, and the services may not be focused on the child's needs.

When the parents flatly reject services or otherwise disagree with the district's recommendations, there is a concurrent erosion of trust. Protracted conflict about classification or required services could lead to resolution through due process, but even if the parent succeeds in avoiding classification or rejecting services the outcome may be counterproductive for the child, because she would still remain in a setting that considers her disabled. The lack of agreement between the school and family could place the child at greater risk especially in cases where the child has been identified as having poor adjustment to the school setting.

Current Trends in Special Education

Thirty-five years after the landmark legislation that established rights for free and appropriate education for children with special needs, the nature of challenges have shifted from universal access to effective education. Most critics of the special education system point to the relatively low quality of instruction and stubbornly high dropout rates, despite its considerable cost. Low graduation numbers, poor preparation for employment, and high rates of incarceration, particularly among poor and urban special education students, continue to spur calls for reform and overhaul.

In the current fiscal and accountability climate, education policy directives are aimed at restricting expensive placements in segregated special education settings. Therefore, administrators routinely discourage referrals for evaluation, and schools tend to provide only the minimum required services for students who are already classified. Although cost cutting has been an incentive for maintaining students with social needs in the general education classroom, advocates for inclusion have argued for such placements on ideological grounds. In their view, disabilities must not be a category of exclusion and marginalization. Instead, they argue for maximum social integration in the regular classroom to give equal access to normative experiences to all children, regardless of ability or disability. Moreover, they point to the beneficial effects of integration on typically developing peers. Emphasis on maximum inclusion most vividly articulates a vision of equal rights despite differences, of full membership despite limitations.

Although it is gaining strength and support from parents and advocates, inclusion as a policy often collides with its philosophical antagonist, the legally stipulated and prescribed continuum of services, which envisions a range of placements and services tailored to the individual needs of children with disabilities. The fundamental premise supporting the continuum is that children may move along this range of services and move progressively toward full mainstreaming as they compensate for their deficits and schools accommodate to their needs. A continuum of services ranges from minimal supports at the regular classroom level—for example, counseling or speech therapy—to residential or hospital placement at the other end of the continuum, where there is little or no contact with typically developing peers.

In special education professional circles there are strong inclusion and continuum proponents who offer sharp critiques of each other's paradigms. Inclusion advocates point to the lackluster record of mainstreaming in public schools. They argue that special education classification is a one-way ticket to restrictive placements and social isolation. Defenders of the continuum model argue that the regular education context may deprive children with specific needs the specialized service and necessary levels of support needed to promote their learning and development. They view full inclusion as an ideological stance that sacrifices the real needs of children rather than a pedagogical approach that meets the individual needs of children.

Critics of the continuum model point out that the low rate of mainstreaming is a consequence of the professionalization of disability services. Thomas Skrtic, in particular, contends that the specialization of workers in special education further isolates the identified children from regular education. By virtue of possessing diagnostic labels, children become subjects of therapeutic interventions, which become codified in their IEPs. Dispensing professional services in a format borrowed from the medical field, special educators prescribe remedial therapies to correct the difficulties previously noted, while freeing regular educators from the awkward challenge of confronting the limits of their accepted instructional practices.

Skrtic also notes that this compartmentalization of education stifles problem solving in the classroom. Because problems presented by classified learners are typically not easily accommodated in regular education pedagogy, they are resolved by turning student characteristics and difficulties into jurisdictional problems. These identified students are subsequently assigned to different sets of specialists, who design specialized interventions. As an alternative, he recommends expanding the problem-solving capacity and knowledge base of regular educators, instead of maintaining a separate education system.

Other critics of special education point to the failure of remediation to address students' learning deficits and the system's failure to stem high dropout rates. The disappointing learning outcomes have spurred a parent-led revolt and a reconsideration of special education pedagogy. Advocating for full inclusion, vocal parents and other advocates demand that children with special needs remain in the regular classroom rather than one served by specialists in segregated settings. Dissatisfaction with the system's outcomes has already spurred significant changes in the reauthorization of the Individuals with Disabilities Education Act, which now places a greater burden on schools to prove that the promised benefits of alternative placements to the regular classroom outweigh potential perils.

Although these arguments are far from settled, emerging practices and legal precedents have opened the door wider for inclusion initiatives while creating more safeguards against inappropriate identification of children for special education services. Both of these trends validate the critical appraisal of special education as a system that has largely failed to return classified children to the mainstream classroom. Seeking to establish guidelines for inclusion, Beukelman and Mirenda proposed a framework for levels of participation. They described four levels as follows:

Competitive participation refers to situations in which classified students are required to meet the academic standards of their peers. Although there may be no need for curricular modifications, students who participate at this level may not be expected to complete every activity. Extended timelines or modified assignments are the most common accommodations at a competitive level. Behaviorally challenged students might be allowed to leave the class to meet with a counselor or benefit from accommodations in the classroom, such as engaging in a soothing activity.

Active participation implies capacity for participation in the general education curriculum; however, these students need not meet the same academic standards as their peers. These students are evaluated according to their individual goals, which are specified in their IEPs, and receive supplemental instruction to develop specific skills. When students are active participants in the curriculum, modifications to daily activities are required. For example, the modified curriculum may parallel the work done by peers but at a level of complexity appropriate for the students' capacity to succeed. A child with pronounced ADHD, for example, may be allowed to hand in shorter or modified versions of the class assignment.

Involvement is a relatively minimal level of participation in classes and activities where the academic content is generally too difficult for the classified student. These students may be offered alternative activities selected from the range of possible tools that the IEP team has suggested. The goal of involvement is to ensure that the student is engaged to the greatest extent possible. A child with autism and moderate cognitive deficits, for example, may be capable of participating in selected classroom activities with the guidance and encouragement of a paraprofessional or other support staff.

Finally, Beukelman and Mirenda refer to *no participation* as a caveat for educators who may consider a placement in which the student is physically present in a general classroom but passive and uninvolved. This level of academic participation, they note, is never acceptable. If a student cannot be productively involved in classroom activities, teachers must ask for help from other team members and administrators.

Clearly, students will perform at different levels on different tasks and under the guidance of different teachers, but the basic premise of this student participation framework is sound and can be used to gauge functional and meaningful learning in inclusion settings. Unfortunately, in the rush to move students into regular classrooms, the nature of their involvement and their needs for adequate supports are often not taken into account. The result could be situations in which the child's teacher and peers become indifferent to or, in extreme cases, even resent the presence of the child with special needs, thereby negating all the potential benefits of such an arrangement. The following example describes a situation of growing teacher detachment from the needs of a child with disabilities.

Ms Lewis's classroom, in an affluent suburban school, was hot and crowded when I visited on a May afternoon. The ninth-graders in her class where busily reviewing material that was likely to appear in upcoming New York State math exams. In the back of the room, near door, Victor sat in his wheelchair, dozing off, while Jim, the paraprofessional assigned to his care, was reading a day-old newspaper. About 20 minutes into the lesson, Victor began to move his hands and make loud noises; this prompted Jim to show him picture symbols in an attempt to quiet him down and ascertain if Victor needed to go to the bathroom. After a few minutes of inconclusive communication, with some of the students taking the opportunity to talk among themselves, Jim helped Victor navigate the power wheelchair away from the classroom. They did not return for the rest of the period. Ms. Lewis commented that she feels sorry for Victor, but sees no benefit to his being in her class. Moreover, she said, he is a distraction to the rest of the class. She explained that there are four other students with IEPs in that class who are making adequate progress. But she related in a low voice that Victor's mother is very active in the school and the district; she said with a smile, "Administration would not dare take her on."

While Victor's case is extreme, it is not altogether unusual. Empowered and well-informed parents may in fact intimidate school administrators. It is often easier to meet the parents' demands than to get involved in time-consuming arbitration or lawsuits that may support the parents' case. Moreover, parents understand that gaining political clout within a district may facilitate access to services for their children and therefore may seek positions in school boards or otherwise pursue access to decision makers.

We may conclude from the previous example that inclusion, when done poorly, is more harmful than when not done at all. In most cases, approaches to inclusion are often more thoughtful and successful than in Victor's experience, both the class and the child with special needs benefit from the placement if they all engage in meaningful work and the classified child is not socially isolated. That was the case for Ms. Lewis' other classified students, who had mild learning disabilities and received in- and out-of-school support services. But the illustration is helpful to appreciate the potential influence that parents may exert on school staff and on the implementation of policies for their children.

Consideration of conflicts regarding access to specific services needs to take into account parental empowerment as well as familiarity with special education law. Conflicts between parents and school staff are relatively common in affluent districts and between highly educated parents in city schools but are relatively rare in poor and immigrant communities. The central issue in these disputes is cost. Parents who know their rights often compel the system to fully fund interventions for their children; while districts tend to offer cheaper and more generic alternatives to less informed parents. The cost of intensive applied behavior analysis for children with autism or private residential schools for students with emotional and behavioral challenges could be prohibitive if such interventions were widely available to all the students who qualify for such services. Moreover, health plans generally fail to cover such costs. As Colin Ong-Dean points out, parents who understand the nuances of the system and have access to resources, including legal counsel, disproportionally marshal costly education and therapeutic services for their children.

Engagement

Engagement in the education process ranges widely across families and schools, from hard-to-reach families who fail to participate in legally required educational planning meetings to families who monitor school services closely and do not hesitate to take legal action to demand specific interventions for their children. Most families fall between these two extremes, and many are satisfied with their children's education and their relationship with school personnel. But as is the case with most children and schools, these relationships tend to fluctuate from year to year based on classroom staffing, district policies, and the developmental needs of the child.

Legislation that extended services for young children and their families in the 1990s emphasized active collaboration, in place of passive consent. Likewise, the latest reenactment of the federal law affecting school-age students expands parents' rights and promotes their engagement in all aspects of the educational process. Research suggests that active and constructive parental participation in school matters is most beneficial for children with special needs; yet, establishing and maintaining collaborative relationships between schools and families remain elusive goals.

Investigations on the sources of conflict and disengagement reveal complex and diverse roots. From the school's perspective, parental demands may appear costly, unrealistic, or impractical; as a rule, school administrators prioritize institutional needs over individual needs. The presence of these differences is anticipated in the law, which provides ample guidance for arbitration. Parents who are most savvy about their legal rights and seek legal representation are best able to win these disputes. As Ong-Dean convincingly demonstrates, affluent and well-educated parents pressure the special education system and generally succeed in channeling disproportional school district resources to address their children's challenges. On the other hand, parents who are ill informed or unable to access adequate representations tend to become quietly dispirited and withdraw from the educational planning process when they disagree with school actions. Beth Harry's research provides vivid portraits of such families. She pointedly documents how puzzling and intimidating the special education process is for disempowered parents. Her qualitative research conducted over the past 20 years documents the linguistic, cultural, and life circumstances that constitute barriers and undermine effective engagement of immigrant, minority, and poor parents As a consequence of their limited knowledge and engagement, their children receive basic and often inferior services.

Trust

Most research on family–school relations has focused on parental engagement and has found high correlations between involvement and student success; fewer studies have focused on the nature of the parents' involvement. Parents' relationships with schools may be assessed in regard to the level of collaboration and trust. An actively involved parent could be someone like Victor's mother, who is highly effective in advocating for her child but whose relationship with staff is undermined by perceived power dynamics and subtle threat. Active engagement, in effect, does not always mean collaboration; families and schools may be intensely engaged in power struggles rather than collaborative relationships. Similarly, there may be low-level engagement where there is mutual trust between parent and school. Alternatively, the relation between parents and school may be distant, permeated by disaffection or hopelessness. We may anticipate that most families will occupy a place somewhere along those two relationship continuums—between positive and negative engagement and between trust and suspicion.

Children with disabilities, and particularly those with psychological disorders, present unique challenges at home and at school; consequently, maintaining cooperative relations may require sustained efforts from both families and schools. The fluid nature of these interactions is clearly evident as children move from grade to grade and from teacher to teacher. Human interactions are complex and changing; a parent might be upset with a service provider but respect the classroom teacher and, over the course of a school year, may come to appreciate the service provider. When parent–school relations are based on an understanding that all parties are committed to helping the child grow and adjust to school, difficulties encountered along the way may be more easily resolved. Trust may be identified as the key ingredient for collaboration; to the extent that trust can be nurtured and deepened, family-school relations may improve to the benefit of children with special needs.

References

Artiles, A. J., & Trent, S. C. (2000). Representation of culturally/linguistically diverse students. In C. R. Reynolds & E. Fletcher-Jantzen (Eds.), *Encyclopedia of special education, Vol. 1* (2nd ed.; pp. 513–517). New York: Wiley.

Beukelman, D. R., & Mirenda, P. (1998). *Augmentative and alternative communication: Management of severe communication disorders in children and adults* (2nd ed.). Baltimore: Brookes.

Bursztyn, A. M. (2007). Multicultural school psychology: Directions for future research (pp. 639–658). In E. Lopez, G. Esquivel, & S. Nahari (Eds.), *Handbook of multicultural school psychology: An interdisciplinary perspective.* New York: Erlbaum.

Harry, B. (1992). *Cultural diversity, families, and the special education system.* New York: Teachers College Press.

Harry, B., Kalyanpur, M., & Day, M. (1999). *Building cultural reciprocity with families: Case studies in special education.* Baltimore: Brookes.

Harry, B., Klingner, J., Carmer, E., Sturges, K., &. Moore, R. (2007). *Case studies of minority student placement in special education.* New York: Teachers College Press.

Losen, D. L., & Orfield, G. (2002). *Racial inequity and special education.* Cambridge, MA: The Civil Rights Project at Harvard University and Harvard Education Press.

Meier, D. (2003). *In schools we trust: Creating communities of learning in an era of testing and standardization.* Boston: Beacon Press.

National Research Council. (2002). *Minority students in special and gifted education.* Washington, DC: National Academy Press.

Noddings, N. (1992). *The challenge to care in schools: An alternative approach to education.* New York: Teachers College Press.

Ong-Dean, C. (2009). *Distinguishing disability: Parents, privilege, and special education.* Chicago: University of Chicago Press.

Skrtic, T. M. (2008). The special education paradox: Equity as the way to excellence. In P. Hick & G. Thomas (Eds.), *Inclusion and diversity in education.* San Francisco: Sage.

Webb, N. B. (2001). *Culturally diverse parent-child and family relationships: A guide for social workers and other practitioners.* New York: Columbia University Press.

Resources

http://www.advocatesforchildren.org/
http://curry.edschool.virginia.edu/sped/projects/ose/resources/legal.html
http://www.schoolpsychology.net/

Index

About the Editor
and Contributors

Editor

ALBERTO M. BURSZTYN, PhD, holds the rank of professor at Brooklyn College (school psychology and special education) and at The Graduate Center, City University of New York (doctoral program in urban education). Dr. Bursztyn's areas of research include psychological assessment of second language learners, family–school relations, multicultural education, and urban special education. He recently edited *Handbook of Special Education* (Praeger Books) and *Rethinking Multicultural Education: Case Studies in Cultural Transition* (with Carol Korn-Bursztyn) Dr. Bursztyn is a licensed psychologist whose doctorate in counseling psychology was awarded by Columbia University. He also holds graduate degrees in science education (Brooklyn College), school psychology (Brooklyn College), and educational leadership (NYU). He has served as vice-president for education, training, and scientific affairs of Division 16 (school psychology) of the American Psychological Association and as its chair of the Committee on Ethnic Minority Affairs. He has also served in the editorial board of the *School Psychology Quarterly.*

Contributors

JEANNE ANGUS, PsyD, is an assistant professor in the School of Education at Brooklyn College, City University of New York, and program head of the graduate program for special education, where she continues her work with students with autism spectrum disorders. While completing her PhD at NYU in psychology, Dr. Angus focused her work on individuals on the autism spectrum and established the first elementary specialty school for high functioning children with ASD in the United States. She has been working with children with special needs and their families for more than 30 years: as a play therapist at Boston Children's Hospital, as a school counselor in both private and public school systems in New York City, and continues to consult and train classroom-integration and behavior management for school systems in the NYC tri-state area.

ELIZA A. DRAGOWSKI, PhD, is an assistant professor at the graduate school psychology program at Brooklyn College, City University of New York. Dr. Dragowski's research interests revolve around issues of social justice in educations. Most recent projects include (1) exploration of bullying and harassment of gay, lesbian, bisexual and transgender students in schools, as well as the educators' willingness and ability to advocate on behalf of these students; and (2) exploration of the social construction of gender and societal mandates about what constitutes abnormal gender expression.

JENNIFER FOSTER, PsyD, is a psychologist working for Perth Amboy Public Schools in New Jersey, where she is a behavioral consultant and coordinator of mental health programming for the district. Dr. Foster received her MS in education and advanced degree in school psychology from Brooklyn College and her PsyD in school psychology from the Graduate School of Applied and Professional Psychology at Rutgers University. Her research interests include the design, implementation, and evaluation of effective school-based mental health programs, crisis intervention and response to trauma, school and community-based supports for youth with severe mental illness, mental health policy, and addressing cultural barriers to accessing mental health services.

DANA FREED, MSEd, is a doctoral candidate in school psychology at Rutgers University. She completed her BFA at the School of Visual Arts and master's of science in education and advanced degree in school psychology at Brooklyn College. Over the years she has worked as a museum educator, violence prevention facilitator, curriculum writer, and school psychologist with children with emotional and behavioral problems. She is currently working at NYC Department of Education District 75 (severe disabilities services), developing and implementing counseling services, assessing individuals with developmental disabilities at the Block Institute, teaching cognitive and academic assessment at Brooklyn College, and developing and implementing programs, including art workshops, for children in foster care and aging out of care.

HAROLD GOLUBTCHIK, EdD, has been a teacher of general and special education students, staff developer, teacher-center director, and school principal during his 30 plus years in public education. Dr. Golubtchik presently teaches graduate-level courses for teachers and administrators and provides training for school districts to create effective school-wide models for their special education and at-risk populations. His forthcoming book, *From Box Cutters to Diplomas: The Transformation of a High School for Throwaway Teens,* describes the journey of educators in an inner-city high school as they search for a philosophy and strategies to meet the needs of students with challenging behaviors.

SUZANNE HUBER, CSW, is a licensed clinical social worker and a certified New York State school social worker. She received her master's in social work from New York University and her bachelor's of arts from the State University of New York at Buffalo. She is currently working as a social worker at The Henry Viscardi School, which is a school for physically disabled and medically fragile children, located on Long Island. She is also the mother of a child with multiple food allergies and is a member of FAAN.

CAROL KORN-BURSZTYN, PsyD, is a psychologist and psychoanalyst, professor of education at Brooklyn College, and is in the PhD program in urban education at The Graduate Center of the City University of New York. Dr. Korn-Bursztyn developed and led the Early Childhood Center Programs, the lab school of the School of Education from 1991–2007. Dr. Korn-Bursztyn began her career as an English teacher and early childhood educator and worked as a school psychologist in New York City public and private schools and in clinical settings before coming to Brooklyn College. She maintains a private practice with children and families and consults with schools. Dr. Korn-Bursztyn is the author of numerous articles on children's narrative; the arts in education and teacher research; and is the co-author, with Alberto Bursztyn, of *Rethinking Multicultural Education: Case Studies in Cultural Transition* (Bergin & Garvey). She is series editor of *Making Sense of Psychology* (Greenwood Press).

YOON-JOO LEE, EdD, is an assistant professor of special education at Brooklyn College, City University of New York. Dr. Lee teaches and supervises master's students in the Graduate Program in Early Childhood Special Education. She had several years of experience in teaching infants, toddlers, and preschoolers in different early childhood special education classrooms before joining the faculty at Brooklyn College. For the past several years, she has served in a board of directors for a nonprofit parent advocacy agency for Korean American families of children with special needs. Her scholarly interests include social experiences of young children with special needs in inclusive settings as well as the experiences of families of children with special needs from culturally and linguistically diverse backgrounds.

AMY L. SANDIGORSKY, MSEd, completed her undergraduate studies at Binghamton University, State University of New York, in 2001, where she majored in English and psychology. She later worked for Puppetry in Practice, a nonprofit, arts-infused literacy program housed in Brooklyn College. In 2010 she completed her MSEd in school p psychology at Brooklyn College, and she is currently completing for her advanced certificate in school psychology while participating in the New York City Department of Education's psychologist-in-training program. Her interest in gender identity disorder was inspired by school psychology program faculty members at Brooklyn College who advocate for LGBT youth and empower their students to promote social justice.

ELIZABETH M. SCANLON, MSEd, is a school psychologist who currently provides in-home behavioral remediation, intervention, training, education, and support to children with disabilities and their families through a nonprofit agency (a real-life Super Nanny!). Her interests include: bipolar disorder; autism; developmental disorders; creating unique individualized behavioral, familial, and academic interventions; child and family advocacy; educational rights; special education; accessibility of psychological and health care for all populations; family therapy; contemporary art; queer culture; music; reading; and writing. She resides with her dog, Dominoe, in Connecticut.

MARÍA R. SCHARRÓN-DEL RÍO received her PhD in clinical psychology from the University of Puerto Rico. After completing her clinical internship at The Cambridge Hospital, Harvard Medical School, in Boston, Professor Scharrón-del Río worked as a child psychologist at the Washington Heights Family Health Center, a primary-care clinic that serves a predominantly Latino and immigrant community in New York City. Currently, she is an assistant professor at the school counseling program in Brooklyn College's School of Education, City University of New York. Her research focuses on ethnic and cultural minority psychology and education, including multicultural competencies, LGBTQ issues, mental health disparities, spirituality, resiliency, and well-being.